FINANCIAL CUSTODY:

YOU, YOUR MONEY, AND DIVORCE

D0877731

by Joan Coullahan
and Sue van der Linden

ALPHA
A Pearson Education Company

International Standard Book Number: 0-02-864196-5
Library of Congress Catalog Card Number: 2001095854

04   03   02   8   7   6   5   4   3   2   1

Interpretation of the printing code: The rightmost number of the first series of numbers is the year of the book's printing; the rightmost number of the second series of numbers is the number of the book's printing. For example, a printing code of 02-1 shows that the first printing occurred in 2002.

Printed in the United States of America

Publisher: *Marie Butler-Knight*
Product Manager: *Phil Kitchel*
Managing Editor: *Jennifer Chisholm*
Acquisitions Editor: *Mike Sanders*
Development Editor: *Michael Koch*
Senior Production Editor: *Christy Wagner*
Copy Editor: *Lisa M. Lord*
Cover Designer: *Doug Wilkins*
Book Designer: *Trina Wurst*
Indexer: *Tonya Heard*
Layout/Proofreading: *Mary Hunt, Michelle Mitchell*
Marketing and publicity, contact: *Dawn Van De Keere, 317-581-3722*

Contents

Introduction

It is a well-known fact that half of all first marriages and many second marriages end in divorce, meaning that 50 percent of this country's population will dissolve marriages and start new lives. But all too often the important legal and financial decisions are being made with incomplete or inaccurate information. Since the focus of the divorce process must be future-oriented while deciding the issues of the present, knowledge and preparation are absolute essentials.

We, as financial professionals, are constantly challenged to help our clients organize and understand the many details of their financial lives so that they can have accurate, complete information on which to base their decisions. That is the reason this book is so necessary. Our intent is for you, the reader, to feel as though we are actually guiding you through the financial portion of the divorce process. Our main goals are to educate and focus your efforts and help you avoid the pitfalls of the divorce process. Our clients will also speak to you. By reading their stories, you will hear their experiences and learn from them.

Right from the start, we want you to know that this is going to require effort on your part. You will have to organize your present financial life and do some soul searching and hard thinking. Helping you become motivated will not be difficult. Just think about this: Whatever assets and debts you receive in the settlement will be the foundation for your future financial life. You now hold the power to shape the rest of your life. You will probably have assistance from professionals such as attorneys, CPAs, or therapists, but they can provide only guidance and advice. You must take the final responsibility. And don't make the mistake of thinking that once the settlement is reached you can sit back and relax. At that point you have ended one financial stage of your life and entered another.

In this book, we cover both stages in your life: before and after divorce. We address the before and after financial aspects of the divorce process with a particular personality and holistic tone that is smart, respectful, punchy, and warm. We hope to give you the tools and encouragement to help yourself now and in the new phase of your life to come. Many of the terms used in the text may be unfamiliar to most of you. A glossary of terms is arranged in alphabetical order in the back of the book so that you can look up words to help you understand the concepts.

Please keep in mind that we are financial professionals. Some of the concepts you will learn about are based on legal actions and advice given to previous clients by their attorneys. However, we do not give legal advice in this book, so reading the chapters and completing the worksheets should not take the place of advice or representation from a legal professional. Reading and understanding the concepts and completing the forms and worksheets will help prepare you if you do retain a professional or if you can complete some of the actions on your own.

Acknowledgments

We are very grateful for the opportunity to work with many special people who were instrumental in the writing of this book. The staff at Alpha Books was a great help with editing, marketing, and publishing. A special note of thanks to Joe Roberts, our agent, who guided us through the experience of writing this book and made our jobs much easier. Nick English, Sue van der Linden's assistant, held down the fort when this project needed her full attention. To our families: Bob van der Linden, a thoughtful husband and gifted author in his own right, and Rich and David Coullahan for their patience, love, and support. Sandra Hester managed client cases and juggled calendars during the writing and editing process. Caryn Lennon and Laurie Forbes provided valuable guidance and expertise to all the chapters containing legal content. Carol Ann Wilson of the Institute For Certified Divorce Planners, Dennis Casty of FinPlan Co., and Nancy and Richard Byrd of Pangean Systems, Inc., allowed us to use their software products in this book. A very special thanks to all our clients, who entrust us with their futures and from whom we have learned so much.

Trademarks

All terms mentioned in this book that are known to be or are suspected of being trademarks or service marks have been appropriately capitalized. Alpha Books and Pearson Education, Inc., cannot attest to the accuracy of this information. Use of a term in this book should not be regarded as affecting the validity of any trademark or service mark.

Chapter 1

You're Getting a Divorce—Now What?

Capsule Outlook

Educating yourself about divorce will be a journey. And you will grow stronger and wiser with each step.

No matter where you are physically, emotionally, or financially, as you start to read this book, you are about to begin a journey. Along the path of your journey you will encounter disappointments, stumbling blocks, personal discoveries and new insights. Your path may even require that you examine and rearrange your priorities. This is because the divorce process results in many types of change. And as we all know, change can result in anxiety and a number of other negative emotions.

The divorce process usually starts from an emotional standpoint: fear of being alone, guilt from leaving the marriage, or anger at being seemingly rejected. From these emotions come expectations of how the divorce process will progress and what the future will be. Those who have become "emotionally divorced" may feel that the process will go quickly with few problems. A spouse who never saw the divorce coming, however, might be angry and expect a long court battle. For them, the divorce process will be like "going to war" to get what they perceive as justice. My parish priest, Father Donald, once said in a homily: "Many people say they want justice when what they really want is revenge." Think about this for just a minute and imagine how your emotional state could affect your expectations. Many times, the reality becomes just what you expect. You make it that way. This is a very important and critical concept to grasp because your expectations should be based on fact, not emotion.

The Biggest Obstacle—Overcoming Fear

Perhaps the most common emotion during divorce is fear—fear of being alone, fear of losing friends because you aren't part of a couple anymore, and fear of not knowing the future. If your role in your marriage was a homemaker, you might not be able to imagine doing anything else. In most instances, the stay-at-home spouse's first emotion is feeling powerless. Your spouse has been the breadwinner, whose career has progressed with steady income from a job he or she already knows how to do. You, on the other hand, must start over. That could mean going to college or technical school to earn a degree or certificate. Just the thought of having to go back to school may be overwhelming.

So if you are having all these fears and feeling powerless, what is the first thing you are going to do? Find someone to be powerful for you! And who would that powerful person be? An attorney who will be strong, fight your spouse for you, and make your spouse do what's right. As you will learn in this book, an attorney is a vital part of a divorce team. But you must also realize that *you* will have to be your own power. You will have to be strong and become educated and focused. You must know your rights and what you need financially to lead an independent life.

It may seem as though that would be an impossible journey to make—to start from where you are now, progress through the emotional, legal, and financial issues of divorce, and finish with the assets, knowledge, and emotional strength you will need for the future. It can be done. But first you must resolve any negative feelings you may be experiencing. By far, those who spent the most on legal fees and who finished the process feeling bitter and disappointed were those who did not confront and conquer their fear and other negative emotions.

The Basic Divorce vs. the Traditional Divorce Process

The best way to confront and conquer fear is by knowing what to expect. By doing this, you will understand the experience you are about to undergo. Traditional divorce can be very complicated and costly. By comparison, using the basic divorce method, many of the required actions are usually done by the two spouses, making this route much less emotionally and financially draining.

The Divorce Process

The divorce process, in its most basic form, is a three-step process.

Step 1: Statements of the facts

Basic information needed for both parties includes names, Social Security numbers, ages, highest education attained, past work history, current state of health, gross monthly income, and average monthly living expenses.

Names, ages, and special needs of any minor children will also be required. Child custody decisions are made separately from decisions concerning the property or asset and debt division. For the property division, a listing of the assets, debts, income, and expenses of both parties is the starting point before any negotiations can take place. This can be as simple as you and your spouse getting together the latest information, such as statements from savings accounts, retirement plans, mutual funds, credit cards, and the mortgage company. Then you need to make a list of where the money goes each month. This is the preferred way to do it.

The opposite, and more expensive, method is each of you retaining an attorney who will file legal papers making your spouse disclose all this information. This is called *discovery* and can be very costly to both spouses. To begin this process, your attorney contacts your spouse's attorney, asking that completed forms and copies of monthly or quarterly statements concerning assets and debts be provided. This takes time and effort, which you and your spouse pay for in attorney's fees. Sometimes discovery is necessary because one spouse won't disclose the information needed. If that happens, you might have no choice but to have your attorney act for you. If possible, cooperation between you and your spouse is definitely the best way to go.

After all the relevant facts have been disclosed, decisions must be made as to the most fair and equitable division of assets and debts. The decision can be made in one of three ways:

❖ **Between you and your spouse.** This is how an agreement is reached in most divorces. There are many reasons this is the most common method. Often minor children are involved, and the parents don't want to inflict any more emotional distress than the divorce may already be causing. Sometimes there aren't many assets to fight over. And sometimes one of the parties just wants out of the marriage and is willing to make sacrifices. Reaching an agreement with your spouse is much more likely to happen when the negative emotions have been dealt with through the passing of time or during counseling with a therapist, priest, or other church official.

❖ **Negotiations between attorneys.** If the two parties can't agree on how the property should be divided, they can each retain an attorney who will negotiate on their behalf. The attorney assesses his or her client's needs and wants, and then talks directly with the other spouse's attorney to try to reach an agreement. Be aware that what you may think is fair might be very different from the legal guidelines or what your attorney is capable of negotiating for you. Many attorneys have disgruntled clients because the clients didn't fully understand the law or their attorney's limitations.

❖ **Decision by litigation.** A judge will listen to the facts of the case and make a decision. This method, often called "going to court," is by far the most expensive and emotionally difficult of the three settlement methods. By going to court, all the facts in the divorce become public knowledge and part of court records. All the "dirty laundry" is aired, so to speak. Many people don't realize they have lost control until it's over. Then, for better and often worse, they must abide by the court's decisions. Those who have taken this route are emotionally and financially drained when it is over. Most look back and wish something had been done to avoid the whole mess. Unfortunately, hindsight is 20/20.

Step 2: Preparing and signing the agreement

The decisions that have been made concerning child custody, payment of child support and/or alimony, the division of assets and debts, and other factors that are important to your particular situation will be formally incorporated into a document called the *settlement agreement.* This document is also called a *marital settlement agreement (MSA)* or a *property settlement agreement (PSA)*, depending on the state where the divorce is granted.

Usually the agreement is prepared by an attorney, but it can also be drafted by a mediator. An attorney can review the agreement for accuracy and completeness. After you have read and completely understand all the conditions, both spouses sign the agreement in the presence of a notary, which makes the settlement agreement a legally binding contract. Although the marital assets are divided when the judge signs the *final decree of divorce,* many couples begin separating checking and savings accounts, investment accounts, personal property such as bedroom furniture, and so on immediately after the agreement is signed. Keep in mind that the divorce must be final before any retirement assets such as a 401(k) account or individual retirement account (IRA) can be divided.

Step 3: Preparing and filing the final decree

The final decree incorporates all the specific issues on which the two parties have agreed. This legal document, signed by a judge, makes the parties officially divorced. Although it is possible to obtain the paperwork from your local courthouse to file for the divorce yourself, it is wise to have an attorney prepare this document. Many times, there are specific conditions you might not think of if you prepare and file the necessary forms yourself. Remember, once these documents are signed, legal action must be taken to amend any portion of the document.

The Traditional Divorce Process

Although a "kitchen table" agreement is the best possible scenario, that might not work out for you. If for any reason you and your spouse are not able to work through the issues and agree on custody, division of assets and debts, and future payments such as child support and alimony, you will likely go through one or more steps of the traditional divorce. There is a generally accepted sequence of events during the divorce process. Since no two divorces are alike, however, some steps may be done out of sequence and some might be skipped entirely. To better understand what could happen during your divorce, the steps are listed in chronological order from start to finish.

1. **Serving summons.** You may be served with a *summons of notice,* which notifies one spouse that the other spouse intends to prosecute and seeks relief. It sounds severe, but it really means that your spouse intends to file for divorce. The opposing attorney responds to the summons by sending a *notice of appearance* stating that he or she has been retained as a representative in the divorce and also asks for a *verified complaint.* Usually while still experiencing the shock of receiving a summons, the spouse who has been served retains an attorney. Keep in mind that the retainer, which an attorney may request, can vary greatly. Some attorneys ask for a modest amount, which could be $300 to $500. Other attorneys might ask for $5,000 to $7,000. Attorneys

ask for retainers because they want to make sure they get paid for their work. A retainer is simply payment in advance. Any work the attorney does is applied against the retainer. You should receive monthly statements, which detail how much time someone spent on your case, the specific work done for which you are being charged, and the total dollar amount charged.

2. **Exchanging pleadings.** *Pleadings,* which state the grounds for divorce, are exchanged between you and your spouse's attorneys. The verified complaint tells the nature of the offenses that have been committed, such as abuse, adultery, and so on. Your attorney can then reply with a *verified answer* in which you admit or deny the allegations. At this point, your attorney can state defenses to the verified complaint or file a *counterclaim* for divorce. After the counterclaim, your spouse can serve a *verified reply* admitting or denying your allegations in the counterclaim.

3. **Getting a financial disclosure.** While some steps in the divorce process can be skipped, a *financial disclosure* is almost always mandatory. All assets and debts must be known before a division can be decided. The first step in the disclosure process is an exchange of statements of net worth, which is done within three weeks of the pleadings described in Step 2. The *statement of net worth* is a form that discloses your income, expenses, assets, and debts. Usually, you must submit a current paycheck and your most recent tax returns. The financial disclosure process can be lengthy and include a *notice of discovery, inspection, and copying,* which entails giving your spouse's attorney bank records, tax returns, mortgage information, auto titles, and so on. These must be original documents. You might have a *demand for interrogatories* in which written questions are answered under oath. Depositions might be taken in which you, your spouse, and other persons may be questioned, under oath in the presence of attorneys and a court reporter. A *Request for Expert Witness* might be prepared that informs your spouse's attorney that you intend to call someone who

has knowledge and experience and will back up your case to testify on your behalf.

4. **Appraising properties.** Any property that is considered valuable might have to be appraised so that its true worth can be stated. Appraisals can be done on houses, land, antiques, collections, and other items. Personal businesses have become very common and discovering their true worth could require the expertise of a business valuator. Sometimes pensions must be calculated to find the expected monthly payment you or your spouse could receive. All of this information is necessary to place an accurate value on the assets.

5. **Filing motions.** At this point, motions can be filed with the court to ask that you be given relief while the divorce proceedings take place. An order called *Pendente Lite* is a request that could include payments such as temporary alimony or child support or ask for temporary custody, visitation with children, or one person to have exclusive use of the marital home. If you or your spouse fails to disclose financial information during discovery, a *Motion to Compel* can be filed to legally force disclosure.

6. **Attempting settlement.** During this time, hopefully you or your spouse has made an attempt to settle the case before it goes to trial. Settlement attempts can be made in a number of ways, including phone calls or letters between the two attorneys, meetings between the attorneys, and even conferences in the judge's chambers before the trial.

7. **Attending a preliminary conference.** If you and your spouse can't agree on all the conditions of the divorce, you may then attend a *preliminary conference,* which takes place at the courthouse. During the conference, the issues of the case are discussed and a schedule for the exchange of financial information can be set.

8. **Scheduling a compliance conference.** To ensure that you and your spouse have completed all the actions that have been requested, a *compliance conference* might be scheduled. During this meeting, your attorney answers questions as to

whether all the financial information has been disclosed and whether anything else needs to be done to settle the case. The trial dates are set at this time.

9. **Scheduling a pretrial conference.** After the attorneys representing you and your spouse have notified the court that they are ready for trial, a judge may schedule a *pretrial conference* in his or her chambers. During this conference both attorneys inform the judge of the facts concerning their clients' positions. The judge might tell the attorneys what he or she thinks is fair and reasonable. Your attorney may then discuss the judge's remarks with you so that you have an idea of what the expected ruling in court will be if the trial proceeds.

10. **Going to trial.** The next step is the *trial,* commonly called "going to court." Both attorneys state the facts and arguments of their clients' cases. The judge might ask for additional information, and expert witnesses can be called.

11. **Reaching an agreement.** The final outcome can be made in one of several ways. A judge can render his or her decision in open court or in writing. Unless an appeal is planned, you and your spouse must abide by the judge's decisions. You and your spouse may settle your dispute and your agreement taken in writing by a court reporter present during the trial. Usually the two parties reach an agreement, which is then prepared and signed.

As you have just learned, there is a big difference between these two methods of divorce. In fact, if most couples read these past few pages, it would likely result in fewer cases being litigated. The basic divorce might cost as little as $1,000, but the traditional divorce usually costs at least $10,000 per person and could run as much as several hundred thousand dollars. At least one of the two parties in the divorce should get to choose which divorce he or she wants. If both spouses decide they want the basic divorce, the costs can be quite reasonable. Unfortunately, if one of the spouses wants the traditional divorce, the cost for the other spouse can increase significantly.

Getting Educated and Focused

Unfortunately, too many men and women go through the divorce process lacking the vital information they need to make smart choices about child custody, alimony, and the division of assets and debts. There is an old saying that "knowledge is power." This is especially true when negotiating your future because that's what a divorce settlement is—the foundation of wealth for the rest of your life. Although this foundation applies no matter what your age, a fair division of assets is even more important for someone if he or she ...

❖ Has been a homemaker.

❖ Has no college degree or specialized training/skill.

❖ Has no recent work history.

❖ Has been employed part-time during the marriage.

❖ Is in ill health.

❖ Is near retirement age.

❖ Has a parent or child with special needs.

Usually women are the traditional homemakers who care for children, parents, or relatives with special needs, and who have not had the advantage of a continuous career progression. And women often feel the most powerless when placed in a divorce situation. Because they may have depended on someone else for income, women are more likely to retain an attorney when their husband asks for a divorce. This reinforces the importance of finding a powerful ally.

Education is a great equalizer. It puts people on a level playing field where no one person has an advantage over another. Education is also a great empowerment tool. Just by knowing more, you feel more confident.

To illustrate this point, the following story describes an experience a friend named Carol had a few years ago. Carol is the car shopper in her family. She loves to bargain and does her homework before entering an auto dealership showroom. She checks the *Consumer Report Guides,* runs the average trade-in and retail prices on KelleyBlueBook.com, and reads the classifieds in the local newspaper to see what private sellers and auto dealers are asking for the particular auto she expects to buy. In short, Carol is an empowered buyer and expects to be treated like one.

A few years ago when her old faithful family car was on its last legs, Carol did her homework and then went to a local dealership. She looked on the lot for about 30 minutes before being approached by a salesperson. Carol was wearing casual slacks and a sweater and looked the part of a stay-at-home mom. The next day, after she had narrowed the choices down to three cars, Carols' husband met her on the dealership lot. He stepped out of his car wearing a white shirt and tie and immediately was approached by two salesmen. These were the very salesmen who had all but ignored Carol the day before. Carol and her husband looked at the three cars and left the dealership, never to return. Because she was educated, she was ready to make a deal. The salesmen at the auto dealership severely underestimated her level of knowledge. Carol went to another dealership and was assisted by a courteous salesperson who recognized that she knew what she wanted and gave her a great deal. Carol has since bought her second car from the same dealer. Because she was empowered by education, Carol could very well walk off the lot. She knew she could get just as good a deal somewhere else.

Many times, women who are not educated feel as though they must accept what they are offered even if it's not fair or not enough.

Educating Yourself

First, educate yourself. Start by learning all the details concerning your particular financial situation. This means listing all your assets and debts, their balances, and whose name they are in. Checking and savings accounts, retirement accounts and pensions, houses, land, personal businesses, autos, and collectibles are all assets and, if earned during the marriage, can be thrown into the pot for division. Debts can be divisible, too, even if your spouse did the spending. If it's a joint credit card and the money was spent before you separated, most likely you will be liable for repaying part of the debt.

Next, find out what most people don't know, which is how much money they spend each month and where it goes. This is a challenge because most people don't track their spending. Don't worry if you are in this majority—by the time you finish this book, you'll not only know your present financial needs but also be able to project your future needs. You need to know your rights, too. This means educating yourself about your state's laws and how they pertain to your specific situation. You'll learn later that most states are *equitable distribution* states, which means specific factors may be taken into consideration when dividing the assets and debts. Sometimes assets are split 50/50 and sometimes they're not. Each divorce is different, and although 50/50 is equal and easy, you should be aware of your needs so you know whether 50/50 is right for your particular case.

The importance of being educated and focused cannot be overestimated and, if you are coping with emotional turmoil, it is absolutely vital as you will see in the following story about Mary Anne.

Mary Anne was married to George for 24 years. Both George and Mary Anne had decided when they were newly married that Mary Anne would take care of the home and the children, and George would continue his career with a local company. Throughout their marriage, Mary Anne raised four children and occasionally took part-time jobs, but none with benefits or the potential for career progression. One morning, to Mary Anne's complete surprise, George told her that he wanted her to leave the house. She was no longer needed to maintain the home and he wanted a divorce.

Mary Anne, having almost no money in her checking account, moved into a small apartment while still hoping that she and George would reconcile. As time went on, Mary Anne came to two conclusions: First, divorce was imminent, and second, she knew almost nothing about their finances. She knew that George had a pension with his company and that they owed a second mortgage on the house. Beyond those bare facts, Mary Anne was clueless. Why? Because George had always told her she didn't need to worry about the finances. He was more than capable of paying the bills and investing the money. Moreover, George also told Mary Anne that it was *his* money and she should be grateful to live in a decent house and have food on the table.

This is a true story that thankfully has a good ending. Mary Anne consulted an attorney, who began the discovery process to learn just what the joint assets and debts were. Mary Anne also retained a Certified Divorce Planner, who helped her organize and list the assets and debts, calculate her present cash flow, project her need for future training and a new career, and prepared spreadsheets and charts that showed Mary Anne how a division of the assets and debts would affect her and George in the years to come. Using this knowledge, Mary Anne and her attorney negotiated alimony and the division of assets so that Mary Anne could have a decent standard of living, get the additional education and training she needed, and be able to save money for her own retirement.

Finding the Proper Resources

There is a wealth of information available from a wide variety of sources, including friends, members of the clergy, books and magazines, and the Internet.

Friends can be a great source of information about divorce. Since one out of two first marriages ends in divorce, friends who have gone through the process can offer helpful advice on the do's and don'ts. Of course, keep in mind that people usually put their own slant on their story. One friend may have a horror story about her attorney, while another friend may want to nominate that same attorney for "lawyer of the year." Because divorce is not a cookie-cutter process, what worked for someone else might not benefit you. Usually, friends who have good experiences are more than happy to pass along their stories and offer referrals to professionals such as attorneys, CPAs, and therapists who helped them. This can be a great starting point, but proceed with caution and decide what is right for you.

Members of the clergy have been trained to deal with marital problems, including divorce. Although divorce may be against the rules of a particular religion, a priest, rabbi, or minister can offer solace, religious guidance, and perhaps a referral to a marriage counselor or therapist. The importance of religious faith should not be underestimated in the divorce process. Many people feel very strongly that divorce should not be allowed. Unfortunately, if your spouse wants a divorce there's probably little you can do to prevent it from happening. But your religious counselor can help you understand your place in the church after the divorce has taken place. Members of the clergy also refer congregation members to attorneys, financial planners, and other professionals as needed.

Books and magazines offer a wealth of information, which is helpful for those thinking about or going through divorce. Since the process entails so many decisions about many different aspects, the topics are endless. Numerous books are available with topics such as the use of mediation in divorce, do-it-yourself divorce kits for various states, guidance on reconciling divorce and religion, co-parenting after divorce, getting control of your finances, general legal advice … and the list goes on. Much of this material is well written and extremely useful. Magazines such as *Working Mother, Self,* and *Psychology Today* often include articles about various legal, emotional, or financial aspects of divorce. A good place to start is your local library.

The Internet offers an almost overwhelming amount of information. Just log on to America Online or another Internet service provider and type in the word "divorce," and you will be offered an endless array of Web sites that provide information and offer links to divorce-related professionals, including attorneys, CPAs, and therapists. The following is a list of Web sites that are a great starting point:

❖ **Splitup.com.** The names, addresses, and phone numbers of divorce-related professionals in your local area are available on this Web site. Links can be used to connect to other materials and books that cover the entire range of divorce topics.

❖ **Divorcesource.com.** This Web site has been operating for several years and offers a large directory of divorce professionals as well as information on each state's divorce laws.

❖ **Smartmoney.com.** Although often thought of as an investment Web site, Smartmoney.com has evolved into a multifaceted Internet stop that has an entire portion devoted to divorce. You can get information on stock options, capital gains taxes, tax filing status, child support, and alimony.

❖ **ABANet.org.** The Web site of the American Bar Association (ABA). Mainly used by attorneys to register for educational courses and obtain other professional information, it also offers a directory of ABA members.

❖ **DivorceResourceNetwork.com.** Is available in the metropolitan Washington, D.C., area. You can read profiles of network members and the services they provide. Online registration is offered for local seminars that feature divorce-related professionals as speakers.

These are only a few of many Web sites, so devote some time to surfing between sites and exploring the various links.

Seminars are a great way to get information concerning divorce from area professionals. Seminars are often held at a local women's center with an attorney explaining the laws of the state. Topics include child support, alimony, division of assets, the basics of the divorce process, and custody arrangements.

Getting Focused

This is the biggest challenge to many people going through a divorce. You or your spouse might be guilty of adultery or abuse, or you may be so concerned about your child's emotional state that you can't concentrate on anything else. As difficult as it may seem, your emotional turmoil must be dealt with separately from the financial and legal issues. In fact, you must get an "emotional divorce" before you can effectively identify and evaluate the other issues. Maintaining your focus could demand that you meet with a therapist at the same time you are consulting other professionals. Keep your eye on the end result, which is getting a fair settlement and building a new life. This is quite easy to say, but it can be tough for the person whose spouse just asked for a divorce. You might have lived in a bad situation and just now feel that you are ready to take action. Whatever your situation, there are professionals who can help guide you through this stressful event.

A Step-by-Step Approach

The information in this chapter is general in nature so that you can grasp the basic fundamentals of the divorce process. As the book progresses, the material will become much more specific. Although the legal aspects of divorce are discussed, the content is offered as a guide and some portions may not apply in your situation. No information should be interpreted as legal advice.

This book has been written to help the reader become educated and focused about the financial elements of divorce. We hope that you feel as though an advisor is with you, explaining the concepts and assisting in the preparation of the essential data.

Divorce is a step-by-step process. Too often, necessary details are omitted and steps are taken out of sequence. Using this book as a guide will help you define your situation and make the most efficient use of your time.

The Bottom Line

You must deal with the emotional part of the divorce situation, but your main focus must be preparation.

Chapter 2

The Traditional Divorce

Capsule Outlook

The traditional divorce has the potential to result in emotional pain and financial hardship that may last for many years to come.

The traditional divorce is, more often than not, bad news. Both parties retain attorneys, sometimes withhold information while trying to gain the upper hand, and fight using their attorneys so that the courts must decide their futures. Why does this happen? First, it must be acknowledged that the divorce process is traditionally an adversarial one. During the marriage, two people who may have thought of themselves as a team change to being opponents when the marriage ends. Someone will be seen as the winner, which means someone has to be the loser. Of course, no one wants to be the loser, so he or she may employ any means possible to gain the advantage. Thankfully, many good attorneys, judges, and legislators are attempting to change the divorce process so that it is more of a compromise and less of a battle.

Another reason for the traditional divorce is a historic lack of knowledge. In the past, spouses had little or no understanding of the legal system. They believed the only way to get a divorce was for each person to hire a lawyer. Also, years ago, divorce was a dirty word. Almost no one did it because society looked down on divorced people. Unfortunately, a great many men and women stayed in bad marriages because of societal pressure.

Our society has changed in the past several decades, and especially in the past 10 years. Knowledge is everywhere, which can be directly attributed to the Internet. People are much more technically sophisticated now. With a wealth of information at their fingertips, individuals are assuming much more personal responsibility than ever before. You only have to look at the huge increase in financial services companies and Internet stock-trading sites to see that people want to assume more control over their finances, careers, and personal futures.

The same can be said for divorce. By becoming more educated about divorce, people are deciding that the traditional divorce process should not apply in every instance. As a matter of fact, professionals are attempting to change the process by introducing other concepts such as "cooperative divorce." Since people know their needs better than anyone else, they should have the information and professional assistance necessary to make the best decisions for themselves and their families. The trend will, we hope, continue so that the divorce process becomes more cooperative and less contentious.

The third issue that contributed to the traditional divorce was the concept of "powerful versus powerless." In the past, women were at a particular disadvantage because they were the homemakers, not the wage earners. This situation has changed drastically in the past 30 years. Women in the workplace are now a driving force behind our nation's economic growth. Women have many more choices and most no longer stay financially dependent in bad marriages. Women now want to have independence in all areas of their lives. Achieving financial independence has been the major source of change.

This economic shift from powerless to powerful has caused a change in perceptions and actions. Today, most couples perceive themselves more as equals, with equal abilities and power. Education through books, Web sites, seminars, and consultations with professionals has leveled the playing field, with both spouses having equal access to information and equal ability to make decisions. Approaching the divorce process as equals eliminates much of the emotional turmoil that results in litigation. Knowledge is power—and both spouses have equal access to knowledge.

Costs and Outcomes

The cost of any action can be measured in many different terms. Unfortunately, financial considerations are usually the measuring stick. Whoever has the most at the end of the game is the winner. In divorce, if you receive more than 50 percent of the assets, it's your right to claim victory. But at what price? The traditional divorce has high emotional and financial costs and causes emotional turmoil not only for the two spouses, but also much more for their children. It also gives most of the control to attorneys and judges, when control should remain with the divorcing spouses.

Emotional Costs

It's also a real shame to let events of the marriage's last few months tarnish all the previous years and the future. At the time of your divorce, you might not share this attitude. However, time and distance have a way of clarifying your thinking. If you have children who are minors, you will almost certainly see your ex-spouse on a regular basis. It is common for children to split their time living with both parents. This shared custody arrangement has become a popular method of child rearing. In most cases, the children benefit from the companionship of both parents instead of just one. In a perfect world, we could all be objective and not let past pain rule our present thinking. But when you haven't reached emotional closure, it is complicated having to explain to your children why they should "play fair" when you and your spouse can't.

Long and difficult court battles often cause a marked loss of self-confidence. Since one party often attempts to demonstrate the shortcomings of the other, it's little wonder the process ends with battered egos on both sides. Financial facts are used to decide the division of assets and debts, but child custody is where personal weaknesses are most often mentioned. It can be difficult to repeatedly hear specific instances of your failure as a parent or spouse without starting to doubt your own abilities. Anyone going through a divorce is emotionally vulnerable and wants reassurance that he or she is a good person, and particularly a good parent. If you and your spouse get into this type of war, be prepared for the consequences. Emotional scars can last longer and have a much more profound effect than any financial inequity.

Financial Costs

Another question begs to be asked: "Would you rather fund your own children's college education and your own retirement, or would you rather do these things for your attorney?" When forced to think about the previous question, most people admit they would rather save the money for their own families. It's not that attorneys don't deserve to be compensated for their services; they most certainly do. But use the services of any professional wisely and for their intended purposes.

The traditional divorce can cost $25,000 or more per person. Yes, that means you and your spouse, together, could spend more than $50,000 in a legal fight. Going through the discovery process alone usually costs each spouse more than $5,000. Add to that the cost of filing legal motions, going to court for temporary support and custody, and then preparing for trial and actually pleading your case before a judge. The costs mount up quickly, especially at $200 per hour. The problem is that costs can increase so quickly that the legal bill is very high before you even see the monthly statement. Then the two parties are put in a position of deciding whether to scrap all the previous work their attorneys have done and try to negotiate between themselves or continue on that same path. Compound that problem with the fact that one or both spouses would have to admit they were wrong in their initial approach, and you have just started to grasp the situation.

Using the traditional approach to divorce, college plans evaporate and retirements are postponed. Before the first step is taken in the divorce process, it benefits both spouses to think about one fact—that whatever assets are left at the end of the process will be their foundation for future wealth. The decision can be made to work cooperatively and preserve assets or use these assets to extract emotional satisfaction. If you get to make that choice, choose wisely.

The following story vividly illustrates the emotional and financial costs of the traditional divorce.

Leeann and Ray had been married for more than 20 years and were parents of 9- and 7-year-old boys. Leeann and Ray had the traditional marriage—she took care of the house and kids and Ray earned the income, took care of the investments, and paid the bills. Unfortunately, Leeann and Ray also had the traditional divorce. Ray perceived himself to be in the superior position because he had an established career with great earning potential. Leeann felt that she was at a great disadvantage. She was being torn away from the house and children, but knew she would have to find a job and take responsibility for her own financial future. Leeann also felt powerless, and saw no alternative but to retain an attorney. Ray saw Leeann's action as a threat, and he also retained an attorney.

And so it went. Ray wouldn't willingly supply statements or other information, so discovery was initiated. Leeann tried to control the process but fought a losing battle. By the end of 13 months, Leeann and Ray were in a serious battle with several trips to court. By the time a settlement was reached, Leeann's attorney's fees were $62,000 and Ray's were $55,000. Leeann did receive permanent alimony, which helped pay her monthly expenses, but a large portion of the assets she received were used to pay her large legal bills. Leeann and Ray's relationship became bitter, and their children were caught in the middle. Leeann could only hope that time would heal some of the wounds that had resulted from the divorce, especially those inflicted on the children.

Difference in Mindsets

Because of the very nature of the two genders, men and women approach divorce with different mindsets. Men often come into this process thinking, "How much is this going to cost me?" Women, by contrast, often wonder, "Am I going to have to live in a box under a bridge when this is all over?"

This difference in mindsets also explains the differing emphasis each spouse places on assets in the property settlement. Women, especially those who have been traditional homemakers, often see the home as a symbol of security. Women are secure in their abilities as homemakers and view the house as a rock of stability during the turbulent time of divorce. Also, women view the house as a permanent residence and may plan to live there for the remainder of their lives. Men tend to be much more objective and view the marital home as a necessary investment that yields tax benefits. The worse the relationship becomes with the other spouse, the more stubborn the resolve to stay in the house. When children who are minors are involved, resistance to uprooting the family becomes even more intense.

Men tend to prize retirement accounts more than other assets. They can see the savings deducted from their paychecks and track the progress of the investments. Retirement assets are symbols of security for men. It's not that women don't recognize the importance of saving for retirement. It's just that they give the emotional aspects of the marital home more importance than retirement assets, which can only be viewed on a piece of paper and whose benefits won't be enjoyed for years to come.

Despite the difference in mindsets, both men and women agree that keeping the children in the home for a year or two after the divorce aids in achieving emotional closure and adjustment. It is becoming more common for ex-spouses to co-own the marital home for a period of time after the divorce. Doing this enables everyone to experience a period of adjustment. Then if the woman still wants to buy out her spouse, she will be making her decision based on economic rather than emotional factors.

Diverse Responsibilities

In marriages of our grandparent's time, men made the money and had careers while women took care of the house, raised the kids, volunteered in the community, and conducted their lives for little, if any, financial compensation.

In more modern times these two worlds converge, as men must assume responsibilities for child rearing and housekeeping while women become wage earners. This can be a disturbing change of circumstances for both, if men are assuming duties in a noncompetitive workplace where there is rarely training or specific expectations, and women are entering or reentering a workplace with well-defined standards. For women who have had a career during marriage, living without companionship or another source of income can be an uneasy, even troubling time. For women who have had little or no employment outside the home, however, this transition most likely will be a major crisis.

The movie *Mr. Mom* (1983) illustrates this point very well. The plot centers on a couple with traditional roles that through necessity become reversed. Michael Keaton loses his job and stays home, performing all the responsibilities of a traditional homemaker, including housekeeping, child care, and grocery shopping. Teri Garr finds a job and enters the corporate workplace, where she does quite well. They both assume duties that are unfamiliar and challenging, which is quite humorous to watch. In the end, they stay married, enjoy a new appreciation for each other's lives, and overcome their difficulties.

If only things ended this way all the time. Women rarely take jobs where they are recognized as marketing geniuses on their first day of work. And men rarely see the humor in changing a dirty diaper in the men's restroom during negotiations with their former boss to get their job back. But then, real life isn't made in Hollywood.

Expand Your Field of Vision

The key to surviving divorce is adaptation. Traditional roles and attitudes must change to meet the demands of new circumstances. Divorce results in unexpected changes. Mothers and fathers must assume different roles in their children's lives. A mother might not be able to acknowledge that her ex-husband is competent enough to care for their sick child, but it happens all the time.

A good example of expanding your field of vision is the story of a couple deciding on living arrangements for the children after the divorce. They were both having a difficult time with adaptation, but the wife much more so than the husband. The main point of contention was physical custody of the two children. Of course, much of the cash-flow analysis depends on the amount of child support to be paid, so the couple was pretty much stuck until they could agree on this point. The wife had recently taken a part-time job and was adamant that the children still needed her at home, even though the children were teenagers. The husband was requesting equal physical time with the children. He wanted a flexible parenting agreement, which would allow at least one of the kids to spend 183 days with him. The wife just could not imagine her future ex-husband rearranging his work schedule so that he could meet the children's scheduling demands. The wife did allude to the fact that if her husband had equal custody of the children, the amount of child support she received would be reduced. The point should be made that the desire for shared physical custody is rarely a result of wanting to pay less child support. In fact, sometimes fathers willingly pay more child support just so they can spend additional time with their children. The husband in this story earned over $140,000 per year, so money was not a main concern.

How did the meeting end? After some tears and raised voices, they agreed on equal physical custody. The wife admitted that her husband was a great father. He replied that the happiness and welfare of the children was his main concern. They left the meeting with the promise that they would ask for their children's input on the shared custody arrangement and then cooperate to make their parenting schedule work.

Write Your Own Ending

You have just learned about the costs and results of the traditional divorce. If your divorce progresses the way most divorces do, you will have some influence over events and decisions. You may or may not need an attorney to negotiate for you. Through education and professional assistance, you can be strong enough to finish the process intact. Your advantage will not be that you beat your spouse and get more assets at the end. The advantage will be that you maintained control and influence over the events and the outcome.

The Bottom Line

Focusing on the true issues enables both spouses to feel that they have received fair treatment and will be able to abide by the terms of their agreement.

Chapter 3

Focusing on Important Issues

Capsule Outlook

Separating the emotional issues from the legal and financial ones is the best thing you can do for yourself.

When going through a long, tedious, and emotionally draining process, some people find it useful to continually think of a phrase or mantra to keep their focus. You may remember that Bill Clinton did this when he ran for president in 1992. His mantra was, "It's the economy, stupid." By thinking these simple words, he was able to focus voters on one of the most important issues of his campaign platform and won the election.

You must be just as focused. It is very easy to stray from the issues which must be decided, especially when emotions cloud your judgment.

The Emotional Side of Divorce

Emotions are powerful motivators. What a person feels is often reflected in his or her actions. This will be an emotional time, since divorce is a major life event. You have to acknowledge and deal with any negative feelings you may have.

Nick had been married to Sharon for 24 years. In his estimation, theirs was a typical marriage with more ups than downs. Sharon had worked odd jobs, but mostly stayed home and raised their two daughters. In Nick's opinion, he and Sharon got along fine. They had managed to save and invest and owned their own home. Then one day out of the blue, Nick was hit by a thunder-bolt. Sharon told him she had reconnected with her old high school sweetheart, John, and they had been exchanging e-mails for several months. Sharon felt that the passion had been long gone out of her marriage and that John was her true soul mate. There was to be no marriage counseling. She wanted a divorce. The next week Sharon moved out and started living with John.

Understandably, Nick was in emotional shock, but decided he shouldn't fight the divorce since it would only make things worse. Secretly, Nick was hoping that Sharon would come to her senses and come back to him. The divorce process started smoothly enough. Then Nick realized Sharon was not coming back. He had gotten over the shock of what Sharon had done and became angry. As a result, Nick wouldn't let Sharon back into the house to collect the rest of her clothes and other possessions. Plus, Nick felt that since Sharon had caused the divorce, she didn't deserve half of the assets. Even though Nick started seeing a therapist, everything became a battle. What should have been a relatively quick process dragged on for over a year. Nick and Sharon's daughter got married during this time, and the wedding was a very painful event for Nick. It took time, but Nick finally worked through the emotional aspects of his situation and came to a resolution. Even though the financial costs were low, the emotional costs were too high.

Marriage is an emotional, financial, and legal union, but in divorce the financial and legal issues are what matter. You must make a choice whether you will use your emotions constructively or destructively. Acting constructively means that you recognize that you can make a life on your own and are willing to educate yourself about your present situation and your rights in your par-ticular state, and will make decisions based on fact. Destructive actions are hiring an attorney to "do battle" with your soon-to-be ex-spouse to make him or her pay for the emotional pain you are feeling. Unfortunately, the majority of the time a judge won't consider that your spouse is abusive, an alcoholic, a bad parent, or emotionally unsupportive. If you can't put a dollar sign on it, it most probably won't have a bearing on who gets what. The facts are the facts and that is what counts most in getting a fair property settlement.

The best way to understand something is to look at it closely, analyze its different parts, and understand its function. So we are going to look at the emotional stages Nick went through and see how each emotion affected his behavior:

❖ **Shock.** This is often the first emotion people feel when confronted by something unexpected. As you read in Nick's story, he was completely surprised by Sharon's news that she reconnected with her high school sweetheart and wanted a divorce. As a matter of fact, Nick was in a state of disbelief. He had thought his marriage was fine and had no hint of how Sharon really felt. Nick was very calm and controlled at the beginning of negotiations. He acted as though he were having a bad dream and hoped he would wake up and everything would be the same as before. Unfortunately, this rarely happens.

❖ **Anger.** After a few weeks, Nick came to realize that there was not going to be reconciliation. Sharon was not coming back. She refused Nick's pleas of marriage counseling and was determined she was going to have a new life, and it wasn't going to include Nick. Nick felt rejected after giving so many years to the marriage. Then, he got mad. Nick was going to get even while still attempting to look like a nice guy. Sharon wanted her clothes and other personal items, but Nick would not allow her in the house. Then he changed the locks since he feared Sharon would come in while he wasn't home and take other items besides the ones she had requested. Nick's anger was slow to subside, which kept him from making any progress toward a property settlement agreement.

❖ **Self-pity.** In divorce, either the husband or the wife rejects the other spouse or the marriage situation as a whole. Nick truly seemed to be a nice guy, and that was the image he had of himself. He couldn't understand how Sharon could reject him when he was such a good person. Nick felt that he hadn't changed, so why didn't Sharon want him? More than a few times, Nick asked, "How could she do this to me?" Then Nick did a very smart thing: He began seeing a therapist. Nick began to analyze his situation and focus on his emotions and what he could do to help himself. Many times, self-pity comes from feeling that you have no control over a situation. The divorce was progressing and Nick felt powerless to stop it.

❖ **Acceptance.** Several months passed before Nick began to realize the divorce was inevitable and he was going to have to face the future without Sharon. Talking with a therapist did wonders for him. He had worked through his anger, examined his feelings, and found that he still thought of himself as a nice guy. Then he really began building his identity as a single person. He wanted to work through the financial and legal issues so that he and Sharon could reach a property settlement agreement.

❖ **Resolution.** It took over 12 months before Nick and Sharon reached an agreement. One of Nick's biggest concerns had always been whether he and Sharon could be at a family gathering without feeling friction or bitterness. The test came when their daughter got married and Nick and Sharon stayed civil to each other. Keep in mind that although the divorce process ends, it rarely has a fairy-tale ending. You may work through the emotions and come to a resolution, but things will not be the same. You and your ex-spouse will have separate identities and separate lives. The best ending for a marriage is one in which there is mutual respect. Sometimes this is possible and sometimes it isn't. It is a goal to keep uppermost in your mind when going through a divorce, especially when children are involved.

The Legal Issues

There is a long list of legal issues that can be relevant to your situation. Remember that divorce is not a cookie-cutter process. Therefore, you should not be particularly concerned with how much money and other assets a friend got in her divorce settlement. Nor should you assume that just because your sister got full custody of her children, your situation will end the same way. Specific topics such as child support, alimony, and division of assets are discussed in later chapters. Although some of these terms were discussed in Chapter 1, "You're Getting a Divorce— Now What?" specific legal actions relating to finances will now be explained in greater detail.

The Pendente Lite Petition

When one household becomes two, one budget becomes two. Different houses, different needs. At the beginning of the divorce process, one of the spouses usually rents an apartment or lives temporarily with friends or family. But the spouse who is staying in the house must still pay the rent or mortgage. Many times, the two spouses come to a meeting of the minds and agree that one of the spouses will make the mortgage payment and pay extra money for child support or alimony. Usually both spouses share the responsibility for paying some of the bills. These payments continue while the property settlement is being negotiated and permanent terms are agreed on.

If the two spouses can't agree on temporary payments, then it might become necessary to retain an attorney to file a petition for temporary support. This petition is called *pendente lite*. This court order is usually used to specify the child custody arrangement, child visitation schedules, amount of child support or alimony, and other payments that either spouse must make. Keep in mind that a pendente lite order might not be necessary. Your particular situation will dictate whether this step is necessary.

We will give you a warning about not having a pendente lite order. If your relationship with your spouse turns from cooperative to hostile, having an order protects you from accumulating debt to meet your living expenses during this time. One client, Alissa, learned this lesson the hard way. Her husband moved out of the house and refused attempts at marriage counseling. He agreed to make the mortgage payments and a small amount for support of the couple's two children. Alissa consulted an attorney to learn her rights. The attorney's opinion was that she shouldn't waste her time going to court for more money. Her husband was paying the mortgage already, and she and her husband would divorce soon, anyway. Therefore, Alissa made no legal attempt toward getting additional money from her husband.

There was a big problem, however. The expenses for keeping up the house and raising the children were far more than what she was receiving from her husband. Things stayed this way for five years. Alissa hoped to reconcile with her husband, all the time accumulating more debt. Finally, her husband filed for divorce. By that time, Alissa was over $90,000 in debt and behind on all the monthly credit card payments. Her credit rating was dismal, and emotionally she was at the breaking point from the stress she was under. When negotiations for property settlement were finished, Alissa did not receive one penny in additional money to pay her debts, even though she had been fairly frugal and only went into debt to pay the monthly living expenses for her and the children. Learn from the mistakes of others. Know your rights. If your spouse is not dependable, it is wise to have a court order. If you are the person who is to make payments to your spouse, do it.

Discovery

One legal step you should avoid, if possible, is discovery. You have probably heard the phrase, "We can do this the easy way or we can do this the hard way." You and your spouse getting all the family financial information together and then sharing this information is the easy way. Discovery is the hard way. It can be quite expensive, too. You and your spouse will be required to complete a 10- to 12-page form that details your assets, debts, income, expenses, employment history, and other information, and then give this information to your spouse's attorney. Your spouse's attorney will use the information you provided in discovery to negotiate the best deal he can for his client, your soon-to-be ex-spouse. Knowledge is power, and if you or your spouse decides to horde power by withholding information, the legal process will drag on and the legal fees will accumulate. A conservative estimate of legal fees, which can be billed during the discovery process, is $5,000 to $10,000 per person.

Motion to Compel

Often, if one spouse is not willing to provide the financial and personal information, a *motion to compel* must be filed. This is a court order that legally requires someone to do something. During divorce, a pendente lite order is often used to force one or both parties to provide discovery information. Although a motion to compel should be sufficient to influence someone to provide information, it isn't always effective. If the attorney who files the motion does not follow through, it can be a waste of time and money.

It is important to remember that you cannot negotiate without complete, accurate information, although many spouses try to do exactly that. Almost without exception, the spouse who refuses to supply information is the spouse who has the most to lose if all the facts are known. However, make sure your attorney uses this legal tool wisely. Several years ago, a woman retained a Certified Divorce Planner for the purpose of assisting her attorney in analyzing the financial data to be used during settlement negotiations. Her attorney was a very nice guy, almost too nice. He had continuously asked the opposing attorney for discovery information, with poor results. Finally, the client's attorney filed a motion to compel. The opposing attorney became so angry when he received this motion that he filed seven motions to compel in response, even though the woman had always provided the requested information promptly. Preparing and filing the seven motions was very costly. The woman did receive some emotional satisfaction from the fact that her husband had to pay his attorney for his wasted efforts.

The Financial Issues

The first important point to remember is *preserve your assets*. This piece of advice may surprise and puzzle you. But, it is much more important to fund a retirement account than to fight in court about who gets the candlesticks. If possible, you should try to view your divorce from that perspective also. It can be difficult to be future oriented when you are operating in the emotional present. We have already talked about some of the emotional issues, however, so let's discuss the financial ones.

There is such a thing as a successful divorce, although many people scoff at the idea. Financially, four needs should be met before a divorce can be deemed successful:

❖ **An appropriate place to live.** This might sound odd, but in many areas of the country right now, renting or buying is a grueling process. There are always areas where the housing prices are high and finding an apartment is hard. To add to this problem, you need to have an assessment done so that you know what the right move is for you to make. Renting could be the answer if you have a low income and little money for a down payment and can't use the tax deductions. On the other hand, everyone has to live somewhere, and it is usually true that if someone earns over $40,000 per year, the deductions for real estate tax and mortgage interest result in a considerable reduction in income tax owed. The hard part is that, as with many things in divorce, there is no cookie-cutter answer. A person with little income but a small mortgage and monthly house payment might be better off keeping the house. There is no pat answer. So before you negotiate to keep the house or decide to sell, find out what effect these actions will have. To know before you act, use a tax software program; consult an accountant, a CPA, or a CDP; or use estimates from a real estate agent or mortgage broker.

❖ **Little or no debt.** Debt is such a challenge in our society. There are people who make $300,000 per year and are drowning in credit card debt. The temptation to use credit cards is so great, and banks and credit card companies make using their cards so appealing. It's no wonder that when many people divorce, deciding who pays which debts is a real problem. As you will learn in Chapter 6, "Cash Flow—the Foundation for Building Wealth," if you overspend or underearn you are heading for trouble. The shame in this situation is that if you have to make credit card payments in addition to paying the essentials, you most likely won't save money. If you don't save and invest, your financial future is put in jeopardy. When educated about the problem, people do realize the effect that making monthly debt payments has on their ability to accumulate wealth. For that reason, using savings and investments to pay off credit cards, cars, and other debts is quite common before dividing the other assets. If you can start debt free and stay that way, it will be much easier to save for college and retirement and have money for those emergencies that always seem to happen when you least expect them to.

❖ **Investments for retirement.** A very common asset division in divorce is for the wife to keep the house and trade away her right to her husband's retirement account. This results in the wife being house rich and money poor. The worst scenario is that after a few years the wife has spent any savings or other investments she did receive and must then sell the house. She traded away real security for what turned out to be false security. Everyone needs money set aside for retirement. It doesn't matter whether you have earned one dollar in your life from a paying job. This is the reason spousal IRAs were invented. Even the federal government knows that saving money is not only a good idea, but also an essential one. In the past 30 years, the federal government has encouraged citizens to take the initiative to save and invest for the future. The Retirement Equity Act of 1984 made retirement accounts part of marital assets, no matter whose name is on the account. So if your spouse saved money in a 401(k), an IRA, or other retirement account during your marriage, you are entitled to a portion of it. Money in a retirement account grows tax-free until you start taking it out. So while you are negotiating your property settlement, just stop and think about all the pros and cons of trading away your right to retirement assets. Even though you will collect Social Security, it will probably not be enough.

❖ **Liquid assets.** Included in liquid assets are stocks, bonds, mutual funds, savings accounts, and money market accounts. In short, any asset that is already cash or can quickly be converted to cash. After divorce, buying furniture is almost always a must. One household becomes two and there are almost never enough beds, tables, chairs, or televisions to go around. Every financial advisor will tell you to have some money saved for a rainy day. The usual recommendation is three to six months of normal living expenses. Owning liquid assets keeps you from having to go into debt if an emergency occurs.

There will always be exceptions to these four needs, but from past experiences, it has been proven those exceptions are very few.

Managing and Controlling Your Divorce

One of the most frustrating situations is when you must take responsibility for decisions made by others. Divorce is the same way. Keep in mind that decisions made while negotiating the divorce settlement will affect you for the rest of your life. It is up to you to make sure those decisions are the right ones.

Going through a divorce can be like being in the funnel of a tornado. Everything is going on around you at once. In the tornado called divorce, what's going on around you is legal, financial, and emotional turmoil. Concepts must be learned and understood and decisions made while trying to keep your feelings and actions in check. It is natural to want someone else to take all the responsibility.

Don't let that happen. You must take charge or you will lose your voice and the ability to influence your own future. The professionals who help you—the attorney, CPA, therapist, or whoever—

are there to assist. You should listen to their advice and use their expertise, but only you should make the important decisions. As with many other life experiences, you must be in control. You must direct the action and "manage" your divorce. Sounds easy, you say, but how exactly can this be done? By breaking down the divorce process into a series of manageable steps. In this way, all the overwhelming details and actions that must be taken are much easier to handle. Each chapter in this book has been written to help you become educated, get organized, and avoid making mistakes. In this book, you will find the tools to create your personal action plan. You should make notes in the margins, copy pages, complete the worksheets, and then share the end results with people who can help you.

A Team Approach

You have powerful allies who can provide education, guidance, and support concerning the emotional, legal, and financial issues you confront. These professionals make up your "divorce team."

First is the attorney, the professional everyone automatically thinks of first. That's because divorce is primarily seen as a legal event, not as a series of actions that produce a legal outcome. Attorneys are educated in specific state and federal laws and licensed to give legal opinions and advice. They should perform the role of counselor. Typically, they help work out child custody arrangements, determine separate property, and review and file necessary documents for dissolution of the marriage. An attorney can be your best ally by being an advocate for you in proceedings with other attorneys or in court actions. Good attorneys should place the client's best interests above all else and should be willing to refer clients to other professionals to get the best possible advice. If your attorney is not "mediation friendly" but prefers litigation, then you should probably look elsewhere. Your first steps toward achieving a fair financial settlement—attempting to get information and negotiating with your spouse—should always be cooperative in nature.

The certified public accountant (CPA) answers vital questions about matters that could save or cost you money in a divorce. The CPA is a tax specialist who keeps current on both federal and state tax laws, can assist you in minimizing taxes you pay, prepares tax returns, and gives tax advice.

A certified divorce planner (CDP) is a professional who has financial expertise in divorce-specific issues, such as calculating child support, preparing cash-flow analyses, and producing spreadsheets and charts that show the results of different asset and debt divisions. The CDP is an objective analyst who, through the use of software programs, can present the factual information divorcing couples need to make the best decisions. Both of the divorcing parties may agree it's best for one person to keep the marital home after divorce, but a cash-flow analysis can actually show the financial consequences of that decision. Information of this nature is invaluable in removing emotions from the financial decision-making process.

Pension experts are knowledgeable about private and public employee pensions. Civil Service Retirement System, Federal Employment Retirement Systems, military retirement pensions, 401(k), and Deferred Compensation and Employee Stock Option Program are plans that become marital property if the money or benefits have been accumulated during the marriage. Therefore, the money and benefits from these plans are often the most valuable assets that must be divided. Pension experts evaluate and calculate the marital portion of these plans and also prepare the court orders and *Qualified Domestic Relations Orders* necessary to divide them.

Members of the clergy are educated and experienced in explaining church policies and procedures that deal with divorce. Most important, clergy offer counsel and guidance. In many faiths, divorce is against the laws of the church. Getting advice on coming to terms with the spiritual consequences and planning for how you will practice your faith after the divorce is invaluable emotional support.

Mortgage brokers, real estate agents, and property appraisers offer services that are vital to settling the division of marital assets. Often the house is the biggest asset people own. It is also an emotional asset; women often want to keep the house since it's a symbol of security and family history. Real estate professionals prepare estimates on mortgage refinancing and home valuation that are used in an analysis of the divorce settlement. If either party needs to buy or rent after the divorce, a real estate agent can help with that also.

The use of a *mediator* can be a great tool in the divorce process. Many times a couple has one or more issues they cannot resolve themselves. A mediator serves as a guide in helping the two parties come to an agreement. Many mediators have backgrounds in psychology, psychiatry, or social work. Depending on state regulations, the mediator can draft a memorandum, agreement, or property settlement agreement that formalizes the financial and legal terms the couple has agreed on. It is best to have only an attorney or qualified mediator draft the property settlement agreement because of regulations about the unauthorized practice of law.

A therapist can help someone going through a divorce deal with the emotional turmoil that often occurs during this time. Anger, guilt, and especially fear can make it difficult to make rational, objective decisions. Decisions about children should be made with a clear head. A stay-at-home mom might have a big problem imagining her soon-to-be ex-husband being a proper caretaker of the kids during overnight visits. The ability to recognize and deal with such anxiety is essential in reaching custody decisions. Therapists educate their clients and help prepare them for imminent lifestyle changes.

You may need the assistance of all or just one of these professionals. The important thing is that you are aware expertise is available if you need it.

The Bottom Line

Keeping your focus now can help you have a solid foundation to build on for the future.

Chapter 4

Getting Organized

Capsule Outlook

You can't get where you want to go until you know where you are right now.

Whether you plan to negotiate the division of assets and debts, child custody, and other details directly with your spouse or have an attorney negotiate for you, you must have a complete and accurate knowledge of your present financial situation. This means knowing about all the assets and debts, whose name they are in, and what they're worth. Many times, one spouse has little or no knowledge about the assets and debts because the other spouse always assumed that responsibility. It is not uncommon for one spouse to manage all the monthly bills, investments, and other financial matters with little or no assistance from his or her partner. That's okay—as long as both spouses know what is going on in the marriage financially. If this doesn't happen, it could cause difficulties when the relationship starts heading for divorce.

Sharing Information vs. the Cost of Not Cooperating

Chapter 1, "You're Getting a Divorce—Now What?" described the traditional divorce method, including all the steps involved if this is the route you have to take. We refer to the basic divorce process as the "kitchen table method" because the kitchen table is where most sharing of information takes place and where most people organize the information needed for the settlement agreement. Often, there aren't many assets accumulated during the marriage, which makes it easy because there isn't much to fight about. It's important to know that disclosing information to your spouse gives him or her some of your power. Yes, knowledge is power. But if you or your spouse refuses to provide the needed information, you could lose—big time, as the following example demonstrates.

Leeann and Rob had been married for 15 years. Leeann had attended college for one year, but left before getting her Associate's degree. She worked on and off at part-time jobs after the marriage. Rob always wanted Leeann to stay home and take care of the family's needs, which Leeann did willingly. During their marriage, Rob controlled the income, spending, and investments, and paid all the bills. Leeann wasn't really interested in the family's investments and ran the house on the budget Rob had given her. When Rob decided he wanted a divorce, Leeann's lack of knowledge about the family's finances proved to be a big disadvantage.

At first, Leeann tried to reason with Rob and asked repeatedly for information about where their money was invested and how much Rob made each month. Rob was reluctant to provide any information. As a result, there were no negotiations. Finally Leeann was forced to retain an attorney. Rob saw this move as a threat to his authority and became more resistant than before. After two years of fighting over everything from child custody to when to sell the house, a judge divided Leeann and Rob's property, set the amount of alimony Leeann was to receive, and decided the child custody arrangements. Leeann was wiser but much poorer after it was all over. By having to defend herself against every legal maneuver her husband started, Leeann's legal bill alone was over $60,000! The judge divided the property 50-50 and was so disgusted with all the legal maneuvering that had happened that Leeann received no attorney's fees from Rob, even though the legal fees she owed were a result of defending herself. No one said divorce was always fair.

Working with Your Spouse

There's an old saying: "Cooperate and graduate." Work together, combine your knowledge and talents, and everyone is successful. This is an old military adage and it is especially true in the divorce process. When both parties disclose all assets, debts, income, and expenses right at the beginning, there is usually no need to retain attorneys to go through discovery. But, when one spouse is not upfront and tries to hide assets or stall the divorce process by not cooperating, discovery might become necessary.

The big problem is that discovery takes time and is expensive. By not providing account statements, an expense form, and other information, the divorce can become costly financially *and* emotionally. If you and your spouse decide you both can put aside any negative emotions and cooperate, your chances of preserving your assets and leaving the marriage financially and emotionally stable are much greater.

Putting Together a Pre-Divorce Checklist

Possessing accurate and complete information is essential to any professional you work with during your divorce. It definitely takes time to assemble this information, but don't procrastinate. When negotiating a settlement agreement, you must take into account all aspects of your life—parental, financial, and legal. Using the following checklist as a guide will help you become organized and make the best use of your time. The personal and legal information you need includes …

❖ Your name and home and business addresses and phone numbers.

- ❖ Name, addresses, and phone numbers of your spouse.
- ❖ Name, address, and phone number of your spouse's attorney.
- ❖ Social Security numbers for you, your spouse, and your children.
- ❖ Dates of birth for you, your spouse, and children.
- ❖ Prior marriages for you and your spouse and details of the divorce.
- ❖ Names and ages of children from prior marriages and custody arrangements.
- ❖ Date and place of marriage.
- ❖ Length of time residing in your state.
- ❖ Prenuptial agreement, if one was signed.
- ❖ Grounds for divorce, if applicable.
- ❖ Date of separation, if applicable.
- ❖ Details of current employment and income for you and your spouse.
- ❖ Education, degrees, or training of you and your spouse.
- ❖ Job history, income potential, employee benefits, and retirement and pension plans for you and your spouse.
- ❖ Joint assets and liabilities.
- ❖ Separate or personal assets for each spouse.
- ❖ Incidences of abuse or threats and relevant court records.

Financial records include current statements from the following sources:

- ❖ Mortgage, debts and loans, credit cards, mutual fund companies, savings accounts and CDs, checking accounts, all retirement accounts, W-2s and pay/salary statements, and tax returns (for the past five years)
- ❖ Family business records that include type of business, shareholders, percentage of ownership of business, bank statements, tax returns, loan applications, income and balance sheets, and financial reports

The Personal Information Form

Appendix A, "Forms," provides a Personal Information Form, which is a great starting point. This form organizes some of the same information listed on the pre-divorce checklist and will serve as a handy reference for your use as well as any professional you may work with. It might seem a bit long, but most of the information you'll know right off the top of your head. The form also asks how you would like your assets and debts divided. It is much better to think about the asset and debt division now than to wait and see what you are offered.

Let's go through this form page by page. We'll provide explanations where necessary. So get out birth certificates, Social Security cards, business cards, retirement statements, and car titles and let's get started:

1. **Your personal information.** If you retain an attorney to negotiate your divorce settlement or prepare the settlement agreement, all the information in this form is vital, especially the dates of marriage and separation.

2. **Your employment information.** How often you are paid determines your monthly income for child support and alimony calculations. If you have a Defined Benefit Pension (U.S. government employees, military members, and some private corporations), your date of hire is essential in determining how much of your pension you must share with your spouse.

3. **Your spouse's personal information.** This information is also needed for your settlement agreement.

4. **Your spouse's employment information.** This information is needed, as is your own, for child support and pension calculations.

5. **Your children's information.** The names, birth dates, and Social Security numbers of any children born during your marriage are included in your settlement agreement when specifying child custody arrangements. Refer to Chapter 5, "Dealing with Child Support and Alimony," to learn more about the different types of custody.

6. **Health insurance information.** Health insurance is one factor included in the child support calculations. Remember, only the premium amount needed to insure the children is included. Only family members are eligible to be covered under an employee's health and dental insurance. Therefore, after the divorce you may be required to pay your own health insurance premiums. If you don't do your homework on the future costs, you could be in for quite a surprise. If you aren't employed now or don't have access to health insurance through your employer, you might be able to be covered under your ex-spouse's insurance for 36 months after the divorce. The only problem is that you will not pay the same rates as your ex-spouse because you aren't an employee or family member. Don't be surprised if the health insurance premiums are over $250 per month. This cost is average for a single person's premium who is not eligible for a group plan.

7. **Mortgage information.** Most of this information is used to calculate the net equity in your home. A professional home appraiser can compare your home with recent sales of homes comparable to yours and give you an estimate of the fair market value. This is the price someone would pay for your home. If you plan to "buy out" your spouse's equity in the home, you definitely need to know the fair market value plus the other information on this page so that you can refinance or assume the mortgage in your own name.

8. **Automobile information.** The net equity in your auto is the amount remaining after subtracting what you owe from the amount it would be sold for. Auto equity is an asset, too, and is often included in the property division. Usually the person who takes possession of the auto after the divorce makes the car payments. You can get a good idea of your car's worth by visiting www.KelleyBlueBook.com, but complete this page first because you'll need all these details to get the retail and trade-in values. An average of these two values is a fair assessment of your car's estimated selling price.

9. **Retirement plans.** These abbreviations and terms might seem foreign to you, but it's important that you understand what they mean. Almost all government employees participate in either the Civil Service Retirement System or the Federal Employees Retirement System. They are defined benefit pensions that pay you or your spouse a certain pension amount every month after retirement for the remainder of you or your spouse's lifetime. The Thrift Savings Plan, or TSP, is a voluntary retirement account that employees contribute to each payday. Members of the Armed Forces do not have a Thrift Savings Plan but earn a Defined Benefit Pension the same as other government employees. The 401(k) plan for employees of public companies allows a portion of an employee's pay to be saved in a special account every payday. Most employers make matching contributions to these accounts. Individual retirement accounts (IRAs) are retirement savings accounts that enable individuals to save $2,000 per year in a tax-deferred account. There are different kinds of IRAs, the most popular two being the traditional and the Roth. The advantages of these accounts and their differences will be explained in Chapter 12, "Now What?"

10. **Separate property information.** This is any property such as land, houses, jewelry, retirement plans, and other assets that you had saved or inherited before your marriage. Make your list now and in Chapter 7, "Dividing Your Assets and Debts," we'll discuss whether you might be able to exclude some of these assets from the division of assets.

11. **Asset information.** Use the information at the top of this page plus your pre-divorce checklist to list all the assets you and your spouse own now. An appraisal may be necessary for some items. Don't guess on the values, especially the selling price of your house or other items that might have appreciated since your marriage. Furniture and other household items are usually considered *personal property* and divided separately from the division of *real property,* such as retirement or savings accounts. It could be determined later that one or more of these items is separate property, but it's

important to know all assets that may be considered for division.

12. **Debt information.** Any credit card balances, auto loans, mortgages, personal loans from friends or family, and loans you have taken from a retirement account should be listed here. *Separately owed debts* are those that you or your spouse have agreed to pay or, in some states, debts accrued after the date you and your spouse separated.

13. **Asset and debt division.** Preferably, you and your spouse can talk about how you want to divide the assets and debts. Many couples use the "kitchen table method" to make a list of everything and sit down and divvy it up. Since you want as much control and input into the divorce process as possible, now is the time to state your wants and wishes. Many couples start with a 50-50 split and then make adjustments depending on the circumstances. Keep in mind that 40 of our 50 states are *equitable distribution* states, which means that all marriage factors are taken into account when deciding the division. Splitting everything equally may work in your case, but it might not.

14. **Future lifestyle.** You should have a say in controlling your own future. Analyzing the information you have assembled should give you a clear picture of whether a particular division of assets, such as keeping the house and giving up a portion of your spouse's retirement assets, is in your best interests. Right now, just put your wants and wishes into words. After finishing this book you'll have a pretty good idea whether these decisions are the right ones for you.

Figuring Out Your Money Situation

Perhaps the toughest task for people when gathering financial information is finding out where all the money goes every month. It's not too hard to make money, but it sure is easy to spend it! But that's exactly what you are going to do: Find out how much you are spending and what you are spending it on.

In Appendix A, you will find a Monthly Income, Expense, and Debt (MIED) form. This detailed one-page form gives you a concise snapshot of your monthly expenditures, fixed debts, and credit card balances that you owe. Spending categories have been included on the form plus some blank lines so that you can adapt this form to include everything for your particular circumstances.

In the top-right corner you are asked to state three amounts:

- ❖ **Gross pay per month.** To get this amount, multiply the gross pay from your latest pay statement by the number of times you are paid each year. Most people are paid biweekly (every two weeks) for a total of 26 paychecks per year. If you are paid twice a month, probably at the middle and end of each month, you will have 24 paychecks per year.

- ❖ **Required retirement.** This is money that is taken from your pay if you participate in a defined benefit plan, such as the civil service plans that are shown. Money contributed to a 401(k) is voluntary and should not be shown on the MIED form.

- ❖ **Any other income.** This includes income from a trust fund, any personal business you have besides your regular employment, and significant interest, dividends, and capital gains from investments.

Now, how do you know what amounts to put in the categories of spending? There are two ways in which this can be done.

Figuring Out Your Expenses

If you use a software program such as Microsoft Money or Quicken, then you already enter your checks in the program and assign the money to categories similar to those on the MIED. Simply print out a categorized transaction report for the past month's—or preferably, an average of the past six months— spending, and use this information to fill in the blanks on the MIED.

If you are keeping track of your finances using your check register, figuring out the various amounts is a bit more time-consuming.

Write down each category from the MIED (it might take several pages). Using the check register from your checkbook, find the first check you wrote six months ago, at the beginning of that particular month. Decide which category each check should be placed into. If you wrote a check to the Honda dealership for repairs on your car, write the amount of that check in the category designated "Automobile—Repair/Tags/Inspection," and so on. Continue categorizing each check until you have reached the most current check. Then add the amounts in each category, divide by six, and write the average amount from each category in the corresponding space on the MIED. The average amount in each category will give you an excellent idea of how much you are spending and on what.

Are you surprised? Most people are because they rarely track their spending as you have just done.

Using the Monthly Income, Expense, and Debt Form

The MIED is used in the divorce process in two main ways:

❖ **Calculation of alimony.** Since alimony is based on need and the ability to pay, the MIED is a valuable tool in determining how much, if any, alimony will be needed to help a spouse live independently. The information on this form should portray reasonable living expenses. The tendency for some people, when completing this form, is to overstate their expenses, thereby making it look like they need more money to live on than is really necessary. This is not wise. If you are using this form to negotiate alimony with your spouse, inflating your living expenses could make your spouse defensive and harm the chances of reaching a settlement. If you must give testimony in court under oath, chances are good that an opposing attorney will ask about your standard of living during the marriage. If there is a significant difference between your prior standard of living and the expense amounts stated on the MIED, the opposing attorney could take this opportunity to question you in great detail and attempt to discredit any previous answers you have given.

❖ **Division of assets and debts.** There are a number of factors all states consider when deciding how marital property will be divided. These factors are discussed in Chapter 7. If one spouse has more disposable income left after paying taxes and living expenses, he or she is more able to invest and accumulate assets quicker, giving him or her the capability to replace any assets given up by receiving less than a 50 percent share. As with alimony, you must present the facts and prove a need.

The following story demonstrates the advantages of being organized and how all this information can be used.

Jean is a woman in her late 60s, smart, professional, and somewhat old-fashioned in her thinking. You see, she knew her husband had strayed during their marriage but always thought that they would stay together despite their problems. One day Jean received a phone call at work. A friend told Jean that her husband had a truck and was moving antique furniture out of the house. Jean came home and confronted her husband. And that's how Jean found out that her husband wanted a divorce.

Jean was one smart cookie. She had saved records from the beginning of her marriage and had lists of expenses, autos, and house records from all the houses they had owned and kept almost every receipt she had acquired during their 25 years together. During the discovery process, Jean's attorney was almost overwhelmed at the amount of information she provided—and it proved very useful. Because Jean had receipts and could prove that her monthly expense statement was accurate and reasonable and could also prove her needs and contributions to the marriage, she received 63 percent of the assets, including half of her husband's pension. Her attorney also negotiated alimony for a period of time. All of this, plus well-placed investments and a reasonable lifestyle, enabled Jean to keep her house, maintain her lifestyle, and still travel several times a year.

The Bottom Line

After completing the forms explained in this chapter, you should have a much clearer perspective on your situation and be ready to formulate a negotiating strategy.

Chapter 5

Dealing with Child Support and Alimony

Capsule Outlook

There is usually a big difference between what people want and what they need.

Some of the most important decisions in many divorce settlements are those concerning future payments such as child support and alimony. These payments are essential to maintaining a decent standard of living for children and ex-spouses as well. This chapter will explain these concepts, offer sample calculations, and provide sources of information so that you may know the laws pertaining to your state.

Defining Child Support

Child support is a dollar amount approximation of the monthly basic living necessities for one or more children. Child support payments cover the essentials: the child's portion of housing, food, clothing, health and dental insurance, and other incidentals. Each state has a formula, often in the form of a chart, for computing child support. Most often the gross incomes of both

parents are added together. Then the number of children is fac-
tored into the formula. Three other items may be added to the
basic support amount:

1. **Unusual medical or dental needs.** The monthly amount
   paid to a dentist or orthodontist for braces is often added
   to the basic amount as well as any unusual medications/
   therapy that are ongoing and require payments above the
   amount paid by a health insurer.

2. **Work-related child care.** Since it is common for both parents to be employed, work-related child care is also added to
   the guideline amount. Work-related child care is the amount
   you must pay to have someone care for your children during your working hours. If both parents individually pay for
   child care, the amount both parents pay is included in the
   calculation.

3. **Medical and dental plans.** Children must be covered under
   medical and dental plans. Therefore, the monthly amount
   paid for these premiums is included in the calculation.
   Whichever parent pays the premiums directly from his or
   her paycheck has the amount of the premium deducted
   from his or her share of child support. We'll illustrate this
   point shortly when discussing the Child Support Worksheet.

The Amount of Child Support

The amount of child support that is actually paid from one parent to the other depends on a number of variables. First, where
does the child physically reside? Does one parent have sole custody of the child or do the parents share custody? If the arrangement is for shared custody, how many days of the year does the
child stay with each parent? If both parents have health and dental benefits from their employment, who should cover the children for these benefits?

Also be aware that child support guidelines are just that—guidelines. Sometimes the parent who pays child support offers to pay
more because of various sports and after-school activities in
which the children are involved. In "Calculating Child Support,"
later in this chapter, we will pin down the monthly expenses for

children so you will have a clearer idea of the amount that's required.

The Duration of Child Support

Child support is usually meant to last until the child becomes self-supporting or is no longer considered a minor. The age at which a child is no longer considered a minor varies by state. In many states it is when he or she reaches age 18. In other states, it is age 21. Many states consider graduation from high school a life event that signifies the child is no longer a minor. Other life events could include joining the military, full-time employment, or marriage.

Custody Considerations

Usually, when people talk about custody they are referring to the living arrangements of the children. But, as any parent knows, there is much more to raising children than just occupying the same residence. This is the reason for two distinct types of child custody.

Legal Custody

The definition of legal custody is the right and responsibility to make decisions about the child's welfare. This right includes making major decisions such as where the child goes to school and what religion the child practices. It also extends to many minor decisions that affect the child's life. The majority of parents share legal custody. Both the father and mother want the ability to influence their child's welfare. If one of the parents is deemed unfit to have decision-making ability, the other parent can petition the court to have sole legal custody. Legal custody continues until the child has reached the age of majority or is otherwise considered to be of age.

Physical Custody

Perhaps the most important decision that is made before the divorce is who the children live with. Many years ago it was almost automatically assumed that children would live with the mother after divorce and the father would have visitation rights. As women entered the workplace in greater numbers, however, many fathers started to assume more active roles in the care and parenting of their children. Although it is still quite common for children to live primarily with their mother, it is also becoming more common for children to live with their fathers or to share the time they reside with each parent. The different types of physical custody are defined by the amount of time the child lives with each parent.

In general, there are three different types of physical custody:

❖ **Sole custody** means the children physically spend the majority of their time with one parent. The other parent usually has visitation rights; the most common schedule is that the child will stay with the visitation parent every other weekend. Other common overnight stays are during summer vacation, Easter and Christmas break, and Mother's or Father's Day.

❖ **Shared custody** is defined as the children residing with each parent more than the defined minimum amount of days per year. Each state is different in its definition of the minimum amount of shared days. Also, many states vary in their definition of a "day." Some states may require that the child be in the parent's physical care for a continuous 24-hour period while other states might require only a certain number of hours per day. The number of hours or overnight stays is then added together to meet the required minimum number of days. Before deciding on shared custody as the most appropriate arrangement for your family, you must know your state's requirement.

❖ **Split custody** means that, in families with more than one child, the children's physical residences are divided between the two parents. Each parent has sole custody of at least one child and visitation with the other child or children. This type of arrangement is extremely rare since children generally prefer to reside together, but it can occur if it is decided to be in the children's best interest.

Calculating Child Support

This is the case of Steve and Jean who have two children, ages 8 and 11. Since Steve does a lot of traveling with his job, it was decided that Jean should have sole physical custody of both children. The following figure shows the child support worksheet for Steve and Jean.

Follow along as we go step-by-step through the form to reach the child support amount to be paid.

A. Gross Income of Parties

1. **Line A1:** Jean earns $3,167 per month and Steve earns $6,083.

2. **Line A2:** There is no alimony to be paid to Steve or Jean.

3. **Line A3:** The adjusted gross incomes are the same as in A1.

4. **Line A4:** Adding Steve and Jean's income together, the total amount of gross income per month is $9,250.

5. **Line A5:** Jean earns 34.2 percent of the combined gross income and Steve earns 65.8 percent.

6. **Line A6:** There are two children, ages 11 and 8.

B. Child Support

1. **Line B1:** Looking at the following Child Support Guidelines, find a gross monthly income of $9,250 in the far left column and then follow this number across until you are in the column for Two Children. You can see the amount is $1,527.

2. **Line B2:** There are no extraordinary medical/dental expenses, so this line is left blank.

3. **Line B3:** Jean pays $225 per month so that someone can watch the children after school until she gets home from work.

4. **Line B4:** Steve has $40 per month deducted from his paycheck to pay the monthly premiums so that the children are covered under his medical/dental plan at work.

5. **Line B5:** Adding B1, B3, and B4 together results in the Total Child Support Need of $1,793 per month.

6. **Line B6:** Jean's portion of the Total Child Support Need will be 34.2 percent, or $614, and Steve's portion will be 65.8 percent, or $1,139. Therefore, Steve will pay Jean $1,139 each month.

CHILD SUPPORT GUIDELINE WORKSHEET

For sole custody support cases with no
spousal support or spousal support
calculated on a separate form.

Smith   v.   Smith

Worksheet of: Steve and Jean Smith

Chancery No.

Date: 4/10/01

A. GROSS INCOME OF PARTIES	Mother	Father	
1. Monthly Gross Income of Each Party:	$3,167	$6,083	**Spousal Support**
2. Spousal Support Payable Between Parties:			
			Spousal Payor
3. Adjusted Gross Income for Child Support:	$3,167	$6,083	☐ Husband
4. Combined Gross Income:	$9,250	Income Shares	☐ Wife
5. Each Party's Percent of Combined Income:	34.2%	65.8%	
6. Number of Children: __2__ Ages: 11, 8			**Custodian:** X Mother / ☐ Father

B. CHILD SUPPORT

1. Schedule Amount for Basic Child Support:		$1,528	From Support Table
2. Extraordinary Medical/Dental Expenses:			
3. Work-related Child Care Costs:		$225	
4. Medical Insurance for Child/Children:		$40	**Child Support Need**
5. Total Child Support Need (Sum: 1+2+3+4):	——————→		**$1,793**
	Mother	Father	
6. Child Support Obligation of Each Party:	$614	$1,179	
(Total Support Need x Income Share)			
7. Direct Payment of Medical Insurance (Subtract):		($40)	
8. Each Party's Presumptive Guideline Share:	$614	$1,139	
			Guideline Child Support
9. Guideline Child Support Payable by Non-Custodial Parent:	——————→		**$1,139**

C. PROPOSED DEVIATIONS FROM GUIDELINE SUPPORT:

1. _____   _____
   _____   _____
   _____   _____

2. Each Party's Proposed share:	$614	$1,139	
			TOTAL CHILD SUPPORT

D. PROPOSED ADJUSTED CHILD SUPPORT: ——————→   **$1,139**

Child Support Payable To   Mother

Submitted by: _____

Counsel for: _____

3/7/00

Child Support Worksheet for Steve and Jean.

Section C can be completed whenever there are deviations, such as sports camps or music lessons.

Child support covers the basic necessities of life, but who pays for new winter coats, allowances, or a $500 bill from the emergency room when Jimmy gets a broken arm playing soccer? How are these "extras" divided? Many people have this question specifically addressed in the settlement agreement. Extraordinary medical/dental or other expenses can be divided in several ways: One parent can pay the entire expense; the expense can be paid *pro rata*, or by percentage of total income (remember Steve and Jean? Jean made 34.2 percent of the combined monthly income and Steve made 65.8 percent); or payment of the extraordinary expense can be divided 50-50. Although this issue is a negotiable item in the settlement agreement, extra expenses are usually divided pro rata, especially if one parent makes a much greater salary than the other.

Whichever parenting arrangement is chosen in your particular case, the children's well-being and happiness should always be the primary reasons for choosing one arrangement over the others.

Now that you know the basics about calculating child support, think about what your opinion would be if you were a judge listening to the following story.

Nancy was married to Jess for 16 years and they had three children. During their marriage, they had made a good living, with a combined income of over $100,000 per year. They lived well during their marriage. They had a lovely home and late-model cars and always sent their children to private schools, courses at area museums, and sports camps during the summer. Nancy and Jess also saved for retirement and always paid off their credit cards every month. Their incomes were enough to pay their living expenses, taxes, some savings, and extras for the children.

When the decision was made to divorce, Nancy expressed her firm opinion that the children should not have to suffer and should have the same lifestyle as before the divorce. This meant private school, museum courses, and sports camps as well as private day care. A big problem arose when child support was calculated with all the "extras" added in. The amount Jess would have to pay to Nancy left little money for his living expenses. Nancy and Jess tried talking it out but always ended up in a deadlock. This went on for over three months, with the kids still attending private school and taking extra courses; all the while Jess barely had enough money to pay the rent on his apartment. By this time, Jess had become quite frustrated because Nancy would not budge on the extras she wanted added into the child support calculations. Jess finally threatened to retain an attorney. The matter was settled shortly afterward in mediation. The compromise was that the kids would attend private school until the end of the term and then transfer to public school the next fall.

Was Nancy unreasonable in her request for private schooling and extra activities to continue, even if Jess couldn't afford to pay for these things and his personal expenses?

Concerning Alimony/Spousal Maintenance

Alimony, or spousal maintenance, is an area that causes a great amount of debate and emotional turmoil during the negotiation of the financial settlement agreement. Most often the receiver of alimony is a woman who has been largely responsible for raising the children and, therefore, sacrificed monetary gain and career advancement. The payer, usually the husband, might feel as though he should not have to "take care" of his ex-wife forever. This is where it really pays to have gotten your "emotional divorce," as mentioned in Chapter 1, "You're Getting a Divorce— Now What?"—the issue of alimony should be based on the financial issues of the marital situation, not guilt or revenge. We have found through experience that this area often lacks guidelines and is open to negotiation. Having the complete facts on your present situation is invaluable.

Alimony According to the IRS

To be designated as alimony, payments must meet *all* the following requirements:

❖ The payment must be made in cash (a check or money order is considered cash for these purposes).

❖ The divorce decree does not designate the payment as *not* alimony. Section 71(b)(2) requires that payments must be made according to a divorce decree or separation agreement. You and your spouse can't agree verbally to these payments and then be able to deduct or claim the payments for tax purposes.

❖ The spouses are not members of the same household at the time the payments are made. This requirement applies only if the spouses are legally separated under a decree of divorce or separate maintenance.

❖ There is no liability to make any payment (in cash or property) after the death of the recipient spouse.

❖ The payment is not treated as child support.

This information was taken directly from Internal Revenue Publication 504, which addresses information specifically for divorced or separated individuals. We strongly recommend that you order this publication and read it several times to thoroughly understand the tax implications of many of the issues you will be dealing with during your divorce. You can order this publication by calling the IRS at 1-800-829-3676 or logging on to the IRS Web site at www.irs.gov. A wealth of publications and forms are available and can be downloaded and printed out directly from the Web site.

Considerations for Alimony

The two factors that are primarily considered in negotiating or awarding alimony are need and the ability to pay. That means the receiver—through pay statements, a monthly expense report, and other means—must show that he or she is presently incapable of providing enough income to meet basic living expenses. The payer, through the same documents, demonstrates that he or she has enough income to afford to pay alimony that enables the ex-spouse to live independently. In Chapter 8, "Putting It All Together," you will actually be completing a Monthly Income, Expense, and Debt form (MIED) that will be the basis of your present financial situation.

Duration of Alimony

One of the most common questions asked when a couple is negotiating the settlement agreement is, "How long should alimony last?" That depends. A number of factors can determine the length or term of alimony, including your particular state laws; whether the details on alimony were negotiated between you and your spouse or were set by a judge in court; you and your spouse's ages, health, and education; the grounds for the divorce action; length of the marriage; any new training or education that might be needed; and earning capacity. These factors vary by state. A consultation with an attorney for a legal opinion may be a good idea at this point. Definitely research the laws in the state where you live. Local libraries have the state code or laws in the reference section. It really pays to become educated about your rights in this area.

The Three Types of Alimony

There are three types of alimony:

- ❖ **Permanent or lifetime**, which continues until the receiving spouse remarries or either spouse dies.

- ❖ **Period or term**, which continues until a certain date, event such as remarriage, or length of time.

- ❖ **Rehabilitative**, which is usually for a shorter duration and awarded so that the spouse earning less can get job experience or attend college or training courses to obtain or upgrade his or her skills and knowledge.

Rehabilitative spouse maintenance is especially important to people who have worked part-time, interrupted their careers, or not received the education necessary to be completely self-sufficient. Many times the divorce process is begun with little notice to one of the spouses. I call this "unexpected independence." The spouse who was not expecting the divorce would probably call it "terror." The thought of being financially independent with little or no notice and with a limited earning capacity is a frightening situation, but becoming educated about your own financial situation definitely relieves some of the anxiety.

How Much Alimony Do I Get?

That's the $64,000 question about alimony. The amount of the alimony payment depends on the laws of the state in which you reside, your personal circumstances, and sometimes on the persuasiveness of your attorney. There are counties and jurisdictions that have guidelines for spousal maintenance, Fairfax County, Virginia is one example. Spousal maintenance is negotiated much more often than child support. One jurisdiction has two formulas, depending upon whether child support is to be paid.

Calculating Alimony Without Minor Children

Let's take a look at the facts about Mary Jones, whose children are grown and who has worked part-time over the past 15 years. Mary makes $1,250 per month at her part-time job. Her husband, Chuck, earns $6,000 per month. As an example of local guidelines, the following alimony calculation would be used to determine support while a divorce suit was pending if Mary and Chuck lived in Fairfax, Virginia:

Chuck's Income:	$6,000 × 30% = $1,800
Mary's Income:	$1,250 × 50% = $625
Recommended Alimony:	$1,175

Using this formula, $1,175 is the recommended amount for Chuck to pay Mary each month.

Calculating Alimony with Minor Children

If Mary and Chuck had a child considered of minor age, the Fairfax, Virginia, formula is as follows:

Chuck's Income:	$6,000 × 28% = $1,680
Mary's Income:	$1,250 × 58% = $725
Recommended Alimony	$955

Factoring in children who are minors, $955 is the recommended amount for Chuck to pay Mary each month.

In many states, if alimony is to be paid, it is calculated first and then child support is calculated. This method is used because alimony increases the receiver's monthly income and decreases the payer's monthly income.

Important reminder: Even if you live in a county or state that has recommended guidelines for the payment of alimony, you must still prove a need (for the receiver) and an ability to pay (for the payer). And just because there's a formula available to recommend a certain amount does not guarantee you will receive that amount. We know by now that you are beginning to understand just how negotiable this issue is. Again, you need to know your financial situation, especially the amount required to pay your basic expenses. Going through all the various details in the divorce process is just like planning for a trip. You must know where you are right now before you can even consider your options for the future. Unfortunately, too many people who get divorced try to skip this step, with disastrous results.

A Lump Sum vs. Monthly Alimony Payments

In most instances, alimony is paid monthly by a check from the payer to the receiver. When a great deal of assets were accumulated during the marriage, however, it may be possible to make one large payment that satisfies the needs of the receiving spouse. A "lump sum" of potential future payments can be calculated by using the present value method. The *present value* is the amount of money needed to be invested in an account now so that the payer can make a specific payment each month for a specific length of time. This method takes into account the monthly payment amount, the number of payments to be made (the total number of months), and the GATT (General Agreement on Tariffs and Trade) interest rate.

A present value calculation is shown for Mary Jones, who calculated that she would need $1,175 each month for 20 years. The GATT Interest Rate used is 5.54 percent.

As you can see by the present value of alimony, although Mary would have received a total of $282,000 if Chuck had paid alimony of $1,175 each month for 20 years, the present value is much less. Ignoring income tax, the transfer of assets that Chuck would pay Mary is now $170,253.

Let's Talk Taxes

Child support payments have no tax effect. Any payments made for child support by a court order are not deductible by the payer or taxable to the payee. On the other hand, by IRS regulations, alimony is deductible by the payer and must be included in the receiver's income. You must know the true cost or benefit of alimony. Since it is income to the receiver, he or she must claim alimony as income when preparing income tax returns.

Tax Tip

Because of the tax effects of alimony and the IRS tax recapture rules, usually the receiver negotiates to receive additional assets equal to the present value amount. This is a one-time transfer of assets and no monthly payments are necessary, therefore there would be no tax implications.

Let's take a look again at the present value of alimony payments illustration used in the preceding section. You can see the marginal tax rates for both Chuck and Mary. Adding the federal and state tax rates together, Chuck is in the 35.5 percent bracket and Mary is in the 20.5 percent bracket. This tax effect of the monthly alimony payments can be seen in the lower left columns of the present value. Two present value amounts are given, one reflecting income tax and another one ignoring income tax. The present value of the 10 years of payments is $170,253 without considering the tax effects. But since monthly alimony amounts are usually taxable, Chuck would really be paying $112,188, and Mary would receive $138,203. That represents a savings to him of $58,065 and a loss of $32,050 to her. What an eye-opener!

What You See Is Not What You Really Get

When an amount of alimony is stated in a settlement agreement, receivers usually focus on that number and don't think about the net amount they will receive after payment of taxes. Ann's story is a good example. Ann has a son who is ready to start college. She and her husband are negotiating their settlement agreement and trying to figure out what would be the best way to pay tuition and other expenses. Either Ann's husband could pay $1,000 per month directly to the college and then claim his son as a dependent, or Ann could receive alimony in the amount of $1,000 per month, pay the expenses, and take the tax exemption for dependents. After the tax implications of the alimony were explained to Ann, she made the decision to let her husband pay the school directly. Why? Because of the tax effects of alimony payments. In reality, Ann would receive about $680 per month after paying federal and state taxes, and Ann's husband would pay about $600 per month because he could deduct the alimony.

Temporary vs. Permanent Payments

Child support and alimony calculations are to be used primarily for temporary payments while the settlement agreement is being negotiated. After all the factors of the case are known, it is much easier to determine the amounts needed for permanent payments. Sometimes different amounts are negotiated or ordered, but often the guideline amounts are used for the permanent payments.

Insuring Child Support and Alimony

Some of the best money you could ever spend is to ensure a future stream of income, whether the money is in the form of child support payments, alimony, or a part of your ex-spouse's pension. It is wise to stop and think about what happens when someone who makes monthly payments from his or her salary dies—the payments stop! Many attorneys always include mandatory insurance for child support in the settlement agreements they prepare, but insuring alimony is one detail in divorce preparations and negotiations that is commonly overlooked. Insurance for a pension will be discussed in Chapter 11, "After the Agreement Is Reached," so let's talk about insuring child support and alimony.

Almost without exception, a clause is included in the settlement agreement that the parent paying child support must maintain a life insurance policy that upon his or her death would be payable to a trustee for the children. In that situation, the life insurance death benefit is placed in an account, and each month money is withdrawn from the account and paid to the parent or guardian. This monthly withdrawal replaces the monthly child support payments from the deceased parent.

Insuring alimony is a little different from insuring child support. First, the person receiving the alimony payments should always be the owner and beneficiary of the insurance policy. Also, the receiver should pay the premiums to ensure that the payments are kept current and the policy doesn't lapse. Disability insurance on the payer can also be used if the payer can't work for a period of time. If the payer has no insurance or income and has to stop working for an extended period of time, he or she would probably try to get the settlement agreement changed, in states that allow modification, so that alimony payments could be reduced or stopped altogether. Even if state law does not allow modifying an agreement to pay spousal support, insurance is a good idea to prevent interruption of an income stream. True, insuring alimony does take a bite out of your monthly budget, but just think about what would happen if the payments stopped altogether and you had no backup plan. This is one reason so many women are in poverty after the divorce. Good planning prevents a bad future!

The Bottom Line

When receiving a future stream of income, such as child support or alimony, you need to know your rights, your needs, and how to protect yourself.

Chapter 6

Cash Flow—the Foundation for Building Wealth

Capsule Outlook

Spending more than you earn is bad. Not knowing that you spend more than you earn is worse.

Building wealth is like building a brick wall. You must stack brick upon brick to make the wall larger. Wealth is built the same way only instead of bricks, you must have dollars available to save and invest. If you spend more than you make, you will never build wealth. The first step in building wealth is knowing where you are right now.

Recognizing Your Financial Reality

The truth is that most people don't know their financial reality. You may be saying to yourself, "I know all about cash flow; the cash flows in and it flows right back out again." The money comes in and quickly goes back out, but where it goes is another matter.

One very common mistake is lack of planning for payment of federal and state taxes. There is usually too much or not enough withheld. One client purposely overwithholds for taxes each paycheck so that he can get a nice "bonus check" the next year. It was gently explained to him that it wasn't a bonus check. This was his own money being repaid to him, and the IRS wasn't paying him interest for the privilege of keeping his money all year. Also, if the correct amount was being withheld from his check each payday, he wouldn't be in debt from charging his groceries on credit cards.

Some men and women are in deep denial about their financial situation. About six months ago, we received an urgent call from a woman who had been referred for a cash-flow calculation. We found that she was desperate to reach a settlement agreement with her husband because she needed his signature to take out another mortgage on the house to pay off $40,000 in debt. It seems that she continually overspent and every two or three years had to declare bankruptcy. Her husband was anxious to have his finances separated from hers because he didn't want to be held responsible for any more of her debts. This couple made a very good living, but the wife continuously spent more than they made. Her daughter was enrolled in one of the most prestigious prep schools in the country, and the tuition was much more than they could afford. The wife refused to think about taking the daughter out of the school, stating that "they could find the money somewhere." To my knowledge, this couple has never settled their asset and debt division. The couple was referred to separate attorneys so they would each know their legal responsibilities concerning repayment of the $40,000 in debts that the wife still owed. The wife was unwilling to break the cycle of overspending.

Knowing Where You Really Are

There's an old saying: "The devil is in the details." This is very true when calculating your cash flow. Earning and spending is much more than just a two-part process. There are many small cogs in your financial wheel that you must be aware of so you can objectively see your situation and plan for your future. You may think you know the complete picture of your finances now, and the changes you will have to make after the divorce. A client also thought she knew, but found out just how wrong she was.

Kelly and Bruce had been married for 11 years and had two children. Kelly and Bruce both earned about $30,000 per year. Six years ago, Bruce changed careers and became a software engineer. As a result, his earning increased at a dramatic rate. Five years after his career change, his salary was $500,000 per year. Naturally, with so much money coming in, Kelly quit her job, took the kids out of daycare, and enjoyed a very lavish lifestyle. Bruce invested the money and paid the bills. Everything was fine until Kelly decided that she wanted a divorce.

Bruce and Kelly negotiated an equal split of all the assets. Bruce readily agreed to pay child support but felt that since Kelly could go back to nursing and earn at least $30,000 per year, she didn't need alimony. Kelly sought professional advice because she needed accurate, factual information to show Bruce that would prove she needed alimony. During her meeting with her advisor Kelly was unable to present a budget but knew that her monthly expenses, including those for the two children, were $2,600 per month. After completing a Monthly Income, Expense, and Debt Form and, after finishing estimating costs for all the categories, her expenses totaled $4,200 per month. Was Kelly ever surprised! She had never thought about how much it would take to live each month, because Bruce always paid the bills. But now, since she was taking the responsibility of establishing a budget and living by it, she became smart about her spending. She took the Cash Flow Worksheet back to Bruce and negotiated alimony that would enable her to pay her bills and save and invest for the future.

Using a Cash Flow Report

In Chapter 4, "Getting Organized," you averaged your monthly expenses, saw where you are spending your money, then completed the Monthly Income, Expense, and Debt Form. Now you are going to see how that information can be used.

The Cash Flow Worksheet is part of a software program called FinPlan. This program—utilized by Certified Divorce Planners, attorneys, Certified Financial Planners, and CPAs—helps clients understand the basics of their financial situation when going through a divorce. The Cash Flow Worksheet is a factual, concise statement of income; federal, state, and Social Security taxes; monthly budget; and a resulting deficit or excess of income.

A Cash Flow Report has the following uses:

- ❖ It helps you to understand your true income, estimated taxes, and disposable income after expenses.
- ❖ It serves as a starting point for future financial planning.
- ❖ It shows your true need for calculation of alimony.
- ❖ It is required for production of spreadsheets and charts showing the results of a property division scenario.

Now you can begin to understand how essential knowing your present situation will be in negotiating the terms of your settlement agreement. You will recall from the alimony discussion in Chapter 5, "Dealing with Child Support and Alimony," that payment of alimony is based on two factors: need and the ability to pay. One of the spouses must prove a need for a portion of the other spouse's income.

The information calculated on the Cash Flow Worksheet can then be used in a software program called Divorce Plan to produce spreadsheets and charts that will show the true situation of both spouses not only for the present, but also on a 20-year timeline. These documents are extremely useful, since the Divorce Plan software program also takes into account future pensions, Social Security payments, and future payment for debts such as houses and autos. This software program was specially written for use in the divorce process. It helps both spouses, their attorneys, and, if necessary, a judge understand the factual results of a property settlement proposal.

Introducing the Components of the Cash Flow Worksheet

In this section, we'll walk you line-by-line through a sample Cash Flow Worksheet.

USE FOR ESTIMATION PURPOSES ONLY - PLEASE CONSULT A TAX ADVISOR

Cash Flow	2001		2002	
Last Name Doe	<u>John</u>	<u>Mary</u>	<u>John</u>	<u>Mary</u>
<u>Gross Income</u>				
1 Salary	0	0	0	0
2 Self-Employment Income	0	0	0	0
3 Social Security Income	0	0	0	0
4 Interest Government Securities	0	0	0	0
5 Other Interest	0	0	0	0
6 Dividends	0	0	0	0
7 Other Taxable Inc	0	0	0	0
8 Tax Exempt Interest	0	0	0	0
9 Other Nontaxable Cash	0	0	0	0
10 Cash Perks	0	0	0	0
11 Other Deductions from Gro	0	0	0	0
12 Alimony Paid (Previous)	0	0	0	0
13 Child Support (Previous)	0	0	0	0
14 Gross Cash Available Spt	0	0	0	0
15 Share of Gross Cash	0%	0%	0%	0%
<u>Less: Cash Flow Deductions</u>				
16 Federal Income Tax	0	0	0	0
17 State Income Tax	0	0	0	0
18 Social Security Tax	0	0	0	0
19 Local Income Tax	0	0 '	0	0
20 Cash Deduction	0	0	0	0
21 Mandatory Pension	0	0	0	0
22 Other Net Deductions	0	0	0	0
23 Net Cash Available for Spt	0	0	0	0
24 Share of Net Cash	0%	0%	0%	0%
25 Children Residing:	0	0		
26 Child Support	0	0	0	0
27 Non-Taxable Maintenance	0	0	0	0
28 Alimony	0	0	0	0
29 Cash After Support	0	0	0	0
30 Other Cash Item (Addition)	0	0	0	0
31 Voluntary Pension	0	0	0	0
32 Cash to Meet Living Expenses	**0**	**0**	**0**	**0**
33 Share of Total Cash	**0%**	**0%**	**0%**	**0%**
34 Monthly Cash Available	**0**	**0**	**0**	**0**
35 Required Cash - Budget	0	0	0	0
36 Cash Over (Under) Budget	**0**	**0**	**0**	**0**

April 16,2001 11:24 AM

A sample Cash Flow Worksheet.

You will notice that there are always two columns, one for each
of the spouses. This program tracks the income, taxes, budget,
and child support or alimony payments made or received.

The Cash Flow Worksheet is divided into two sections: Gross Income (lines 1 through 13) and Cash Flow Deductions (lines 16 through 31). The *Gross Income* section identifies the many sources from which money can be received, including salary, wages, Social Security payments, interest, dividends, cash perks, child support, and alimony. The *Cash Flow Deductions* section includes any items that are subtracted from line 14, Gross Cash for Support. These items may include payments for taxes, mandatory pension, child support, and voluntary pension such as a 401(k) or 403(b). Usually, only mandatory pension contributions are allowed as deductions. Any contributions to a 401(k) or other plan are voluntary and considered optional savings.

Three of the largest deductions are payments required for taxes. Taxes include the amount of federal, state, and Social Security payments that are owed in a given year. Line 16 on this Cash Flow Worksheet shows the exact amount of federal income tax that will be owed for the years 2001 and 2002. It's very important that you are aware of the different factors that affect the amount of taxes you will owe in a given year. While these factors aren't on the Cash Flow Report, they are input into the FinPlan software program and used in all the calculations.

Filing status

Filing status determines whether you can claim certain deductions and credits. Your filing status is your marital status on the last day of the tax year. Here is a brief description of the four categories:

- ❖ **Single.** This is the correct status for someone who has never married or is divorced or widowed.

- ❖ **Married.** Unless you have received a decree of divorce or annulment before the last day of the tax year, you are still considered married for tax purposes, even if you have lived separately from your spouse.

- ❖ **Married Filing Separately.** If you and your spouse have lived apart or, if for any other reason you do not wish your income and exemptions to be filed with your spouse's, you may use this status. There are certain rules concerning itemized deductions that must be obeyed. Also, the tax rates are higher for married persons who file separately.

❖ **Head of Household.** If you provide more than half the cost of keeping up a home that was the main residence for a child or other relative, you can file with Head of Household status. The cost of keeping up a home includes paying more than half the amount of rent, mortgage interest, taxes, insurance, repairs, utilities, and food. There are very specific rules that must be followed when determining that someone is your dependent. Usually you must be single to file as Head of Household, but if you have lived apart from your spouse for more than the last six months of the previous tax year and paid more than half the cost of keeping up a house for a qualified person, you can be eligible to be considered in this status.

Someone may have three different filing statuses in three consecutive years. In the 2000 tax year, both spouses may have filed as Married Filing Jointly. In the tax year 2001, if the spouses lived apart during the last six months of the year and the custodial parent paid more than half the cost of keeping up the home, he or she could file as Head of Household and the other spouse would file as Married Filing Separately. This couple will likely be divorced by the end of 2002. Therefore, the custodial parent will continue to file as Head of Household and the other ex-spouse must file as Single. Whenever there is a change in filing status you must estimate the amount of federal and state taxes you will owe. Generally, filing as Head of Household results in a substantial tax savings while Married Filing Separately results in more taxes owed.

Taxable exemptions

Taxable exemptions enable you to deduct a specific amount from your income. There are two types of exemptions, personal and dependency. A personal exemption is the one you take for yourself if no one else claims you as a dependent. A dependency exemption is allowed if the person you wish to claim lives with you for the entire year, is related to you, is a U.S. citizen or resident, does not file a joint tax return with you, does not earn $2,800 or more in the tax year, and if you provide more than half of the person's total support for that calendar year. In 2000, the dependency exemption was worth $2,800.

Important Tip

The custodial parent who the child lives with for a greater portion of the year is generally treated as the parent who provided more than half the child's support and takes the dependency exemption for that child. This means that even if you are receiving child support from your spouse, you can claim your child as a dependent. As you will see when we discuss Steve and Jean's Cash Flow Worksheet, Jean allowed Steve to claim the two children because the tax savings for Steve would be greater than for her. The custodial parent files a Form 8332, Release of Claim to Exemption, to allow the other parent to claim the child as a dependent. The Release of Claim to Exemption can state how long the custodial parent is transferring the exemption. The period can be for one year, for a specified period of time, or for all future years that the child will be a dependent. Many times, if there are two or more minor children, the dependency exemptions will be split between the two parents.

State taxes, which is the amount owed on line 17, are determined partially by the adjusted gross income from your federal tax return and the variables of the state in which you reside.

Social Security taxes (line 18) is the amount saved for future Social Security benefits that you will receive after reaching the minimum retirement age set by the federal government. Included in Social Security taxes is Medicare, which is the government's health benefits plan for retirees. In 2001, 6.2 percent of your earnings up to $79,200 will be paid in Social Security tax and 1.45 percent in Medicare tax.

Itemized deductions

Itemized deductions are different categories of expenses that you have paid throughout the year, which can decrease the amount of federal and state taxes you will have to pay. Itemized deductions allow the amount of certain items to be subtracted from adjusted gross income before calculation of the amount of taxes owed. The most common deductions are those for medical expenses, property tax, local income tax paid, mortgage interest, and charitable contributions.

It is very common for people to ask if they can deduct the costs of getting the divorce. These costs could include attorney's fees and the advice and services of a therapist, Certified Divorce Planner, CPA, mediator, or other professional. You *cannot* deduct legal fees and court costs for actually getting the divorce, but may be able to deduct legal fees paid for tax advice in connection with the divorce and legal fees paid to get alimony. You may also be able to deduct fees you pay to appraisers, actuaries, and accountants for services in determining your correct tax or for help in getting alimony. In other words, you can only claim attorney and professional fees that are paid for receiving income such as alimony or tax advice. Deductible fees can be claimed only if you itemize on Schedule A.

Again, we will mention IRS Publication 504, Divorced or Separated Individuals. Reading this publication will help you greatly in understanding the tax implications of divorce before you sign the settlement agreement. It is best to consult with an accountant or CPA if you have tax questions, especially about filing status and dependency exemptions. It could mean the difference between paying and saving a lot of money in taxes.

You can also check the IRS Web site at www.irs.gov for the most recent Tax Rate Schedule. Just go to the "Tax Rate Tables and Schedules" section of the site and check out "Schedule Z—Use if your filing status is Head of Household." The information in this table shows the tax bracket based on the amount of taxable income from the Form 1040.

The Cash Available section (lines 32 through 36) shows your true cash-flow situation. Cash to Meet Living Expenses (line 32) is the yearly amount of money available after paying or receiving child support and alimony and payment of taxes. Required Cash—Budget (line 35) has been discussed in Chapter 4. The monthly budget is the total amount shown on the Monthly Income, Expense, and Debt Form that you should have completed. Line 36 really tells the story. This is the amount of money, if any, left after paying everybody and everything. Line 36 is important. This line indicates whether you under spend or over spend your income.

Cash Flow Worksheet for Steve and Jean

Now that you have a working knowledge of the components, let's take a look at the following figure—Steve and Jean's cash-flow situation.

❖ Lines 1 through 3 show their annual taxable income from salary.

❖ Lines 5 through 6 show the interest and dividends paid yearly from the Fidelity and Chevy Chase accounts.

❖ Line 9, Other Non-Taxable Cash, is the yearly amount that Steve and Jean have withheld from their paychecks for payment of medical premiums. These premiums are not taxable but do count as income.

❖ Lines 16 through 18 show the correct amounts that should be withheld from Steve and Jean's paychecks to pay taxes for the year 2001. These taxes were calculated based on Steve filing as Married Filing Separately, Jean filing as Head of Household, Steve claiming the two children as dependents, and Jean deducting the real estate taxes and mortgage interest because she was buying out Steve's equity in the house.

❖ There are no deductions for items listed on lines 19 through 22.

❖ Line 26 indicates that Steve will pay Jean $13,668 per year in child support.

❖ Lines 32 and 34 show the net amounts per year and per month available to pay living expenses and invest for retirement.

❖ Line 33 shows that after paying taxes and child support, Steve has 46 percent of the total disposable income and Jean has 54 percent.

❖ Line 35 indicates the monthly budget amounts for Steve and Jean based on their completing the Monthly Income, Expense, and Debt Form.

❖ Line 36 shows that in 2001 Steve has an excess of $972 per month and Jean has a deficit of $170 per month.

USE FOR ESTIMATION PURPOSES ONLY - PLEASE CONSULT A TAX ADVISOR

Cash Flow	2001		2002	
Last Name Smith	Steve	Jean	Steve	Jean
Gross Income				
1 Salary	72,040	37,400	74,201	38,522
2 Self-Employment Income	0	0	0	0
3 Social Security Income	0	0	0	0
4 Interest Government Securities	0	0	0	0
5 Other Interest	492	0	492	0
6 Dividends	788	0	788	0
7 Other Taxable Inc	0	0	0	0
8 Tax Exempt Interest	0	0	0	0
9 Other Nontaxable Cash	960	600	960	600
10 Cash Perks	0	0	0	0
11 Other Deductions from Gro	0	0	0	0
12 Alimony Paid (Previous)	0	0	0	0
13 Child Support (Previous)	0	0	0	0
14 Gross Cash Available Spt	74,280	38,000	76,441	39,122
15 Share of Gross Cash	66%	34%	66%	34%
Less: Cash Flow Deductions				
16 Federal Income Tax	12,398	2,242	12,912	2,412
17 State Income Tax	3,648	819	3,772	891
18 Social Security Tax	5,511	2,861	5,676	2,947
19 Local Income Tax	0	0	0	0
20 Cash Deduction	0	0	0	0
21 Mandatory Pension	0	0	0	0
22 Other Net Deductions	0	0	0	0
23 Net Cash Available for Spt	52,723	32,078	54,081	32,872
24 Share of Net Cash	62%	38%	62%	38%
25 Children Residing:	0	0		
26 Child Support	(13,668)	13,668	(13,668)	13,668
27 Non-Taxable Maintenance	0	0	0	0
28 Alimony	0	0	0	0
29 Cash After Support	39,055	45,746	40,413	46,540
30 Other Cash Item (Addition)	0	0	0	0
31 Voluntary Pension	0	0	0	0
32 Cash to Meet Living Expenses	**39,055**	**45,746**	**40,413**	**46,540**
33 Share of Total Cash	**46%**	**54%**	**46%**	**54%**
34 Monthly Cash Available	**3,255**	**3,812**	**3,368**	**3,878**
35 Required Cash - Budget	2,283	3,982	2,354	4,062
36 Cash Over (Under) Budget	**972**	**(170)**	**1,014**	**(184)**

April 10,2001 06:31 AM

Steve and Jean's Cash Flow Worksheet #1.

The Meaning of the Bottom Line

Now that we have taken a look at Steve and Jean's cash flow, you can see that Steve will do fine. He has money left over to invest, especially in his 401(k). Jean however, can't make ends meet. She has two options. She can either reduce her spending to make up for the deficit, or she can accumulate debt by charging groceries, clothing, and anything extra that she or the children may need on her credit cards. Neither option is good. Even if Jean reduces her spending and doesn't go into debt to live, she still is not saving for retirement and doesn't have extra cash available for emergencies. If Jean uses credit cards to make ends meet, eventually her debt will be so large that she will have to sell the house. Whichever way you look at it, Jean's situation isn't good. But don't worry about Jean. You will see how her story turns out in Chapter 8, "Putting It All Together."

Accumulating Wealth

In most instances, wealthy people did not receive their money through inheritances. It may seem as though they did because of intense advertising from financial services companies. Every day you see ads on television for brokerage houses talking about the huge transfer of wealth that will take place when our parents die and leave us with large amounts of assets. We hate to break the news to you, but most likely any wealth you enjoy will be because of your efforts, not your parents.

Accumulating wealth is done the old fashioned way: slowly over a period of time. This means that your pennies do count because they make dollars that can be invested for the future.

As you just saw in Jean's case, she doesn't enjoy the luxury of having pennies to save. She is spending her income and then some. She may enjoy living in the house, but the cost of doing so is much too high. She is jeopardizing her future to live in the present. We're not saying that you must become a penny-pinching Scrooge. You should always enjoy the moment. But in our experiences we have seen far too many people, especially women, trade away their futures for what they perceived to be security. And then that symbol of security was eventually lost.

Using the Cash Flow Worksheet in Negotiating Alimony

As Sergeant Friday used to say, "Just the facts ma'am." Keep that phrase in your mind. You already know about the concept of need and the ability to pay. This is where that concept is proven. Using the information provided by Steve and Jean, the Cash Flow Worksheet clearly shows that Jean has too little income for her present financial needs, and Steve has excess income for the foreseeable future. It is at this point in working with a financial professional or attorney that the two spouses start having a serious discussion about the amount and term of future alimony payments.

There are a few factors in Steve and Jean's case that you should keep in mind. First, Jean did stay home the first five years of their marriage to raise their kids during their early or "tender" years. Second, Steve and Jean both think it's a very good idea to keep the kids in the house for a year or two so they can adjust to the divorce. True, Jean did want to keep the house, but Steve encouraged her to do so.

If Jean used an attorney to negotiate the terms of her financial settlement, her attorney would take a great interest in the Cash Flow Worksheet, because the bottom line proves that Jean has a need for a portion of Steve's income. And since the bottom line is based on fact, it may be very difficult to argue to the contrary. We will see how Steve and Jean resolved their situation in Chapter 8.

The Bottom Line

Knowing that you spend more than you earn and continuing to do so puts your financial future in jeopardy.

Chapter 7

Dividing Your Assets and Debts

Capsule Outlook

Doing your own research and getting professional advice is invaluable in deciding your property settlement.

If a marriage is a union, then a divorce is a disunion. What was once joined together must now be set apart. That means everything purchased, saved, and received during the marriage is subject to division. Each state has its own laws concerning who gets what. Before you can begin to make a list of your wants and wishes concerning the division of marital assets, you must know the specific rules or laws of property division.

As a test of what you may already know, see if you can answer the following questions. Are you living in a community property state or an equitable distribution state? Since your 401(k) is in your name only, do you have to split it with your spouse? How do you divide the silver service you both received as a wedding gift? What about the stock that Aunt Victoria left you in her will? If you didn't know the answers to any of these questions, don't feel bad. The vast majority of people wouldn't either. Most people never think about these things until divorce is a real possibility. Then they start getting educated as fast as they can.

Knowing the State You're In

Where you live can make a difference in how your assets and debts are divided. There are resources, including Web sites listed in the back of this book, which are great sources of information on issues such as these. *Community property* means that unless it is otherwise agreed, all jointly held assets or property are divided equally between the spouses. Courts sometimes award more assets to one person if it's determined that economic or other situations warrant an unequal split. *Equitable distribution* means that how assets and debts are divided can vary with each situation. There are factors that could result in an unequal division of assets. The following is a general list of factors that might be considered if you live in an equitable distribution state:

❖ The contributions, monetary and nonmonetary, of each party to the well-being of the family

❖ The contributions, monetary and nonmonetary, of each party in the acquisition, care, and maintenance of marital property of the parties

❖ The duration of the marriage

❖ The ages and physical and mental condition of the parties

❖ The circumstances and factors that contributed to the dissolution of the marriage

❖ How and when specific items of marital property were acquired

❖ The debts and liabilities of each spouse, the basis for these debts and liabilities, and the property that may serve as security for debts and liabilities

❖ The liquid or nonliquid character of all marital property

❖ The tax consequences to each party

❖ Other factors as the court deems necessary or appropriate to arrive at a fair and equitable monetary award

Divorce should never be approached as a "cookie cutter" process. Your marriage is different from your friends and family's marriages. That's one reason reading and completing the worksheets explained in Chapter 4, "Getting Organized," is so essential. Getting organized helps you clarify the facts about your own situation.

Dividing assets and debts should not be done without giving thought to the circumstances of both spouses and their standard of living during the marriage. There are professionals such as attorneys, therapists, mediators, certified divorce planners, and accountants who can give you information that will help with making settlement decisions. But only attorneys are authorized to suggest that your assets and debts be split a certain way, and can make recommendations if you or your spouse needs help with property settlement issues. That's why it is best to educate yourself about your rights through seminars, reading materials, and Web sites, and by consulting divorce-related professionals so that you can make the best decisions possible.

The following story illustrates how each person must make their own best decisions.

Jane was the mother of a three-year-old boy and a five-year-old girl. She had a thriving career and had worked throughout her nine-year marriage. As a matter of fact, Jane earned a larger salary than her husband, Michael. In recent years, several of Jane's family members had died and left her large sums of money as inheritances, which had been deposited in an account in only Jane's name. Besides the house and two cars, Jane's inheritances were about the only assets they had. When it became clear that the marriage was heading toward divorce, Michael made a list of everything they owned down to and including the dishtowels. And Michael said he wanted half of everything.

Jane had attended a pre-divorce seminar where an attorney had explained the difference between marital and separate assets. Jane knew that any money that she had inherited was hers alone and she didn't have to split it with her husband. Jane also realized that, since she was going to have shared custody of the two children with Michael, she was going to have to see him frequently. Jane didn't want her custody arrangements to become a battle because Michael felt he didn't receive a fair share of the assets. Jane consulted a divorce professional and discussed the pros and cons of hiring an attorney and negotiating the property settlement. Jane then made the decision to give Michael $50,000 in cash so that he could make a down payment on a house of his own. Michael also received one of the cars and an amount equal to one half of the equity in the house. Jane had become educated, consulted a professional, and then made her decision. By law, she didn't have to share her inheritances with Michael, but she did. Just like Jane, you have to make your own decisions—the decisions you believe are the right ones for you.

In our experiences with divorcing clients, we have found that when spouses negotiate their own property settlement, they are very aware of their own needs and those of their spouse. In fact, about 60 percent of the time they agree to an unequal division of assets and debts. The clients realize that many factors are involved in their situation and judge for themselves whether a certain asset division is fair.

Community Property and Equitable Distribution States

The first step in planning your property settlement is knowing how your state divides marital property. Here is a listing of all 50 states and their classifications:

❖ **Community Property:** Arizona, California, Idaho, Louisiana, Nevada, New Mexico, Texas, Washington, and Wisconsin.

❖ **Equitable Distribution:** Alabama, Alaska, Arkansas, Colorado, Connecticut, Delaware, District of Columbia, Florida, Georgia, Hawaii, Illinois, Indiana, Iowa, Kansas, Kentucky, Maine, Maryland, Massachusetts, Michigan, Minnesota, Missouri, Montana, Nebraska, New Hampshire, New Jersey, New York, North Carolina, North Dakota, Ohio, Oklahoma, Oregon, Pennsylvania, Rhode Island, South Carolina,

South Dakota, Tennessee, Utah, Vermont, Virginia, West Virginia, and Wyoming.

❖ Mississippi is a **"lone title"** state, which means you keep everything in your own name and then divide the other assets.

Types of Assets and Debts

Most states recognize that there are two types of assets and debts. Assets and debts accumulated during the marriage are classified as being *marital*. That's an easy definition. But it's a little more complicated than that. It depends on the way your state, and maybe even your county, defines an accumulation period. Some states define "during the marriage" as the period from the date of marriage to the date of divorce, or the date when the division is being negotiated. In other states, the accumulation of marital assets and debts may stop at the date of separation. The separation date is most commonly the date that the spouses began living in separate locations. To complicate matters more, some jurisdictions could recognize two people living separately in the same house as being separated if they both agree on a specific date when they stopped living as a married couple. There are many specifics that could make a big difference in the assets you're entitled to and the debts for which you must take responsibility.

Separate assets are those you owned before the marriage or that were gifts or inheritances from someone other than your spouse while you were married. Separate debts are amounts owed before the marriage or debts accrued after separating from your spouse.

Assets that are part marital and part separate are considered *mixed assets*. If you had money in a 401(k) before you were married and continued your contributions after the marriage, that account would be considered a mixed asset. The separate portion must be deducted from the marital portion to determine the amount you might have to split with your spouse.

Valuing Assets and Debts

Usually assets and debts are valued as to the amount of each item or account that was acquired during the marriage. Money invested in a 401(k), IRA, money market account, or savings account is valued as of the balance on the latest statement.

Equity in the marital home is the biggest asset some people own. Therefore, it is common to have the house value determined by a professional appraiser. The appraiser looks at current and recent sales of homes comparable to yours and then inspects your home to check for additions or custom features you may have installed. The amount that an appraiser calculates your house is worth is called *fair market value.*

Personal businesses, artwork, and antiques are other items that frequently require an appraisal. Other professionals might also be needed to determine the value of marital assets.

Asset Classes

Assets can generally be placed in one of several classes. The distinction between the classes of assets is essential since each class has its own characteristics. The favorable and unfavorable consequences of trading assets are discussed in Chapter 9, "The Negotiation Process."

Real estate is land or any dwelling placed on a plot of land. The marital home, beach condominium, timeshares, farmland, and investment property are included in this class.

Personal businesses have rapidly become a source, and sometimes the only source, of income for the family. Both spouses often work for the business. The value of the business goes beyond what you can touch and see. Desks, computers, machinery, and autos are tangible assets, but the value of a business also includes goodwill in the community and the amount of gross receipts. Professional business valuators can use cash-flow and profit-and-loss statements to determine a business's true value.

Career assets such as professional degrees, certifications, and licenses can be valued, too. The most common example of a career asset is a professional degree to practice as a doctor or lawyer. In some states, if one spouse can prove that his or her contributions of time, money, or effort helped the other spouse earn a degree or otherwise further his or her career, a monetary value of the career can be determined and considered a marital asset.

Retirement assets can be accumulated in several different types of accounts. The most common retirement accounts are 401(k)s and IRAs. Other accounts, such as 403(b)s (nonprofit organizations), Deferred Compensation, Simplified Employee Plans Individual Retirement Accounts, Savings Incentive Match Plan for Employees, and profit-sharing, are also included in this class. Defined benefit pensions such as Civil Service Retirement System, Federal Employee Retirement System, military, and private company pensions are also included.

Know Your Defined Benefit Plans

Some defined benefit pensions are *not* divisible. Plans which can not be divided include some law enforcement and other local government agencies. It is vital that you or your attorney check to make sure that any pension of this type can be divided in a divorce settlement. If a plan cannot be divided, the entire division of assets will be affected.

Liquid assets include brokerage accounts, mutual funds, savings accounts, certificates of deposit, money market accounts, savings bonds, cash value of life insurance policies, and cash. Stock options have become a major source of compensation and bonus income, especially for employees of Internet companies. Stock options can be fully vested, partially vested, or unvested, depending on the terms of employment and vesting requirements. They are also either nonqualified or incentive based. Options are difficult to value and can actually be a large income tax liability. If you or your spouse has been awarded stock options, it would be wise to consult a certified public accountant, certified financial planner, or certified divorce planner to fully understand the complexities before considering a division of these assets.

Other assets can include autos, boats, jet skis, campers, recreational vehicles, stamp and coin collections, artwork, frequent flier miles, season passes to professional sports events, and collectible items.

What About the Furniture?

Furniture, clothing, small articles of jewelry, and other household contents are generally considered personal property. Think about the contents of your living room. Besides the furniture, you've used lamps, pictures, and knickknacks to decorate this room. Now think about adding together all the items in your house, especially the kitchen. You probably have quite an accumulation of contents.

Many people attempt to place a monetary value on every major item in their home. Doing this takes a lot of time and usually has inaccurate results. Realize that you have lived with and used the contents of your home. If you bought the dining room set for $3,000 10 years ago, it probably isn't worth anything near that amount now. Therefore, consider not using estimated prices as a factor in dividing your personal property.

The most practical method of dividing personal property doesn't consider an item's monetary worth. It's called the *alternate selection method* and the process goes like this: First, make a list of the major items in your home. Then you and your spouse find common ground, which means selecting items that one of you wants but the other spouse doesn't. After those items have been chosen, the remaining items on the list are the ones both of you want. Flip a coin, then both of you call either heads or tails. You can even do the best two out of three. The winner gets to choose the first item. The other spouse chooses the second item, and the process is continued until all the items on the list have been chosen. Is this rocket science? No. Does it work? Yes.

To show you the alternative to the simple approach just discussed, we're going to tell you about how Joanne and her husband approached this task.

Joanne and her husband, Rich, had relied on their attorneys to work out the details of their property settlement. In fact, after almost two years, they finally settled the division of the pension and other assets while standing on the courthouse steps. Neither Joanne nor Rich had first worked through the emotional part of their divorce. As a result, both had bitter feelings toward each other that continually surfaced whenever they tried to negotiate. Joanne had been an antiques dealer and had furnished their home with rare and valuable items. Naturally, Joanne felt that since she had done all the work selecting and buying the antiques, she should get more than half the items.

Unfortunately, Rich didn't feel that way and neither did his attorney. List upon list of items were made. Rich put a dollar value on each item that Joanne felt was either ridiculously high or low. The bartering went on for two days, while they each paid their attorney $200 per hour to argue about who should get a particular item. At the end of the second day, even the attorneys were weary of the process. It was decided that the alternate selection method would be used to divide all the items that were still in dispute. After 40 minutes, the last item had been chosen and the process was finally finished. But the story doesn't end there. When Rich came to the house to get the items, Joanne had hired someone who checked each item off the list as it was taken out the front door. The fees for each attorney were over $2,000, but Joanne and Rich paid a much higher emotional price for not working cooperatively.

The Bottom Line

Sometimes even if you win, you lose.

Chapter 8

Putting It All Together

Capsule Outlook

Guessing about your future is very unwise. You must know how settlement decisions will affect you before signing the agreement.

In Chapter 6, "Cash Flow—the Foundation for Building Wealth," we introduced the Cash Flow Worksheet of Steve and Jean Smith. The results of the Cash Flow Worksheet showed Steve and Jean's financial reality. After all payments were made, Steve had a $972 per month excess and Jean had a deficit of $170. Year after year, Steve saved more money and Jean went deeper into debt. If Jean were like most people, she wouldn't have known the effect that keeping the house would have on her monthly cash flow. Unfortunately, this situation happens in most divorces. People make settlement decisions without knowing the specific outcomes and consequences of those decisions.

We're not going to let that happen to Steve and Jean, however. We are going to use their Cash Flow Worksheet and see how it fits into the whole picture that makes up their property settlement agreement. First, you need to know more about Steve and Jean's case. So let's look at all the details, see the outcome of their proposed settlement, and review any adjustments that Steve and Jean agreed on to make their settlement an equitable one.

The Case of Steve and Jean Smith

Steve and Jean are a young couple. They have been married 12 years and have a son, age 11, and a daughter, age 8. As we mentioned before, Steve and Jean make a very good living. Steve earns $73,000 per year in his job as an engineer, and Jean earns $38,000 per year as an executive assistant. Jean became pregnant soon after the wedding and, they decided it was better if Jean stayed home and cared for the children while they were babies. Jean did return to work seven years ago. Since Steve's job requires regular out-of-town travel, it was decided that Jean would have sole physical custody of the two children but would have shared legal custody.

Asset Listing

Now let's look at the specifics of their assets. This asset listing is typical for a couple of Steve and Jean's ages with their working histories. Usually, there is some equity in the marital home. One important concept: When listing the value of any assets, and especially before negotiating the division of assets, all debt owed on any assets must be subtracted from that asset's fair market value. Fair market value is the amount for which an asset can be sold or the amount of an account, such as a 401(k) or savings account.

In Steve and Jean's case, the house has $41,582 in equity, which means Steve and Jean could sell the house for $225,000. After deducting what they owed on the mortgage, they would receive $41,582, which doesn't reflect any selling expenses. The normal calculation of net equity doesn't include selling expenses if one spouse is keeping the house and buying out the other spouse's equity. Definitely check the usual calculation of net equity in the state and county where you reside. In many cases, deduction of selling expenses is a negotiable item. Of course, that means the spouse who is leaving the home and receiving his or her share of equity would get more money. In most cases, if one spouse were staying in a residence, he or she would assume responsibility for these costs, if and when the home is sold.

Steve and Jean both have 401(k) plans at their place of employment. Steve's is larger because he makes more money and can contribute more each payday. Also, Steve continued working during the time Jean stayed home caring for the children.

They also have some liquid assets: a Fidelity mutual fund and a Chevy Chase savings account. There are two autos: a 1996 Ford Explorer and a 1998 Honda Civic. Keep in mind that before negotiating or trading assets during negotiations, the values that are placed on assets should be net values, meaning that all debt and other incurred expenses have been deducted from the fair market value.

Steve and Jean have done what many couples try to do before dividing assets in a divorce settlement. They have paid off their credit cards and other debts. There are no loans on their 401(k)s and the only asset on which debt is owed is the marital home.

Asset Listing for Steve and Jean Smith

Asset	Value
Home FMV $225,000	$41,582
Mortgage $183,418	
Interest 7.5%	
Term 30	
401(k)—Steve	$34,156
401(k)—Jean	$15,445
Fidelity Fund	$16,574
Chevy Chase Savings	$6,290
1996 Ford Explorer	$9,593
1998 Honda Civic	$9,600
Total	$133,240

Proposed Division of Assets

Let's take a look at how Steve and Jean have agreed to divide their assets. Jean keeps the house; Steve and Jean each keep their own 401(k) account; Steve receives the Fidelity mutual fund and Chevy Chase savings account; Steve gets full title to the Honda Civic; and Jean gets the Explorer. The asset listing now reflects how the assets will be divided.

Asset Division for Steve and Jean Smith

Asset	Value	Steve	Jean
Home FMV $225,000	$41,582		$41,582
Mortgage $183,418			
Interest 7.5%			
Term 30			
401(k)—Steve	$34,156	$34,156	
401(k)—Jean	$15,445		$15,445
Fidelity Fund	$16,574	$16,574	
Chevy Chase Savings	$6,290	$6,290	
1996 Ford Explorer	$9,593		$9,593
1998 Honda Civic	$9,600	$9,600	
Total	$133,240	$66,620	$66,620

Child Support

Let's look again at the following Child Support Worksheet, introduced in Chapter 5, "Dealing with Child Support and Alimony." Using the gross monthly income for both Steve and Jean, the suggested amount of support for the two children, which Jean will receive, is $1,139 per month.

For financial planning purposes only, we calculated the amount of child support Jean would receive when her son graduated from high school and her daughter was still living with her. Child support payments would decrease to $632 per month. In reality, both Steve and Jean's incomes would have changed, so child support would be recalculated using their incomes at that time.

CHILD SUPPORT GUIDELINE WORKSHEET

For sole custody support cases with no
spousal support or spousal support
calculated on a separate form.

_____ **Smith** _____ v. _____ **Smith** _____

Worksheet of: Steve and Jean Smith

Chancery No. _____

Date: 4/10/01

A. GROSS INCOME OF PARTIES	**Mother**	**Father**	
1. Monthly Gross Income of Each Party:	$3,167	$6,083	**Spousal Support**
2. Spousal Support Payable Between Parties:			
3. Adjusted Gross Income for Child Support:	$3,167	$6,083	**Spousal Payor**
4. Combined Gross Income:	$9,250	Income Shares	☐ Husband
5. Each Party's Percent of Combined Income:	34.2%	65.8%	☐ Wife
6. Number of Children: 2	Ages: 11, 8		

Custodian:
X Mother
☐ Father

B. CHILD SUPPORT			
1. Schedule Amount for Basic Child Support:		$1,528	**From Support Table**
2. Extraordinary Medical/Dental Expenses:			
3. Work-related Child Care Costs:		$225	
4. Medical Insurance for Child/Children:		$40	**Child Support Need**
5. Total Child Support Need (Sum: 1+2+3+4):		⟶	**$1,793**
	Mother	**Father**	
6. Child Support Obligation of Each Party:	$614	$1,179	
(Total Support Need x Income Share)			
7. Direct Payment of Medical Insurance (Subtract):		($40)	
8. Each Party's Presumptive Guideline Share:	$614	$1,139	

Guideline Child Support

9. Guideline Child Support Payable by Non-Custodial Parent: ⟶ **$1,139**

C. PROPOSED DEVIATIONS FROM GUIDELINE SUPPORT:

1. _____   _____   _____
   _____   _____   _____
   _____   _____   _____

2. Each Party's Proposed share:	$614	$1,139	

TOTAL CHILD SUPPORT

D. PROPOSED ADJUSTED CHILD SUPPORT: ⟶ **$1,139**

Child Support Payable To Mother

Submitted by: _____

Counsel for: _____

3/7/00

Child Support Worksheet for Steve and Jean.

Cash Flow Worksheet

In Chapter 6 we calculated Steve and Jean's monthly cash flow, shown in the following figure.

USE FOR ESTIMATION PURPOSES ONLY - PLEASE CONSULT A TAX ADVISOR

Cash Flow	2001		2002	
Last Name Smith	Steve	Jean	Steve	Jean
Gross Income				
1 Salary	72,040	37,400	74,201	38,522
2 Self-Employment Income	0	0	0	0
3 Social Security Income	0	0	0	0
4 Interest Government Securities	0	0	0	0
5 Other Interest	492	0	492	0
6 Dividends	788	0	788	0
7 Other Taxable Inc	0	0	0	0
8 Tax Exempt Interest	0	0	0	0
9 Other Nontaxable Cash	960	600	960	600
10 Cash Perks	0	0	0	0
11 Other Deductions from Gro	0	0	0	0
12 Alimony Paid (Previous)	0	0	0	0
13 Child Support (Previous)	0	0	0	0
14 Gross Cash Available Spt	74,280	38,000	76,441	39,122
15 Share of Gross Cash	66%	34%	66%	34%
Less: Cash Flow Deductions				
16 Federal Income Tax	12,398	2,242	12,912	2,412
17 State Income Tax	3,648	819	3,772	891
18 Social Security Tax	5,511	2,861	5,676	2,947
19 Local Income Tax	0	0	0	0
20 Cash Deduction	0	0	0	0
21 Mandatory Pension	0	0	0	0
22 Other Net Deductions	0	0	0	0
23 Net Cash Available for Spt	52,723	32,078	54,081	32,872
24 Share of Net Cash	62%	38%	62%	38%
25 Children Residing:	0	0		
26 Child Support	(13,668)	13,668	(13,668)	13,668
27 Non-Taxable Maintenance	0	0	0	0
28 Alimony	0	0	0	0
29 Cash After Support	39,055	45,746	40,413	46,540
30 Other Cash Item (Addition)	0	0	0	0
31 Voluntary Pension	0	0	0	0
32 Cash to Meet Living Expenses	**39,055**	**45,746**	**40,413**	**46,540**
33 Share of Total Cash	**46%**	**54%**	**46%**	**54%**
34 Monthly Cash Available	**3,255**	**3,812**	**3,368**	**3,878**
35 Required Cash - Budget	2,283	3,982	2,354	4,062
36 Cash Over (Under) Budget	972	(170)	1,014	(184)

April 10,2001 06:31 AM
(c) Copyright 1990, 2000 by FinPlan Co. All rights reserved.

Steve and Jean's monthly cash flow.

Because Steve's filing status will change over the next several years, it was necessary to calculate his taxes in 2000 as married, filing separately. In 2001 and the following years, Steve will file as single. The important item to focus on is line 36 on this page. You will see that Jean has a monthly deficit of $170 in the year 2001 and $184 per month in 2002. The deficit keeps increasing because she spends more each month than she is earning. Either Jean will attempt to cut her expenses so that she breaks even, or she will start charging monthly expenses on her credit cards. If she can't cut her expenses, she will start going into debt just to meet her living expenses.

Net Worth

The old saying goes that "a picture is worth a thousand words." The following "Net Worth" figure illustrates both Steve and Jean's net worth over the next 20 years based on the division of assets in the preceding figure. Someone's *net worth* is simply the value of assets he or she owns after deducting any loans still owed on the assets. The calculation of net worth took into account every aspect of their future financial lives. Salary, expenses, debts, rate of appreciation of assets such as 401(k) accounts, and future incomes such as Social Security are all included to produce this chart showing the increase in both Steve and Jean's net worth.

Both Steve and Jean seem to be doing fine. Both are above the break-even line and each one's net worth increases over time. Keep in mind that Steve's net worth will always be more than Jean's because his salary is larger and he has an excess of income each month.

Working Capital

Working capital is the result of subtracting the amount you spend each month from the amount you earn, after taxes have been deducted. An excess of working capital means you have money to save and invest. A shortage of working capital means you spend more than you earn. All the information on the Cash Flow Worksheet is reflected on the "Working Capital" figure on the next page. This chart shows the result of Steve having a monthly excess of income and Jean having a deficit.

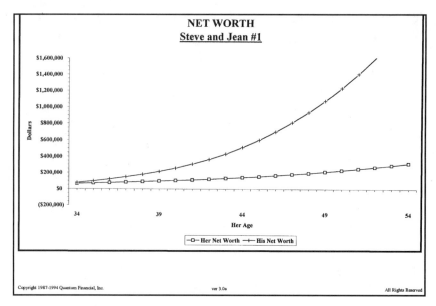

Net worth of Steve and Jean (1).

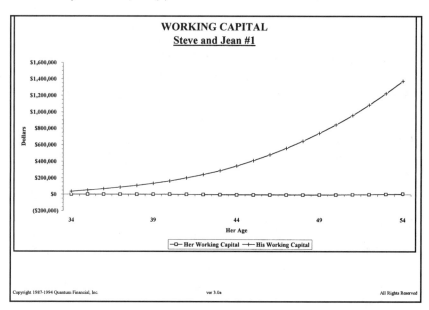

Working capital of Steve and Jean (1).

This chart shows a picture of the reality of Jean's cash flow. Notice how a small monthly deficit affects Jean over a period of time. Jean is barely under the break-even line. She never has working capital to invest. That means Jean will never accumulate retirement assets, but will always accumulate debt. More important, let's discuss the cause of Jean's problem. Jean really wants to keep the house. To her, as to many people, the house represents security, but that security has a very large cost. If Jean and Steve divided their assets in this way, most of Jean's wealth would be tied up in the house. She would have no liquid assets and a small retirement account. That's not so bad. What causes Jean's long-term decline is that she cannot afford the house with just her salary. In Jean's case, keeping the children in the house after the divorce is a great idea, but it's just not feasible for any length of time.

Back to the Drawing Board

Although Steve had a pretty good idea of where he would be financially, Jean was surprised. Steve had agreed with Jean that keeping the kids in the house was a good idea because the children needed time to adjust to the divorce. But after seeing the effect this arrangement would have on Jean's financial future, Steve and Jean agreed that adjustments needed to be made.

First, Steve agreed to give Jean half of the Fidelity mutual fund and Chevy Chase savings account. These liquid assets represented ready cash that could be used in the event of an emergency. This meant that Jean would be receiving more than half of the marital assets. Steve then offered to pay Jean $600 per month in alimony for five years so that she would not go into debt each month by staying in the house. These two actions helped Jean start her new financial life on a positive note. Jean realized that the house was too expensive for her to maintain by herself, so she developed a plan to sell the house after two years and buy a less expensive home. Steve saw the effect that renting would have on the amount of federal and state tax he would owe and also decided to buy a house in two years.

Quite a bit different scenario than what was originally proposed. But remember that future financial plans often change when the true picture is seen.

Effects of the Settlement Changes

As a result of the changes Steve and Jean made to the terms of their settlement, other financial aspects changed also. Child support will be reduced to $1,023 per month because of the shift in income when Steve starts paying $600 per month in alimony.

Look at the following Cash Flow Worksheet. Note the changes that occur because of Steve's payment of $7,200 per year in alimony to Jean, which is shown on line 28. Lines 16 and 17 show that Steve now pays less income tax because he is able to deduct the alimony payments. Jean's federal and state taxes increase because she must claim the alimony as income. The biggest changes are the ones on line 36. Jean no longer has a monthly deficit. Steve originally had a cash excess of $972 per month before any settlement changes were made. Now, after paying $600 per month in alimony, Steve still has $655 left over each month in 2001 because alimony is a deductible payment. A real eye-opener, isn't it? These are the little details that aren't thoroughly discussed during settlement negotiations. It's only when all aspects of the cash flow are analyzed that the true cost or benefit of alimony is known.

The biggest changes are the ones that occur over time. The following chart shows the new net worth chart based on the changes Steve and Jean made to their financial settlement. Note how both Steve and Jean increase their net worth after the third year for the reasons explained in the previous section. Jean doesn't go into debt each month staying in the house. She will sell her present home at the end of 2002 and buy a less expensive home at the beginning of 2003. Steve will pay less money in income taxes because he will buy a house at the beginning of 2003 and be able to deduct the real estate tax and mortgage interest.

USE FOR ESTIMATION PURPOSES ONLY - PLEASE CONSULT A TAX ADVISOR

Cash Flow	2001		2002	
Last Name Smith	Steve	Jean	Steve	Jean
Gross Income				
1 Salary	72,040	37,400	74,201	38,522
2 Self-Employment Income	0	0	0	0
3 Social Security Income	0	0	0	0
4 Interest Government Securities	0	0	0	0
5 Other Interest	246	246	246	246
6 Dividends	394	394	394	394
7 Other Taxable Inc	0	0	0	0
8 Tax Exempt Interest	0	0	0	0
9 Other Nontaxable Cash	960	600	960	600
10 Cash Perks	0	0	0	0
11 Other Deductions from Gro	0	0	0	0
12 Alimony Paid (Previous)	0	0	0	0
13 Child Support (Previous)	0	0	0	0
14 Gross Cash Available Spt	73,640	38,640	75,801	39,762
15 Share of Gross Cash	66%	34%	66%	34%
Less: Cash Flow Deductions				
16 Federal Income Tax	10,203	3,350	10,666	3,521
17 State Income Tax	3,197	1,269	3,321	1,342
18 Social Security Tax	5,511	2,861	5,676	2,947
19 Local Income Tax	0	0	0	0
20 Cash Deduction	0	0	0	0
21 Mandatory Pension	0	0	0	0
22 Other Net Deductions	0	0	0	0
23 Net Cash Available for Spt	54,729	31,160	56,138	31,952
24 Share of Net Cash	64%	36%	64%	36%
25 Children Residing:	0	0		
26 Child Support	(12,276)	12,276	(12,276)	12,276
27 Non-Taxable Maintenance	0	0	0	0
28 Alimony	(7,200)	7,200	(7,200)	7,200
29 Cash After Support	35,253	50,636	36,662	51,428
30 Other Cash Item (Addition)	0	0	0	0
31 Voluntary Pension	0	0	0	0
32 Cash to Meet Living Expenses	**35,253**	**50,636**	**36,662**	**51,428**
33 Share of Total Cash	**41%**	**59%**	**42%**	**58%**
34 Monthly Cash Available	**2,938**	**4,220**	**3,055**	**4,286**
35 Required Cash - Budget	2,283	3,982	2,354	4,062
36 Cash Over (Under) Budget	**655**	**238**	**701**	**224**

Steve and Jean's monthly cash flow (after settlement changes).

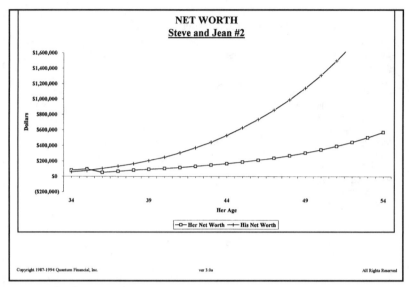

Net worth of Steve and Jean (2).

The real change can be seen in the next chart, which shows Steve and Jean's working capital. Jean's original deficit has been eliminated; therefore she never goes below the break-even line. The adjustments Steve and Jean made will allow Jean to live within her budget and accumulate money and invest for the future. The working capital chart also shows that in 2003, Jean's excess increases dramatically because she sells the house and buys a less expensive home. Steve's cash flow excess also increases in 2003 because he buys a home and deducts the mortgage interest and real estate taxes.

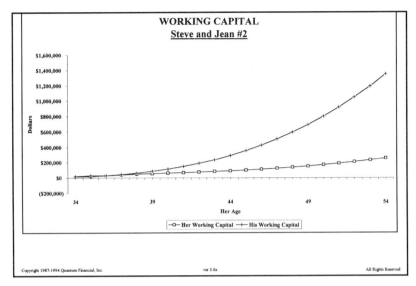

Working capital of Steve and Jean (2).

Is This Settlement Equitable?

Steve and Jean used facts in negotiating the terms of their settlement agreement. They reached what they believed was an equitable division of assets and future income. The outcomes shown on the previous charts may not look fair to you. In fact, you might think that Jean received too little. Remember that Steve earns more than Jean and he also spends less. Therefore, the two lines on the Net Worth and Working Capital charts will never merge as long as their financial situations remain the same. Equitable does not always mean equal, however; it means fair. Steve and Jean are happy with their settlement because it enables them to live within their means and maintain a fairly good standard of living.

If this case had been litigated, would the outcome have been the same? No one could predict that. But using the facts, Steve and Jean defined what they believed was equitable. If a case is litigated, the judge imposes his or her version of what's equitable.

Sometimes, after exhausting all other settlement methods, litigation is the only way a divorce case can be settled. If this happens, having your situation defined and based on fact is vital.

Assistance from Professionals

Just as studies have shown that women are much more likely to ask someone for directions if they are lost, women are also more likely to seek the assistance of professionals when unsure of the correct action to take. It's okay to do a lot of the organizing yourself, but when you are unsure of something, seek advice.

Deirdre had a simple situation and did seek advice. She and her husband had agreed on almost all the details of their property settlement, but were unsure of which method to use in paying for their son's college expenses. Deirdre's husband had offered to pay $1,000 per month and thought the best method would be to pay Deirdre monthly alimony of $1,000. Deirdre could then pay the $1,000 for his expenses and claim her son on her tax return since he lived with her during semester breaks. Therefore, she would get the tax exemption for dependents. Deirdre learned from her advisor that receiving alimony would increase the taxes she would pay. Of every $1,000 she got, she would really be receiving $720 and her husband would really be paying about $600. Deirdre decided this arrangement wasn't the answer to her situation. Since her son resided with her during semester breaks and she provided money for tuition, room, and board, she was already entitled to claim her son as a dependent. Her husband wasn't trying to take advantage of Deirdre; he just didn't have all the facts when he made his offer.

After reading this chapter, you have long ago realized the point being made: Get the facts and know the consequences of your potential decisions before you act.

Of Ownership Rights and Mortgages

There are two elements in home ownership: the title and the mortgage. The *title* names the person or persons who have ownership rights to the property. Ownership rights include selling a portion or all of the property, taking loans against the property's value, renting, or remodeling. Debt on a home is how much owed on the *mortgage,* which is a financial contract in which one party, usually a bank or mortgage company, lends the person or persons named on the title a certain amount of money.

When Jean buys out Steve's equity in the house, two actions should occur. While they are sitting at the settlement table, Steve should execute a *quitclaim deed* giving up all his ownership rights to the property. As a result of Steve signing the quitclaim deed, Jean can change the title to reflect that she is the sole owner. Jean then signs the new mortgage contract taking Steve's name off the mortgage. Although it's rarely allowed, it may be possible for Jean and Steve to sign a letter stating that Jean has bought out Steve's interest in the house, that Jean is solely responsible for repayment of the mortgage and all other costs, and that Steve is relieved of responsibility for payments of any kind relating to the house. This is often called a *hold harmless letter.* If the mortgage company or bank that holds the mortgage accepts the letter, they can retitle the mortgage in Jean's name only. Then if Jean defaulted on the loan, Steve would not be held responsible. As we stated before, this situation is rare. In fact, we have seen just one instance in which it occurred. In most cases, the person taking sole title to the house must refinance the mortgage in his or her name only. In the event of foreclosure, Jean would then be solely responsible for the debt and Steve would be protected.

The Bottom Line

Make informed decisions now, and you will have no regrets in the future.

Chapter 9

The Negotiation Process

Capsule Outlook

Know your rights, your needs, and your "bottom line" before starting to negotiate.

The accumulation of marital assets can be compared to making soup. You put a lot of different assets or ingredients into a big pot, where they all blend together and simmer for a number of years. When the soup is done, both spouses are entitled to a share. So what is the definition of a "share"? Do both spouses get the same number of bowls? Or because one spouse is larger and consumes more calories, should that spouse receive more than the other?

In most households, the person with the greatest need gets the most bowls. Unfortunately, during divorce, emotional stress often clouds the ability to see the issues clearly. If you need more bowls of soup from the pot, you must be prepared to justify that need.

Do Your Homework

All the previous chapters have been devoted to educating and preparing you to make informed decisions about your future. By now, you should have a clear sense of where you are emotionally and financially. We must stress again that financial preparation is the key to a fair settlement. You might still be trying to come to terms with events in your marriage that could have caused your divorce. A therapist is cheaper than an attorney. Use one if necessary.

Specific actions you should be working on at this point include

- ❖ Assembling statements and other financial information.

- ❖ Completing the Personal Information Form in Appendix A, "Forms," which supplies much-needed information to any professionals whose services you may use.

- ❖ Averaging your monthly expenses necessary for completing the Monthly Income, Expense, and Debt Form.

- ❖ Determining values for assets such as your house, land, autos, personal business, vacation timeshare, art, antiques, and collectibles.

- ❖ Making a tentative plan for your lifestyle after the divorce is over. (Be realistic; there is only one Ivana Trump and she still earns a living!)

- ❖ Educating yourself about the divorce process by finishing this book, attending seminars, scanning divorce Web sites on the Internet, or inquiring about information and resources at your local women's center.

The following story is a great reminder that each marriage is a unique set of circumstances. Taking a "cookie cutter" approach to dividing assets and debt could definitely result in an unfair property settlement. Fifty-fifty is easy and equal, but it is not always fair.

Aileen had been married to Jeff for 22 years. She had stayed home during the last 10 years of her marriage. She wanted to slowly transition back into the workforce and had recently taken a part-time job so that she could work and still be home in the afternoon for their then 13-year-old son. Aileen did what most people only think of—she hired a private investigator to follow her husband when she suspected him of having an affair. Unfortunately, Aileen's intuition was correct. The private investigator followed Jeff one night and collected evidence that Jeff was seeing someone else. Aileen knew that her marriage would end and was apprehensive about the future. Even though she now had a job, her work history was spotty at best. To compound this, she had her son to think about.

Aileen was more scared than she was mad. It didn't take much to convince her that she should focus on her financial future instead of attempting to get emotional revenge through the divorce process. Aileen worked with her attorney and provided all the information, statements, and documentation her attorney requested, and more. Aileen was determined to present the facts and prove her needs. In fact, when Aileen retained a certified divorce planner (CDP) to analyze her financial situation, she requested that the CDP prepare the spreadsheets and charts with her receiving 65 percent of the assets and her husband receiving 35 percent. Her thinking was that since her husband made six times the salary she earned, after the divorce he would be able to accumulate assets much more quickly than she would. Also, she had made substantial nonmonetary contributions to the marriage and felt that 65 percent of the assets would be adequate reward for her efforts of 22 years.

There were both negative and positive aspects to Aileen's case. The bad news is the case did go to trial and a judge decided the property division. The good news is that Aileen received 63 percent of the assets, permanent alimony, and payment for all attorneys' fees. The judge's reason was that Aileen clearly had proved her need for alimony and a greater share of the marital assets. You must know and prove your own need, just as Aileen did. As you read each successive chapter, you will have a much clearer picture of your resources, needs, and desires for the future. Use a highlighter, make notes in the margins, dog-ear the pages, and use Post-it notes as tabs. This book is going to be the basis of your action plan. In the negotiating process, you must have a plan, or you won't have a reference point to start from.

Important Financial Issues to Consider

The two biggest mistakes that can be made when negotiating the asset division are not realizing the tax implications of assets, and not knowing how certain assets must be distributed.

You and your spouse might decide to divide an account that contains $100,000 in stock. At first glance, it seems easy: You get shares worth $50,000 and your spouse gets the same. But the true value of the shares might not be the same. If the shares of stock your spouse receives were bought for $48 per share and are now worth $50 per share, very little tax will be due if the stock is sold. If you receive shares of stock that were bought for $15 per share and are now worth $50 per share, you will be paying a large amount of capital gains tax. In effect, if you must pay $7,000 in capital gains tax when the stock is sold, you are actually getting stock worth $43,000, not $50,000. The sale of rental property also has tax implications. A woman was negotiating a settlement with her husband and as part of the division of assets, he offered to let her have sole title to the house they owned and had been renting out for the past 17 years. Her husband told her the house was worth $150,000 since it could be sold for that amount and no mortgage was owed on the property. Omitted from the offer was the fact that the cost basis of the property had been greatly depreciated; if she sold the house, she would have to pay approximately $28,000 in capital gains tax since she had not lived in the house for two of the previous five years and could not claim it as her principal residence.

Another common mistake is not knowing how some assets must be distributed. If you are giving your spouse a portion of your 401(k), you or your spouse must pay an attorney to draft and submit an acceptable *Domestic Relations Order* to the pension administrator at your company. The pension administrator ensures that the order meets all the requirements and then qualifies the order as acceptable for processing. Only then can money be taken from your 401(k) and distributed to your spouse. This cost for drafting and submitting the court order can range from a few hundred to a few thousand dollars, depending on the time required for the work to be done and the attorney's hourly fee. Also, in many states these orders can be submitted to the judge only after the divorce is final.

Computing taxes and drafting court orders are often complicated tasks and should be done only by qualified professionals. We highly recommend that both you and your spouse have an attorney read any settlement proposal before signing the document.

The Basics of Negotiation

Some people love to negotiate and some hate it. In essence, the act of negotiation is two or more parties coming to agreement over the value of a good or service, but there's a lot more to it than that. Each party is working from a reference point, meaning each party has already attached a value to whatever is the subject of the negotiations and knows the *breakpoint,* the lowest value he or she will accept.

If you have ever lived in a foreign country you have probably had the experience of negotiating a sale price when you were shopping. Korea is one country where almost everything is subject to negotiation. Some people love to bargain and some hate it. We have friends who were assigned to a post in Korea. The wife loved to shop and bargain. She always did her homework by seeking out the merchants with the best quality goods at the lowest prices. By doing this, she knew her breakpoint, or the highest price she would pay for something. She also had a negotiating style that worked very well. Almost always when the deal was done, she paid a reasonable price that she considered a bargain and that enabled the storeowner to make a profit. Everyone was happy, and she could return to that store many times and always be treated fairly.

Aileen, whose story is related above, also knew her breakpoint very well. After consulting with the CDP, Aileen knew that she didn't want to start with a 50-50 division of assets and then negotiate lower. During the months before the trial, Aileen's attorney made several attempts to negotiate with the opposing attorney, but the opposing attorney would not discuss any terms that gave his client less than 50 percent of the assets. Aileen's breakpoint was 60 percent of the assets and she would have settled for that amount, but nothing less. She stuck to her guns and received more than she actually hoped for because she had the facts.

Negotiation as an Act of War

It is always fascinating to watch negotiations take place. Each person has a style he or she thinks will work best in that particular situation. In divorce, the approach to negotiations usually has an "us versus them" mentality. You and your attorney are "us" and your spouse and his or her attorney are "them." The divorcing parties have forgotten that their marriage used to be an "us" situation. All that goes out the window.

Several things can happen during this scenario. You may come to the bargaining table prepared with the facts. All the assets and debts have been listed, child support calculated, and monthly expense statement completed, and you are willing to supply documents supporting all your numbers. If the opposing attorney is unprepared, he or she might go into "attack mode." This recently happened to a client. The client and her attorney had completed the required forms and prepared the latest statements of the assets and debts. An analysis had been done based on a proposed division of assets and debts. The client and her attorney were prepared to negotiate with the facts at their disposal. The opposing attorney came to the meeting completely unprepared and assumed he could negotiate off the cuff. When he saw the prepared documents, he immediately tried to discredit the information offered. He threatened to appeal to the court so that the client would have to pay alimony to her husband. He ended the negotiations by walking out of the room.

Your spouse and his or her attorney might withhold information. You may remember a document mentioned in Chapter 1, "You're Getting a Divorce—Now What?" called a *motion to compel*. Filing this motion should be sufficient to force someone to provide the necessary information. One negotiating tactic is to ignore the motion and see whether the filing attorney applies more pressure. Sometimes when a proposed property settlement is prepared, the document lists only assets and doesn't mention the value of each asset. Since the first step in the divorce process is a statement of financial facts, you cannot begin to negotiate until you have accurate, complete financial information.

Negotiating with an incomplete settlement proposal

Negotiating with an incomplete settlement proposal is also common. A woman received a proposed settlement from her husband, who was a successful real estate attorney. The proposal was all words with no values attached to any of the assets. The client had faxed the proposal to the CDP she had arranged to meet with and asked the CDP to read it to ensure there were no financial pitfalls, such as potential capital gains taxes, that she should be aware of before signing. As the CDP read the proposal, she began to sense that something was missing. The proposal offered to let the wife keep the first $1,000,000 from the sale of the marital home. This was a generous gesture, but since their relationship had turned combative, it seemed somewhat out of place. When the CDP met with the woman, the first question the CDP asked was, "What does your husband do for a living?" The woman then told about her husband's practice. The CDP immediately understood the reason for the generous offer of the house equity. Although the law practice was started during the marriage and was definitely a marital asset, it had been purposely omitted from the assets mentioned in the proposed agreement. The CDP advised her client to hire a business valuator, who would be able to analyze the law practice and place a value on this asset. Until the entire asset values are known, the woman could not effectively evaluate her husband's proposal.

Using children as emotional hostages

The CDP's client you just read about also had to deal with another common negotiating tactic: using the kids as emotional hostages.

Yes, unfortunately this happens. Her husband told her that if she did not agree to his terms and if she asked for more alimony or a greater share of the assets, he would tell the children it was their mother's fault he couldn't pay for their college education. During their marriage, she and her husband had established a high standard of living, but they could afford it. Child support had already been computed with income from the woman's part-time job of $2,000 per month and her husband's income of over $44,000. Yes, that's $44,000 per month. The woman's expenses were over $5,500 per month. So you do the math. Fortunately, the woman could do the math and realized she was being manipulated. Her attorney has since assumed negotiations with her husband.

Using the "water on rock" technique

The "water on rock" technique is also used in negotiating as an act of war. Your spouse and his or her attorney might not be openly combative, but will continually go over and over the same points until your patience has been exhausted. Of course, the goal is for you to get to a point where you just give up. Also, any concerns or objections you have may be trivialized and treated as petty or unimportant. If your emotional baggage has not been checked, this technique can be quite effective. Just the relief of not having to undergo a constant barrage of objections could be enough to force you to surrender.

Lucy was 65 years old and had recently undergone a heart bypass operation. She was physically frail, which weakened her emotional state. Lucy's husband had retained an attorney who viewed negotiations as adversarial with little or no room for negotiation. Lucy was continually barraged with requests for information. In addition, Lucy's husband suddenly stopped paying the mortgage and Lucy had no income because of her recent surgery. It was clear that her husband and his attorney were gradually wearing Lucy down so that she would agree to their settlement terms. However, she never surrendered. She complied with the requests for information, but never gave in. After 18 months, she and her husband negotiated a settlement and Lucy received a much higher share of the assets.

If you are a victim of the "water on rock" technique, we strongly advise that you review your financial facts, especially your Monthly Income, Expense, and Debt Form. Giving up monthly alimony payments now could make a big difference when you have to pay your own health insurance after the divorce.

Settling before the trial begins

Settling on the courthouse steps happens all too often. In fact, it is the preferred technique of some attorneys. You see, testifying in court is intimidating. Many people would rather go through a root canal without Novocain than appear before a judge. You or your attorney may have made numerous attempts to settle before the court date, but the opposing attorney refused. Imagine that in 30 minutes you are scheduled to appear in the courtroom and have a judge decide the settlement terms. If you reach an agreement now, you will know what you are getting. If the judge decides, it is anyone's guess how things will turn out. An opposing attorney can use this pressure to his or her advantage. In fact, most cases scheduled to go to trial are decided in the courthouse before the trial begins. The pressure is intense, so you might agree to just about anything just to have relief. Therefore, you settle.

There are two problems with this scenario. One, you probably will agree to terms that are less favorable, so you will not get the alimony or assets you might truly need. Second, you still have to pay your attorney's fees for all the time spent preparing for trial and the time spent in court that day.

Unfortunately, the divorce process brings out the worst in some people. It might be because divorce is traditionally seen as an adversarial process in which you must fight to get what you believe should be rightfully yours. It may also just be that the people who make negotiations into a war-like process have that mental mindset about life in general. You know yourself, and hopefully you know your spouse. If you believe you will confront any of the situations just described, mental and financial preparation is essential. You may be left with no choice but to retain an attorney to assist in the negotiations.

Negotiation as an Act of Good Faith

Now that we've looked at the dark side, let's look at the more positive alternative.

If this were a perfect world, there would be no wars, all people would be respected equally, chocolate would cure all ailments, and divorce negotiations would always be approached with honesty and fairness. Judging by the experiences we just described, we can safely say that our world is not perfect. But we can definitely work toward that goal.

Negotiating as an act of good faith is much simpler and has much lower emotional and financial costs than negotiating as an act of war.

Negotiating a settlement agreement should be a three-step process:

1. **Both parties give complete cooperation and full disclosure.** Use the "kitchen table" method of arranging the statements and listing all your assets and debts. This method was discussed in Chapter 4, "Getting Organized."

2. **Both parties consider the needs of the entire family.** Above all, list in detail the needs of any children. If possible, ask for their input before deciding the custody arrangements. You are much more likely to have well-adjusted children after the divorce if they have a say in who they live with and the visitation schedule of the other parent.

3. **Both parties construct an agreement that truly reflects the needs of the entire family.** You and your spouse know your needs better than anyone else. Use this knowledge to craft an agreement that will benefit everyone. Remember, you were a family before the divorce and you will still be a family afterward. The parent-child relationship remains, even if the parents no longer reside in the same house.

Negotiating Strategies That Work

Many divorcing couples work out the details of their settlement agreements between themselves. Several strategies have been proved over and over again to work the best.

Splitting the Assets and Debt

Starting with a 50-50 split can be effective, especially if working with a CFP, an accountant, or a CDP who can use software to show the results of various settlement options. Since this asset division is usually seen as a worst-case scenario, giving each spouse exactly half of the marital assets and debts gives a good picture of how this split will affect both parties. If one spouse earns much more than the other, usually the higher earning spouse sees his or her net worth and liquid assets growing while the lesser earning spouse barely accumulates assets or goes into debt just to meet basic living expenses. After the true picture is known, adjustments can be made that result in a much more equitable settlement. Assets and debts can be shifted from one spouse to the other, and paying or receiving alimony can be considered as an alternative.

Splitting the Difference

Splitting the difference often results in a win-win situation. Since negotiation is often seen as a game of one-upmanship, splitting the difference levels the playing field. A good example of this technique is if you want $100,000 of the assets and your spouse offers $75,000. The difference between the two amounts is $25,000. Your counteroffer could be to split the difference by dividing the $25,000 in half and giving up $12,500. You would then accept $82,500 instead of $100,000. That way, you both are forfeiting an equal amount, and there is no loser.

Trying on Each Other's Shoes

A third negotiating method enables the two parties to view the property settlement from their spouse's position. The wife selects assets for the husband and vice versa. More important, each person states the reasons for his or her choices. While some might think this is an exercise in futility, it does offer each spouse insight into the motivation behind the behavior and often results in moving the negotiations toward settlement.

The alternate-selection method, described in Chapter 7, "Dividing Your Assets and Debts," is used commonly in the last stage of property settlement: dividing the personal property. Personal property such as furniture, jewelry, and artwork is part of the history of the marriage and often has sentimental value. An example is a couple who had a tense relationship, yet the wife wanted to keep jewelry the husband had given her because it represented the good times in their marriage. This method of division works well because it is fair and each person gets some of the items he or she really wants.

These negotiating methods have been tried and proved to be effective, as long as both spouses are willing to make the attempt. You might find that one method suits your situation better than others. That's fine; the important thing is to attempt to negotiate first and litigate only if all other methods fail.

Separating Want from Need

Many times, what people think they want at the beginning of the divorce process is completely different from what they know they want at final negotiations.

Take the case of Martha and Sam. They had been married for 28 years. Sam had been a military officer and Martha had moved with him from place to place during his career. After Sam retired, he accepted a well-paying job. Martha, now settled in one place, renewed her career in real estate. They had been married a long time and their marriage had been stable, but not particularly happy. Through a coincidence, Martha found that Sam had been having an affair with someone for the past 10 years. Martha saw it as a betrayal that made most of their marriage a lie. Sam and Martha both wanted to end their marriage with as little cost as possible. They retained a professional to value and list their assets and debts, analyze their cash flows, and produce the charts and spreadsheets showing several asset and debt division scenarios.

During the first meeting to begin their financial analysis, Martha stated very strongly that she wanted Sam to pay her $3,000 per month in alimony for the rest of her life. In fact, Martha pounded on the table when she made that statement. She also remarked that she was willing to go to court and spend whatever it took to ensure she received this amount of alimony. Many different asset and debt division scenarios were produced, and Sam and Martha carefully studied them all. After Martha had been shown the true benefit of alimony and realized she would, in fact, be able to spend only $1,998 of the $3,000 because of income taxes, she retreated on her initial demand.

How did Sam and Martha settle their property division? After two months of analyzing seven different asset division scenarios, Martha declared that she did not want alimony. She would rather have a higher share of the assets, which she could invest. That was fine with Sam since he never wanted to pay alimony. Sam and Martha settled their property division by using the facts and negotiating between themselves. Even with their almost hostile relationship, they would rather have talked to each other than pay attorneys to fight in court.

This story yields a great lesson: Eventually, facts triumph over emotions. It took two months of constant work, but Martha finally realized that extracting revenge by making Sam pay $3,000 per month was not really in her best interest.

Most disagreements arise when there is a difference between want and need. The importance lies in reconciling these two issues. In divorce, there is a choice. Two spouses can negotiate based on the true needs of both parties, they can retain attorneys who can negotiate for them based on what their attorneys' experience and the law views as fair, or a judge can determine the needs of both parties. By doing your homework and objectively determining your real needs, you can help prevent the last two choices from occurring.

In closing this chapter, the bottom line is words of wisdom spoken by Lynn Brenner, a wonderful attorney with more than 20 years of experience in the practice of family law.

The Bottom Line

When negotiating the division of your assets and debts, be realistic and don't expect the negotiations to go any better than your marriage. If you fought then, the chances are very good that you will fight now.

Chapter 10

The Settlement Agreement

Capsule Outlook

Your future will be defined by this document for many years to come.

The settlement agreement is a roadmap for your life after divorce. All the hard work you have done by becoming educated, organized and fully involved is about to pay dividends. You are almost finished with the most difficult part of the process.

The Purpose and Scope of the Agreement

After you have decided the legal issues, such as child custody and visitation, and the financial issues, such as division of marital assets and debts, alimony, and child support, you will have these issues formally stated in a document. Depending on the state, your agreement may be called a property settlement agreement (PSA), a marital settlement agreement (MSA), or simply a settlement agreement.

The purpose of the agreement is to formally and legally record the terms of the separation. The scope of the agreement concerns actions that have occurred from the date of the marriage until the date of the separation, legal filing, or divorce. What's important is that the agreement binds both parties to perform specific actions that will occur after the divorce is granted. That's the legalese version. The settlement agreement basically describes who gets what, who pays what, and where the children will reside after the marriage has ended. In most states, the settlement agreement is incorporated into the final decree of divorce so that all the terms you and your spouse have previously decided on become part of the decree.

Keep in mind that signing the agreement does not mean you are granted a divorce. In fact, you and your spouse might sign the agreement months or years before filing the documents necessary to legally end your marriage.

Understanding the Settlement Agreement

The terms you and your spouse negotiate and the document itself might be very creative, depending on your specific situation. If it suits your needs to use the yacht every other Sunday during the summer, then so be it. Remember that you will have to abide by the terms you negotiate.

As creative as your document may be, certain terms and sections, described in the following sections, are included in every settlement agreement.

Recitals

The first section of the agreement starts with a statement citing the date and names of the two spouses and may include their Social Security numbers. The recitals section also states the date and place of the marriage and names of the children and their dates of birth, may contain the date the spouses separated or started living apart, and states that the parties want to enter into a legally binding agreement and be governed by the agreement's description of terms of child custody, alimony, and all financial and property matters.

Child Custody and Visitation

The parenting plan, which the two spouses have agreed to, is described in this section. The type of physical custody is described as sole, shared, or split, and the visitation schedule is defined. A common visitation schedule is that the child or children stay with the noncustodial parent every other weekend, two or three weeks in the summer, and a portion of spring and Christmas breaks. If the mother and father live within a short distance of each other, the noncustodial parent can have the child stay overnight during the week and make sure the child is taken to school the next morning. Visitation can be on a loose schedule with room for deviation, depending on the needs of the children and the parents, or it can be a very specific plan.

Many times, when clients work with a certified divorce planner (CDP) they will ask that the CDP read the settlement agreement before they sign to ensure that all the financial information provided during their analysis is included and correctly stated. A very bitter and contentious divorce settlement agreement is usually also the most specific concerning details such as the child visitation schedule. Every pickup and drop-off time for the children can be exactingly stated down to the minute. There can also be provisions and penalties if one of the parents was more than five minutes late.

This section also addresses the amount of child support to be paid, when the payments will be made, and when payments will end. In some states, child support is paid until the child reaches age 18, graduates from high school, is married, or is otherwise emancipated. In some states the age is 21. Be sure to check the age limit in your state.

Since it is important that the child's welfare be the main consideration during divorce, language concerning how the mother and father should conduct themselves after the divorce could be included. Specifics include keeping each other fully informed about the children's health and consulting with each other on major problems and decisions. These decisions might include education and private schooling, religious training, health care, and discipline methods. Also, a statement can be included mandating that both the mother and father make every reasonable effort to maintain free access to the children and not hamper the parent-child relationship.

One of the most common clauses included in this section addresses planning for future college costs. Keep in mind that in many states, the court does not require the parent or parents to pay these costs. College tuition, room, board, fees, and other expenses are not considered essential to raising the child to the age of majority. Given all this information, most parents still want their children to have a college education. A compromise that's used frequently is including a clause in the agreement stating that "after all scholarships, grants, work/study program income, and loans have been considered, any remaining costs will be borne by the parents in some proportion." Usually, the remaining costs are paid on a pro rata basis, which means by percentage of income. If the mother earns 75 percent of the parents' total income, she pays 75 percent of the remaining costs and the father pays 25 percent. Most likely, a sentence will be added stating the age at which any parental obligation for college expenses will end. In Chapter 13, "Understanding the Fundamentals," the concept of goal setting and balancing your children's need for higher education against your need for retirement funds will be discussed. Read that chapter carefully and take to heart the advice that is given.

The extra expenses that always arise can be addressed in the agreement, too. These costs can be stated as nonreimbursed expenses or as extraordinary medical, dental, or other expenses not already included in the child support calculation. No matter what language is used, defining responsibility for future costs now causes much less friction when these bills have to be paid.

Health and Dental Coverage

If your state requires that children who are minors must be covered by medical insurance, the settlement agreement states which parent will be responsible for maintaining this coverage. The premium amount for health and dental benefits is included in the calculation of child support payments. Spouses are usually allowed to remain covered by an employer's plan until the divorce is final. After the divorce, a husband or wife can still retain medical coverage under their ex-spouse's plan, but do not pay the same rate because he or she is no longer considered a family member. Under the COBRA legislation, ex-spouses may retain medical insurance from their former husband or wife's employer for as long as 36 months after the divorce. The average monthly COBRA premium varies, but plan on paying at least $250 per month.

Spousal Maintenance/Alimony

If no alimony will be paid or received by either spouse, a clause can be inserted stating that they both forever waive any right to receiving alimony.

As with the conditions for child support, alimony provisions should state the monthly or yearly amount to be paid, when the payments are to begin, and the term or length of payments. If alimony is to be event specific, the terminating action or event must be described. If alimony is to be paid for a certain term, the number of years or months must be stated. Permanent or lifetime alimony usually stops if the recipient or payer dies or the recipient remarries, whichever occurs first. We have read an agreement that contained alimony provisions that were a combination of term and permanent. The wife would receive alimony for nine years. If the wife remarried any time during the first three years, the alimony payments would still be paid but would stop after three years.

A common clause included in this section addresses whether the alimony payments can be modified. Usually, child support and alimony are modifiable. If the wife is to receive alimony but wins the lottery, for example, shortly after the divorce, the ex-husband can petition the court to have the alimony payments reduced or stopped. Remember that alimony is based on need and the ability to pay. If the recipient has sufficient income on his or her own and no longer has a need, the court can decide whether alimony payments from the ex-spouse are still necessary.

A Word of Caution

As with many things, alimony is a double-edged sword. Nonmodifiable alimony does not change if your ex-spouse becomes wealthy and could easily afford to pay a larger amount. On the other hand, if alimony is modifiable and your ex-spouse loses a job through no fault of his or her own and can't earn a living, then alimony payments can be ordered to stop completely. Making alimony modifiable is an area that should be carefully considered. Consulting an attorney could ensure that the agreement clauses on alimony are described as you fully intended.

The following story has two morals. A local attorney was retained to plead a case for a man who had been divorced for five years. The settlement agreement, which he and his ex-wife had signed, stated that he would pay alimony of $500 per month. It seems that the ex-wife's attorney had prepared the agreement and the man decided he didn't need an attorney to read the agreement to make sure his rights were being protected. The settlement agreement stated only that the man would pay his ex-wife $500 per month. There was no time limit or event that stated when the payments would end. In the meantime, the ex-wife had married a doctor who earned a large salary, so the man reasoned that since his ex-wife was enjoying a better lifestyle, she no longer needed the alimony to be self-sufficient. "Wrong," said the court. No conditions were agreed on as to when alimony would end. Therefore, the man had to pay his ex-wife $500 per month for the rest of his or her life, whoever died first.

The two morals are first, know what you are agreeing to, and second, secure the opinion of a professional to ensure you know what you are agreeing to. Most certainly, if the man had paid an attorney to read the settlement agreement, the attorney would have made sure his client knew the implications of signing the agreement without the clause for terminating the alimony.

Life Insurance

Protection should be included for income provided by future payments. If a father is to pay child support from his salary but then dies, the child support payments would stop. We have never met a parent who did not want to make sure their children have the same standard of living after the parent's death. Often, the most effective and inexpensive way to add this protection is by maintaining a term life insurance policy on the life of the payer. If the payer dies, a portion of the lump sum death benefit would be paid to the surviving parent or guardian to be used exclusively for the children.

Although life insurance is almost always included for child support, it is often omitted when planning for continuation of alimony. Anyone who receives alimony depends on this income the same as wages or any other source of income. The settlement agreement can guarantee the right to an insurance policy, but usually the person receiving the alimony payments makes the premium payments. If the receiver pays the premium, he or she can ensure that the policy remains in force. It happens all too often that the policy lapses and an ex-spouse receives nothing when the payer dies.

We highly recommend that a provision be included that addresses the need for disability insurance for one or both of the parties. The intent is the same as the need for life insurance. Payments for child support and alimony are made from current wages and salary. If the payer is incapacitated and unable to work, a plan for substitute income must be in place.

Division of Property

Deciding who gets what should already be a done deal by the time the agreement is prepared. Specific paragraphs address how the assets will be divided. Real estate, including houses, land, and rental properties, is usually listed first since these assets are the most valuable. Also, this section specifies who must pay any remaining mortgage balances. As we stated in Chapter 7, "Dividing Your Assets and Debts," whoever receives an asset almost always assumes responsibility for any debt associated with that asset.

If the marital home is to be sold, specific actions should be addressed, such as when and who will list the property, how the net proceeds of the sale will be distributed, and how disputes over the listing price or other aspects of the sale should be addressed. It might be possible to use a mediator, or the court can make the final determination. A full description should be included about how the costs from settling the dispute will be paid.

Retirement assets such as 401(k)s, pensions, and IRAs are mentioned in a separate paragraph and repayment of any loans on these accounts should also be addressed. Since a *Qualified Domestic Relations Order* or other court order might be needed to transfer money from one account to another, the agreement should mention who will take the responsibility for paying for these orders to be prepared. This issue is rarely discussed and often seen as a secondary action or something to be done after the divorce has been granted.

The agreement also describes the disposition of personal property, savings and investment accounts, and autos and other vehicles.

Debts and Other Pledges of Credit

Just as the assets are divided, the debts must be divided also. As we previously stated, usually the person who receives the asset assumes the responsibility for any debt associated with that asset. Still, to make sure there are no misunderstandings, each debt should name the person responsible for repayment. Each spouse should confirm that there are no other outstanding debts he or she is liable for.

Tax Matters

The couple is usually still married after the settlement agreement has been prepared and signed. If they are still married at the end of the year, they will be able to file income tax as Married Filing Jointly, even though they have a settlement agreement in force and intend to divorce. If one spouse has sole custody of the children and wants to file as Head of Household, the other spouse must file as Married Filing Separately and, as a result, pay more taxes. How the couple files income taxes is a negotiable item. Also, if the couple has children who are minors, it should be stated who has the right to claim the children as dependents for tax purposes. Usually, the parent the children live with claims the exemption. However, this right can be waived and transferred to the noncustodial parent.

The settlement agreement can specify whether alimony is deductible for the payer and taxable income for the receiver. Also, since few facts are usually known about the future sale of assets, courts may consider potential taxes in dividing the marital property. The attempt at computing taxes is complicated and might be beyond the court's authority. Therefore, a clause can be included stating that each party will have the responsibility for any taxes incurred in selling or otherwise transferring any of the marital assets divided in the agreement.

Release and Waiver

This section addresses the right of either spouse to make a claim against the estate of the other. Since all marital property is divided and distributed by the settlement agreement, any property accumulated after the agreement is executed is deemed separate property. This clause does not prevent either spouse from filing for Social Security benefits as a former spouse or widow/widower. The right to receive survivor benefits from retirement plans is not affected by this statement.

Additional clauses can address actions such as the reconciliation of the spouses, claims for payment of attorney's fees, bankruptcy, right to independent counsel, and incorporation of the agreement into a decree of divorce.

Seeking Professional Advice in Creating the Settlement Agreement

Many people negotiate their own agreement and also file the paperwork for dissolving their marriage. Sometimes this works, but many times it is a mistake.

Since the financial and legal aspects of divorce are so complicated, seeking out and using the advice of professionals while negotiating and preparing your settlement agreement can be a wise investment. Sometimes wording omitted from the agreement is more damaging than any inaccuracies the document might contain. A good example was given in the previous section "Spousal Maintenance/Alimony." The omission of a few words from the agreement forced a man to continue paying alimony, even after the need no longer existed.

Especially important are any tax implications that arise when assets are sold. Before signing the agreement, a CPA or accountant should be consulted, especially when complicated assets such as rental property are involved. A depreciated tax basis on a beach house that has been rented for many years could result in a high tax bill when the property is sold. CPAs can also assist in estate planning and reducing taxes when transferring property to your potential heirs.

The advice of certified financial planners and investment advisors is usually sought after the settlement has been signed, but the delay in getting their advice could be a big mistake. It is best to show any proposed settlement agreement to your financial advisor before signing. These professionals are knowledgeable about investments and asset allocation. Even though you might get a portion of your spouse's retirement account in cash, you must know the details of specific actions you should take to avoid paying unnecessary taxes and fees. If you are to receive stocks, bonds, mutual funds, or other investments from the property settlement, you should know in advance which of these assets would benefit you the most. Consulting with an advisor before the settlement is signed will give you a much better understanding of the assets you may receive.

Of course, using the advice and skill of professionals should not take the place of educating yourself about the divorce process. Internet sources such as www.splitup.com and www.divorce-source.com can be invaluable in giving you the big picture about financial and legal issues. Contact the Internal Revenue Service about the various pamphlets available that explain some of the tax implications of divorce. The IRS Web site, www.irs.gov, offers a wealth of information, and you can download forms and publications right from the Web site. You can also place an order for information to be mailed to you or e-mail a specific question and IRS personnel will make sure you get an answer.

Anne's story is a good illustration for the bottom line in this chapter.

It had been a long and stressful day for Anne, even before she met her attorney at the courthouse at 9:30 A.M. As a result of anticipating her court testimony, Anne had slept poorly the night before and was feeling mentally and physically weak as she stood on the courthouse steps with her attorney and financial advisors. As expected, her husband's attorney made another offer minutes before the trial was scheduled to start. Anne was under a great deal of pressure to make quick decisions in hopes of settling her case. Both attorneys made several offers and counteroffers before Anne and her husband agreed on the terms of their settlement. After all the details concerning alimony and the asset division had been worked out, Anne felt a great deal of relief. The opposing attorney requested that Anne, her attorney, and her husband stay in the area while his secretary typed the settlement agreement. Then they could meet in his office to sign the papers.

They all went their separate ways to have lunch and then met to sign the agreement. The next day Anne read the agreement again, and was horrified to discover that some of the terms she had agreed to at the courthouse had been changed or left out of the agreement altogether. The biggest change was the disposition of the house. Anne had traded her right to her husband's retirement so that she could keep the house. But the agreement stated that if she died within three years, her soon-to-be ex-husband would get half of the proceeds from the sale of the house. Of course, this discovery caused Anne more emotional distress, but there was nothing she could do. Even Anne's attorney had not caught the errors when he read the agreement. If Anne had gone home, gotten a good night's sleep, and then returned the next day to sign the agreement, she would have noticed these changes. But she yielded to pressure because she just wanted to get it all over with. Fortunately, Anne has lived more than the required three years since signing the agreement and can dispose of the house as she wishes.

The Bottom Line

Make sure you understand every aspect of your agreement thoroughly before signing.

Chapter 11

After the Agreement Is Reached

Capsule Outlook

You are not done yet; make sure the agreement contains every detail you negotiated.

Congratulations. By the time you've reached this point, you've made it through the toughest part of the divorce process. Let's recap for a moment to see how far you've come:

- ❖ There are complete and accurate listings of your assets and debts, how they are titled, and their values.

- ❖ An agreement has been reached on the type of custody you and your spouse will have for your children. Also, you have a framework of days, weeks, or months to serve as a schedule for where the children will be living.

- ❖ All of the children's immediate medical, dental, and extraordinary needs have been assessed and these items have been included in the child support calculation.

❖ Provisions have been made in your agreement for any other extraordinary expenses for children who are minors.

❖ The amount and term of alimony has been agreed on.

❖ A realistic monthly budget has been created that shows your present living conditions and projections for anticipated future changes after the divorce.

❖ You know how changes in your income tax filing status will affect the amount of federal and state taxes you pay for this year and the next two calendar years.

❖ Using the preceding information, you know all sources of income, what payments of taxes and expenses need to be made, and whether you will have a deficit or excess cash to invest.

❖ You and your spouse have reached an agreement on the division of assets and debts.

Much effort and thought has gone into preparing for a successful transition from your present lifestyle to your future one. If you have reached this point in the divorce process, you should take great satisfaction in the knowledge and control you have gained from your efforts.

A Word About the Intangible

We hope you and your spouse have been able to work cooperatively during this time. If this is the case, you will have preserved not only your assets, but also your potential future relationship. Being able to maintain cordial relations should always be a goal during divorce, especially when children are involved. If this period has been traumatic and difficult, you would be wise to take the time now to evaluate whether you need the services of a therapist. Even if your negotiations have been fairly easy with no bickering or emotional blackmail, you might need to take an emotional inventory of how well you are enduring the inevitable changes during this time. Everyone feels stress, whether they show it or not. The emotional effects of divorce could affect you at any time during the process. It's important to recognize that this part of your life is in the past, and you must now live in the present and plan for the future.

Preparing the Settlement Agreement

After all the financial and legal details have been worked out, a formal, binding contract must be prepared that is acceptable to the court. We discussed the different portions of the agreement in Chapter 10, "The Settlement Agreement," so you can use that chapter as a checklist of what must and what can be included.

Seek Professional Advice

An attorney usually prepares the agreement—that is, drafting the document and ensuring that all the important details are included. In some states, mediators can draft the agreement, and this is especially helpful if the two spouses have used the services of the mediator who has in-depth knowledge of their particular situation.

We urge you not to attempt to prepare a settlement agreement on your own. There are many small but important details that must be included to protect both you and your spouse. Remember the story of the man in Chapter 10, who thought he didn't need an attorney to read the agreement before he signed and, as a result, wound up paying his ex-wife $500 per month in alimony for the remainder of their lives? This is just one example of how spending a little money right now could produce big savings later on.

Check and Double-Check

By the time you've reached this point in the divorce process, the tendency is to relax and not pay close attention to the details. Don't make this mistake. The attorney or mediator who drafts the agreement is not a mind reader. Make sure they have all the details that were agreed on.

Since you have taken the time and effort to complete the forms in this book, use them as part of a checklist to make sure no details are accidentally left out of the document.

Start with the Personal Information Form, which is described in detail in Chapter 4, "Getting Organized." When completing this form, you are asked to list all your assets and debts, as well as their values and present balances. Make sure your agreement names each asset, its value, and who gets that asset. Also, each debt should be stated, along with the amount of each debt and who has payment responsibility.

Child custody and monthly child support and alimony payments should have already been calculated and agreed on with your spouse. Specific dates or events must also be mentioned that determine when child support and alimony payments will end. The agreement should include a specific plan for paying the children's extra expenses and also state which parent claims the children for income tax purposes. Remember that your agreement should specify whether alimony is modifiable or nonmodifiable. Payments for child support and alimony usually begin immediately after the agreement is signed by both spouses and notarized. If this is not the case, a starting date should be included.

The specifics of tax deductions and exemptions must be included. If your children live with you most of the time, but you are willing to waive your right to the exemption by completing Form 8332, you must also state whether your spouse can claim the children for one year, a number of years, or indefinitely. If you are to pay or receive alimony, your agreement should state whether the alimony is tax deductible for the payer and taxable income for the receiver.

Your agreement should state whether one or both spouses will maintain insurance policies to replace child support or alimony payments, in the event of the payer's death. Information on other insurance policies, such as health insurance covering minor children and disability insurance for continuation of child support or alimony payments in the event of the payer's inability to work, should also be included.

A final word to the wise—read through all your notes, checklists, and other documents to make sure every detail you and your spouse agreed to is included in the settlement agreement.

Preparing a Domestic Relations Order

If you are to receive a portion of one or more of your spouse's retirement accounts, most likely you need to have a court order prepared called a Domestic Relations Order (DRO). The Internal Revenue Service has specified that most employer-sponsored retirement accounts, such as a 401(k) and 403(b), are tax-qualified plans. Because of this tax-deferred designation, these accounts must be transferred or divided only by court order. The DRO should be prepared as soon as the asset division has been agreed on. Ideally, the recipient should retain an attorney to prepare the DRO so that it can be sent to the judge for signature at the same time as the final decree of divorce. After the DRO is signed by the judge, your attorney should forward it to the company pension plan administrator. He or she will look it over carefully and make sure that it contains all the necessary information and can be accepted for processing. When the DRO has been accepted, it is given the status of being qualified and the DRO then becomes a Qualified Domestic Relations Order (QDRO). One distinction about division of retirement accounts must be made: In most cases, your divorce must be granted before you can submit a DRO or divorce decree to any institution requesting that an account be divided because of the property settlement.

Separating Accounts

It is common for the division of assets, other than retirement, to begin immediately after the settlement agreement has been signed. The rationale is that the agreement is legally binding and therefore pretty much set in stone. Most couples close joint accounts and open new separate accounts by transferring funds or shares of stock, mutual funds or other investments from the old accounts. Also, it is common for the house to be put up for sale immediately after the agreement is signed, if that is what the couple agreed on. If one spouse buys out the other spouse's equity, the spouse remaining in the home begins refinancing and at the refinancing settlement the other spouse executes a quit-claim deed, transferring his or her ownership rights. Autos must be retitled and investment accounts divided by transferring shares from a joint account to new individual accounts.

Debts such as auto loans and credit cards must be separated and retitled, if necessary. This could get somewhat tricky since auto loans are usually made in both spouses' names. If this is the case, the institution that issued your loan might want the joint loan account to be closed and a new loan issued only in the name of the spouse who is assuming that debt. This reissuing could result in the new auto loan having a higher interest rate than the previous loan. It is easier if each spouse can assume responsibility for debt that is titled in his or her own name only, but this might not be possible. Balances from joint credit cards can be transferred to new accounts in only one spouse's name. This method seems to be the easiest way to divide credit card debt. There are banks and other credit card lenders who will remove a spouse's name from the account. It is best to ask each lender how it handles dividing accounts.

Signing Your Settlement Agreement Makes It a Valid Contract

You may think the above statement is a little too obvious—that after all the effort and expense you would be more than willing to sign on the dotted line. Well, it might not be too obvious after all. There are people who don't sign the agreement immediately after it is prepared. Sometimes, they never sign.

Consequences can result from not promptly signing your agreement. Some time ago, we helped a very nice couple with the financial portion of their divorce. They had no children and therefore had to wait only six months before filing their petition for divorce. They were a pleasure to work with and were fair in respecting each other's needs and opinions. Their analysis was finished quickly, and they retained a mediator who prepared their settlement agreement.

A problem arose about a year later, when the wife called to ask what to do about the transfer of funds from the husband's retirement account. When they had negotiated the asset division, the wife was to receive a major portion of one of the husband's IRAs. But in the time the couple had delayed signing their agreement, the stock market had dropped significantly. When the couple finally thought about signing their agreement, the portion of the

IRA the wife had negotiated to receive was more than the total amount of money remaining in the entire IRA account. After consultation with an attorney, the couple agreed that the wife would receive the amount that had been negotiated, or the entirety of the account, whichever was smaller. As it turns out, the wife received all shares in the account. The husband received nothing, even though they had agreed he would receive $25,000 of the account. This is a good example of how waiting can be costly.

The last thing to do before signing your agreement is to discuss it with an attorney. By doing this, you ensure that someone with experience and knowledge is looking out for your best interests. Also, by reading the document, the attorney can catch errors and discuss with you any clauses or statements that might seem out of the ordinary. It's a good way to make sure your true intentions are stated in the agreement.

Legal Actions After Signing the Settlement Agreement

After the settlement agreement has been signed by both parties and is witnessed by a notary, it can become part of the final decree of divorce. A judge reads the agreement, especially when the couple has children who are minors, to ensure that an acceptable amount of child support has been set for future payment. The judge then signs the decree and it is entered into the court record. Your attorney gets the signed final decree of divorce from the clerk's office at the courthouse and then sends a signed copy to you. Your divorce is not final until the decree is signed and any period for filing appeals has expired.

Don't forget about any court orders needed to transfer retirement funds from one spouse to the other. If funds are being transferred from a Defined Benefit Plan, such as a private employer pension, or Defined Contribution Plan, such as a 401(k), Thrift Savings Plan, profit-sharing plan, Money Purchase Plan, Keogh, tax-sheltered annuity, or Employee Stock Ownership Plan, a Domestic Relations Order must be prepared. Other plans, such as those covering police and fire personnel and state and city government employees, require a court order. Plans covered by the Employee Retirement Income Security Act of 1947 require a DRO, too. Other plans require another type of court order. These orders should be prepared immediately after you and your spouse negotiated the division of assets and debts. The DRO or other court order should be submitted to the court at the same time as the final decree of divorce. That way the judge can sign all the documents at the same time. When your attorney receives the signed DRO or court order, he or she should immediately submit that document to the pension plan administrator at your or your spouse's place of employment. The plan administrator reviews the DRO, accepts it as complying with the requirements of that particular company, and then qualifies the order. The order then changes from a Domestic Relations Order (DRO) to a Qualified Domestic Relations Order (QDRO). The plan administrator contacts whichever spouse is to receive the funds so that the necessary documents can be completed, and the transfer of the funds can then take place.

We can't emphasize strongly enough that, if you are getting money from your spouse's retirement account, the DRO or court order should be prepared and submitted promptly. We have a friend whose divorce has been final for several years. When asked about her DRO and when she was to receive the money from her ex-husband's retirement account, she just shrugged her shoulders. Her attorney had prepared the QDRO several months after the divorce was final, but it was never submitted. It was then explained to her that she was the owner of that money and should have control of it. As long as the money remained in her ex-husband's account, he controlled the investments. Her ex-husband's investment style is much more aggressive than hers, and that meant her money was not invested in funds that would benefit her the most. Unfortunately, the stock market has since dropped significantly and the investments she was supposed to receive have lost value. If the money had been transferred to her IRA, she would have invested it in mutual funds with much less risk.

These are issues most people never think about. Not taking action can really hurt.

The V-8 Experience

You might remember the television commercials for V-8 Juice: The man or woman is drinking a beverage, sees someone drinking V-8, and slaps him or herself on the forehead and exclaims, "I should have had a V-8!" The gesture and phrase was used for many years afterward when someone should have thought before they acted. This happens in divorce, too. Sometimes, through error or intent, something is left out of the settlement agreement.

Modifications or changes can be made to portions of a settlement agreement. Child support is most often modified when one of the parent's income increases or decreases significantly. The same can be done with alimony payments, if the payments were previously agreed to as modifiable. Child custody can be changed if one of the parents moves from the local area or if the children's needs change as they grow older.

Some states allow modification of the agreement if an asset or clause was accidentally omitted. If assets were intentionally omitted or not disclosed during the negotiations, one party can petition the court to change the agreement.

Some parts of the agreement may not be modifiable, specifically those clauses dealing with the division of assets. If you change your mind and want more assets or different assets after the agreement has been signed, it might be too late. That's one reason to take your time, know what you want, and understand your rights and responsibilities before signing the agreement.

Enforcing the Agreement

Most people willingly live up to their responsibilities under the settlement agreement, but not everyone. The two areas where problems usually arise are payment of child support and child visitation. If your ex-spouse does not obey the agreement, you could be forced to take legal action, which might include garnishing your ex-spouse's wages or bank accounts or having a sheriff seize property belonging to your ex-spouse so it can be sold. A spouse can be held in contempt of court if he or she doesn't turn over property as specified in the agreement or violates the child visitation clauses, and those held in contempt of court can be jailed or fined.

Taking Action After the Divorce

Some people don't want their ex-spouse to be the beneficiary of their retirement accounts or insurance.

Your state may have laws that change your estate plan immediately upon a divorce. If it does, your ex-spouse would no longer be a beneficiary. At the very least, check your state's law before your divorce becomes final.

The best course of action is to complete a review of all accounts, titles, and ownership documents before the divorce is final. Beneficiaries for retirement accounts cannot be changed until the divorce is final, unless the spouse who is the beneficiary signs a notarized statement acknowledging that he or she agrees to the change. Once the divorce is final, you can change your designation of beneficiaries for any and all assets and accounts, other than those agreed to in your settlement agreement.

Legal documents that must be changed include wills, trusts, and powers of attorney. Perhaps we should say *especially* powers of attorney since they are used while you are still living. A General Power of Attorney authorizes someone to take any actions that usually only you could take. These actions include buying and selling property, accumulating debt, and withdrawing funds from bank accounts. Even a limited power of attorney should be changed.

A Healthcare Power of Attorney or Advance Medical Directive gives someone else the right to make medical care decisions for you if you are physically incapable of doing so. This directive can even include the decision to start, continue, or discontinue life support. It is important to not only designate someone else to act on your behalf, but also to ensure that whoever you designate will carry out your wishes.

If you are to receive funds from your spouse's 401(k) or IRA, make sure the DRO or court order is submitted to the pension plan administrator, or the final decree of divorce is submitted to the trustee of the bank or mutual fund company so that money can be transferred between retirement accounts.

The Bottom Line

Attention to detail and follow-through ensure that your divorce has a successful ending.

Chapter 12

Now What?

Capsule Outlook

This is the beginning, not the end. Your new financial life starts when you start taking action.

Once a divorce is final, many people are unsure what to do next to begin building a secure financial future. In this chapter, we discuss issues that need to be dealt with immediately following a divorce. The urge to procrastinate is strong, and you probably feel physically and emotionally exhausted. But this is not the time to collapse. Take a couple of days to collect yourself. Then begin the process of building a successful financial life for yourself and your family.

Don't feel that you have to get everything done immediately or all at once. Instead, focus on knowing what issues you need to deal with and learning how to handle them effectively.

By the time you finish this chapter, you will have a much clearer picture of what you want to achieve with your money. In this section, we attempt to demystify the process of goal setting and investing. If you have a better understanding of what you need to do, the more likely you are to follow through and make concrete progress toward achieving your financial goals. This is the process we call "post-divorce financial recovery."

You've just left the courthouse. It's over. You thought you'd feel relieved at this point, but it's more like confusion and lack of direction. And one thought keeps crossing your mind: "Now what?" The answer is, "Everything!" Don't take this enthusiasm the wrong way. We're not glad you were in the position where your only alternative was to get a divorce. However, we're glad you are now in a position where you can call your own shots, set your own priorities, and focus on making your own financial dreams a reality.

What a Woman Needs

Mary Kay Ash of Mary Kay Cosmetics is credited with a saying:

> From birth to 14 a woman needs good parents and good health.
> From 14 to 40 she needs good looks.
> From 40 to 60 she needs personality.
> From 60 on she needs cash.

Are you doing what you should to have the cash you will need to do what you want?

Beginning Your Financial Success Is a Simple Process

Creating your own financial success is a simple process:

1. Earn money.
2. Save money.
3. Invest money.

The most critical piece of this process is to actually do it. Thinking about saving won't get you any closer to your goals. And permanently parking all your money in a money market account while you procrastinate about decision-making won't get you anywhere, either. The secret to success is to take action!

Remember: Earn, save, invest. You can handle the earning part. You go to work every day and earn your paycheck. The saving part is pretty straightforward, too. You have a budget, which accounts for how you spend that precious paycheck. Hopefully there's a little bit left over each month, which you dutifully set aside. (We'll talk about how to do this most efficiently in Chapter 13, "Understanding the Fundamentals.") However, investing is where things get confusing. You know about savings accounts and certificates of deposit (CDs), but you also know that savings accounts and CDs that earn barely more than the inflation rate won't get you very far.

And then there are all these strange-sounding terms like "asset allocation," "risk tolerance," and "market volatility." Foreign languages are not limited to French and Spanish. Finance and investing can seem like a foreign language, too. Ultimately, you just want to know if you're behind on your goals, whether you're making the most of your money, and if you'll have to take a job as a greeter at Wal-Mart after you retire to make ends meet.

Use this fresh start as an opportunity to begin your financial life anew. Consider making it a group project with your friends or your children. They might have a perspective on something you hadn't thought about before. Plus, they are great for keeping you on schedule. It's tough to look at your friends or your kids (like your teachers in school) and tell them that you haven't done your "homework." Your relationship with them will help you hold your own feet to the fire. These people are the reason you have goals in the first place. But remember, the decisions we're talking about making are ultimately yours. Your kids can lobby hard for that new car to be your first priority, but you know that you have to save for retirement. So in that case, the retirement plan comes first.

Before you begin, understand that financial planning and goal setting are processes. To be successful, you should commit to a written plan, including a list of your specific goals and the detailed steps you intend to take to achieve them. This plan should not be written in stone. It should be treated as a living document that can be adapted as your circumstances change. As time passes, your thoughts, ideas, and goals will probably change. You will achieve some of your goals and replace them with new ones. You are allowed to change your mind. But don't change the entire plan on a whim or in the heat of a moment.

Setting the Ground Rules

As with any endeavor, there are some ground rules that need to be followed. You won't find them carved in stone anywhere. In fact, these are just reminders of some commonsense items. You will need them to keep you from feeling overwhelmed, and to keep you making forward progress. Our clients have found it very empowering to have this track to run on. We hope it gives you some general direction in your planning, and the positive outlook that will see you through the rough spots you may encounter while creating a plan of your own.

Know That You Are Not Alone

Nearly 50 percent of all first marriages and around 60 percent of second marriages end in divorce. With numbers like that, you are one of an estimated 19 million people who are dealing with taking control of and responsibility for their own money (source: *Divorce Magazine* statistics from 1998). Think of it this way. The next time you are at the office, or the post office, or any other public place, look at the person to your left and the person to your right. Odds are, two of the three of you will be divorced, so you are not the only one to deal with these issues.

Check Your Guilt at the Door

This is not about "could have," "should have," "wanted to," or "if I had known." Check your guilt at the door. Claim checks will not be given!

You don't have just one divorce. You have three: emotional, legal, and financial. Ideally, you take them in that order, mastering the emotional issues first before they master you. When you have achieved the emotional divorce, moving past issues like guilt, anger, or resentment, you can then take up the legal and financial items that apply to your situation with greater confidence and a much-improved chance of success. By addressing the emotional issues first, you can be far stronger, know what you need and want, and avoid having others do things like use your children as weapons against you or play on feelings of guilt or self-doubt. To be most successful at legal issues, it is critical that you have dealt with your emotions.

Your money is no different. It is a highly useful servant, but it's a lousy master. And if you are not clear about which of you is the servant and which is the master, money has a way of doing the deciding for you. So to be most successful, deal with the emotional issues first and then tackle the legal and financial ones. If you don't, you will carry emotional baggage into your financial world. This will cloud your judgment and impair your ability to make well-founded and sensible decisions. This advice was true during the divorce process, and it is equally true after your divorce is final.

If you need counseling to deal with your emotional issues, then do it. The decisions we are going to talk about require you to be clear-headed and objective. If you are still wrestling with emotions like guilt, anger, and resentment, you will be making your decisions from a position of weakness, not a position of strength. Ultimately, that position serves as a weak foundation for your financial house. You deserve a strong, healthy financial future. So make your decisions from a position of strength.

At this point, your divorce is final. You have your property settlement agreement done, and we are talking about your situation as a single individual. Now we take what you have and move forward.

Take Action

While we're flattered that you have chosen to read this book, it is only your first step toward financial independence. It cannot be the only step, or you will never make anything constructive happen. You must take action. Write out a list of activities, and set a schedule for doing them. The hardest part is making yourself stick to it. If you have made this a group project with a friend or your children, ask them to help you hold yourself accountable. Get them to help you stick to your activity schedule. Maybe you set out to do one thing a day, one a week, or one a month. We'll admit it won't be easy. Like a good workout, it is demanding, but it's the only way to make progress. You deserve an improved and fulfilling financial future. And in the end, this success will be worth the effort you put into it now.

Find Out What You Know and What You Don't Know

Any time you deal with the issues raised by a divorce, you're bound to come across a lot of things you are unsure about or just plain don't know the answer to. That's okay. As you gather information, you will find it falls into two categories: things you need to deal with (like retirement planning), and things that don't apply to you (like college planning if you don't have kids).

Of the issues you need to deal with, again, there will be things you know relatively well and things you just don't have any idea about. Make a list of the issues that apply to you. Choose one or two items you need to become more informed about. Now you know what subjects you need to focus on, so you can make a more concerted effort to learn about them.

You don't have to become an expert at all this, but we are talking about your dreams. You should at least be familiar with the concepts that apply to helping you make those dreams a reality.

It's like going to the doctor's office for a blood test. You need to know generally that the nurse is going to stick your arm and draw blood, which gets sent off to the lab to be tested, which tells the doctor if you're sick. You don't necessarily need to know all the chemistry and biology that's involved. If you do, then you're that much more informed. But you do need to understand the basics.

Make Planning for Your Future a Priority

Most people spend more time planning their annual vacation than they do planning their financial future—talk about having your priorities backward! You're going to spend only a week, maybe two, on vacation. That's not very long. The goals we're talking about here last a lot longer. A college education takes four years. A nursing home stay averages around two years. And the average retirement now runs close to 30 years. You're going to be retired for a whole lot longer than you'll be on that vacation, so you should put significantly more effort into planning for these goals.

Besides, you get up and go to work every day in pursuit of these goals—whether you consciously acknowledge this or not. Even if you love your job, you probably don't go every day just for the joy of working. Considering you're putting in so much effort, don't you think you deserve to achieve your financial goals? Look at retirement. By the time your working life is complete, you will probably have been working toward retirement, for 30 or 40 years. And, as the retirement age increases, you will work more years during your lifetime. It is said that childhood is the best time in your life. We suggest that retirement should be pretty darn good, too, because you will have put an incredible amount of work into becoming retired.

Action Steps—Where to Begin

When you decide to go on vacation and you call a travel agent, her first question is "Where do you want to go?" And the second question is "Where are you now?" It is important to know these things, because where you are now and where you want to go determine how you should travel to get to your destination. Some methods of travel work better than others, and some might not be possible.

For instance, if you're in Chicago and want to go to Milwaukee, you'll probably go by car. You could walk, but it wouldn't be your first choice. Plus, it would probably take longer to get there than you planned. If you want to go to New York, you could go by train or plane. But if you want to go to Paris, you could sail or fly, depending on how long you have to get there. But to get from New York to Paris, walking is out of the question.

Financially, these questions are the equivalent of "What are your goals?" and "What do you already have?" The question of "How do you want to get there" will largely be answered by how long you have to achieve a particular goal. Time is a critical factor in determining whether stocks, bonds, or cash will be the better way to get to your goals.

Get Organized

What you need now is a budget and a net worth statement based solely on you as a single person, not half of a couple. Use the Cash Flow Worksheet you completed in Appendix A, "Forms," as an outline for your new budget. Many people find a financial program, like Microsoft Money or Quicken, helpful in keeping organized and updated. These programs allow you to sort your income and expenses into specific categories to make tracking your money easier. You have to know where your money goes to control it and take charge of your spending.

Cash flow and net worth are the most basic indicators of your financial health. A *cash flow statement* shows exactly what you take in and what you spend. Perhaps more important, it shows *where* you spend your money. When you put your own cash flow statement together, be careful not to let much get thrown into the "miscellaneous" category. Try to categorize as much as you possibly can. This exercise can be very useful, and a little bit scary. You'll probably be amazed at how much you spend on some tiny little thing like buying lunch out every day you're at work. If you spend $5 a day, that works out to $1,250 a year. That's a lot of money for a sandwich! And it totals over half of what you could be putting into an IRA (in 2001).

A *net worth statement* shows how much you are worth. The basic formula is as follows:

How much you own – what you owe = net worth

Or:

Assets – liabilities = net worth

For instance, if you own a home worth $100,000, it appears on the asset side of the statement. The $80,000 mortgage you have on the house appears on the liabilities side. So the value of your home minus what you owe on it results in a net worth of $20,000.

Remember, these statements won't be of any use if you don't include everything. So dig through all your statements and include each and every item on your books.

Decide What Issues You Need to Address

What financial-planning areas apply to you? Here's a general list of topics to get you started. Think about which of these areas apply to you and which don't. This way, you can focus your time, energy, and money on those plans that fit your life, and you won't waste energy, time, and money on items that don't fit your life. Use this list as a starting point to identify the issues that are important to you:

* College planning for yourself
* College planning for your children
* College planning for other relatives (nieces/nephews, grand-children, godchildren, etc.)
* Retirement planning for yourself
* Long-term-care planning for yourself
* Long-term-care planning for your parents
* Long-term-care planning for other relatives
* Estate planning for yourself
* Pay off credit cards
* Pay off student loans
* Pay off other debts
* Buy a house
* Buy a car
* Buy a vacation home (beach, mountains, etc.)
* Take a special vacation (trip around the world)
* Other goals

Choose Whether to Use an Advisor or Do It Yourself

Depending on what else is going on in your life, how comfortable or uncomfortable you are dealing with investment and financial-planning issues, and how disciplined you are in sticking with your plan, you may choose to work with a financial advisor. Or you might choose to do things yourself.

With the explosion of information on the Internet, many people feel confident about their ability to navigate the fields of financial planning and stock trading successfully. If you are one of those people, great! There is a wealth of information available to help you: in the public library, at local colleges, and on the World Wide Web. Take advantage of these resources, and use them wisely.

On the other hand, you could be one of those people who are overwhelmed by this flood of information. Too much data often leads to paralysis because you can't make sense of all of it. Surfing the Web can often leave you feeling like you've been hit by a tidal wave of information. If this is the case for you, then you might be better off working with a professional financial advisor.

Think of this advisor as a coach. He or she will help you get organized, spell out your goals, develop a plan for achieving those goals, and implement and maintain that plan. Even more important, your advisor can serve as your conscience, reminding you of your goals and bringing you back to the plan when you start to stray.

Reality Check

Don't confuse having a lot of information with knowing what it means and how to use it. With the advent of the Internet, a great deal of information is available at the touch of a button. But just because you have the information doesn't mean you have the knowledge, wisdom, or experience to put that information to good use.

Think of it this way: You can look up how to do open heart surgery on the Internet. And it's really a pretty simple concept. You could study the articles for a while. But the question is, "Would you trust yourself to do your own heart surgery with that level of knowledge?" Probably not. You would probably prefer the knowledge, wisdom, and experience of a first-rate doctor. In our view, your financial health is no less important than your physical health. So consider your choices in the investment area with the same care as your medical choices.

Build Your Own Advisory Team

You might choose to build your own brain trust—your own team of financial professionals. Different advisors can help you with various aspects of your life. Who you need to include on your team varies depending on your particular situation:

- ❖ Are you self-employed, or do you work for someone else?
- ❖ Do you have a simple portfolio or a complex one?
- ❖ Do you own investment real estate (apartment building, vacation property, and so on)?
- ❖ Are you a trust fund beneficiary?
- ❖ Are you a trustee of someone else's trust fund?

The more complex your financial life is, the bigger your team will probably be. It will likely include people such as the following:

- ❖ An accountant
- ❖ An attorney
- ❖ A financial planner
- ❖ A stockbroker or investment manager
- ❖ A private banker
- ❖ A real estate agent
- ❖ A mortgage broker
- ❖ A property and casualty insurance agent
- ❖ A life insurance agent
- ❖ Someone whose advice you trust (like a parent or close personal friend)

You might not need all these specialties, or you may need someone who isn't on this list. So feel free to customize your own team.

Remember, too, that one person can wear several of these hats. This is entirely proper. Just be sure to confirm that the person you are dealing with has the appropriate training, credentials, and experience to give you the kind of service you're looking for.

Probably the best way to build a team for yourself is to ask other people for suggestions. For instance, if you like your real estate agent, ask her for recommendations if you need a mortgage person. The people she refers you to are likely to provide the same quality and level of service you get from her.

Set Specific Financial Goals

Take a few minutes, and write out your financial goals on a piece of paper. We gave you some suggestions earlier to get you started. Now create a list with any other goals you may have. Anything that has to do with money is fair game. And don't worry how long your list is. Just get all your goals down on paper. This is your time to dream, so go for it!

Now go back to that list and make every single goal precise, exact, and specific! For instance, don't just say, "I want to buy a house." Instead, break that idea down into its component parts: time, cost, starting point, and contribution. As you work through the resulting math, you will be able to tell whether you're close to your goal and how far off you are if you're short. This information tells you whether that particular goal is realistic. If it's too much of a stretch, don't abandon it, but try changing some of the pieces. For instance, if you're trying to save for a new Mercedes and were planning on putting away $100 a month, you will quickly find out that you're not putting enough aside. So change the goal a little bit. Now, instead of aiming for a 500S, go for the smaller C Class. Or maybe you're willing to skip going out so often so you can save more. Ultimately, the goal is a new car. It's up to you to figure out exactly how that happens. Maybe it's that Mercedes, maybe it's a Honda, but either way, it's still a new car!

So that goal of a new home now becomes: "I want to buy a house in two years (time). I am willing to pay and able to afford a

$100,000 mortgage (cost). I already have $2,500 saved in a money market account that pays 5 percent (starting point). And I'm able to save about $100 a month (contribution)." With this information, you should have just under $5,300 in two years. Using that for your down payment and closing costs, and taking out a $100,000 mortgage at 7 percent interest, you would have payments of $665/month for 30 years. Is that reasonable for you? If so, that's your goal. If not, then go back and revise some of the parts and see how that affects your goal. And when you're looking at financing a large purchase, be sure to check on interest rates regularly. You don't want to plan on getting a loan at 5 percent and find out late in the game that you can only get the loan at 8 percent. The difference in your payments could be dramatic.

Goal Worksheet

Priority _____

Goal description _____

Time remaining _____

Cost (current dollars) _____

Cost (future dollars) _____

Existing nest egg (current dollars) _____

Current savings rate _____

Estimated growth rate _____

Needed nest egg (future dollars) _____

Estimated nest egg (future dollars) _____

Overage/shortage _____

Time Value of Money

The *time value of money* is a fancy way of saying that a dollar isn't worth what it used to be. As time passes, things go up in price because of inflation. For instance, if you bought a nice family sedan in the mid-1960s, it probably cost around $3,000. To buy a comparable car today would cost you nearly $30,000. So as you plan your goals, remember to factor in the time value of money.

The time value of money is a fairly easy concept to understand. Anyone who buys something repeatedly understands it well. For instance, the price of the gallon of milk you buy every week has generally gone up in price over the years. The math can get a little complicated if you work it out by hand, and we don't intend for you to become a math professor. So we suggest you use one of the many goal calculators available on the Internet. Nearly every mutual fund company and brokerage firm has one on its Web page. It might take a little bit of digging to find them. We suggest you find one you are comfortable using, and stick with it. A list of various mutual fund, bank, brokerage firm, and other Web sites is provided in Appendix B, "Resources," for your reference.

When you've identified your goals in specific terms, write them down on index cards—one goal per card. Then number each card. Now, line those cards up in chronological order, according to the date at which you want to reach each goal. Which goals happen sooner, and which goals happen later? For instance, let's say you're 35 years old and planning to retire at age 65. That's 30 years from now. But your daughter is 10 years old and will be going to college at age 18. That's only eight years from now, so your college funding goal happens before your retirement goal. Write down the number from each card in order of when they happen from soonest to latest. Keep this order in mind as you go through the next steps.

Prioritize

Now let's prioritize those goals. Take the same cards and line them up in order of how important they are to you (just you, and no one else). Make a note of the cards' order now. See why we said "no guilt"? You might find that you just can't pay for that dream vacation to Disney World, *and* pay for all your kids' college educations, *and* retire at age 65. To do the college and vacation would mean working until you're 75, and you just don't want to do that. That's fine! These are *your* financial goals. Decide what you want and what you're willing and able to do. You may decide that your retirement is the most important goal and that you can cover only half of your kids' expected college costs, which means you should put off Disney World for a while.

Go through this exercise several times. Review the order you have put your goals in, and see if you still feel the same way tomorrow, next week, or next month.

Working with an Advisor

There are advisors of all kinds. Some specialize in trading stocks and bonds. Others specialize in preparing written financial plans. Still others do both tasks. There are also specific licenses and credentials for these different specialties. Your first job is to determine what kind of advisor you need and want.

When interviewing advisors, see if you feel comfortable with them. You need to be able to tell them anything and everything without fear. And while you might not like their answers to your questions, you need to find an advisor who can give you both good news and bad news. Your initial consultation should be a two-way trial: you checking to see if the advisor fits your needs, and the advisor checking to see if you fit his or her practice. Personalities, communications, and relationships are crucial here. Pay attention to what your intuition tells you about the advisor you are talking to.

Many advisors have formed teams to better serve their clients. The advantage of a team is that you have specialists in each area: planning, investments, insurance, trust services, and the like. You may need several of these specialties. When working with a team, make sure you have a consistent point of contact so you and your plan don't get the runaround.

Recognizing Licenses and Credentials

Once you have determined what kind of advisor you are looking for, ask the advisors you interview what kinds of services they provide, what licenses they hold, and what credentials they have. Particularly as the financial services industry becomes more competitive, you will find more and more firms and practitioners working to be one-stop shops that give clients access to all financial services.

To be licensed to buy and sell certain types of securities, advisors must have a license from the Securities and Exchange Commission. For example, the Series 7 license allows an advisor to deal with stocks, bonds, and mutual funds, but the Series 6 permits an advisor to deal only with mutual funds. Those who deal with privately managed portfolios hold a Series 65 license and are called *registered investment advisors.*

A variety of professional organizations offer certain credentialing programs. Here are just a few of the ones you are likely to run into:

CFP	Certified Financial Planner
ChFC	Chartered Financial Consultant
CLU	Chartered Life Underwriter
LUTCF	Life Underwriting Training Council Fellow
CIMA	Certified Investment Management Analyst
CIMC	Certified Investment Management Consultant
MSFS	Master of Science in Financial Services

Paying for Your Advisor's Services

Today, most advisors offer a broad array of products and services. However, there are essentially two ways to pay for them: commissions or fees.

If you choose to work with your advisor on a commission basis, you pay for each transaction you make. If you have a long-term buy-and-hold strategy, it could be the most cost-effective way for you to pay. However, some people feel there is an inherent conflict of interest in paying this way. Since in a commission-based relationship the advisor gets paid each time he buys or sells a security, some people wonder whether a particular trade is really necessary, or if the broker is just trying to generate commissions. If you choose to work on a commission basis, you will need to be very comfortable with your advisor's transaction recommendations. If you're going to be questioning his motivation, then perhaps you should look for another advisor, or consider using a fee-based account.

Also, if you don't have many transactions, you might not get as much attention from your advisor as you would like. If this is the case, work with your advisor to create a way for both of you to be rewarded by the relationship. It may require a little more work from you. By necessity, an advisor spends more time with clients who compensate him the most—he has to make a living, too. On a commission basis, those clients are the ones who trade the most. This is where it's important to be a good client.

If you choose a fee arrangement, your portfolio is assessed a percentage of the total account value. Typically, this fee is on a sliding scale (the more you have in your accounts, the lower the percentage), and depends on your portfolio's size and complexity and the level of service you require. Some people object to this arrangement because the fee is paid regardless of how many transactions are made and fees are paid even if the account loses money. However, these reasons are also the main attractions of this type of arrangement for other clients. Trading more does not mean you will make more money. And in non-IRAs, heavy trading can create tax problems. So a fee-based account allows you to make trades when you need to, without being hampered by the idea that the trade will cost anything more. Also, since fees are based on the account's value, if the account loses money, the fee goes down and the advisor is paid less. This way, you both have the same incentive—to make the account worth more! Last, being on a fee basis allows your advisor to advise you to buy, sell, or do nothing, whatever the most appropriate action may be. They are compensated for giving you their best advice, not for making a trade.

Bringing the Team Together

A good financial advisor asks about other advisors you might have. Be prepared to let her know who else you may be working with, including your attorney, accountant, banker, mortgage lender, real estate agent, and insurance agent. Remember, getting all the advice you need is a team effort, so don't be bashful about having all the members of your team working together for your benefit.

How to Be a Good Client

If you choose to work with a financial advisor, be prepared to be a good client. This means ...

- ❖ **Completely disclose all your assets to your advisors when asked.** They will ask you for a great deal of information, all of it extremely personal in nature. They aren't being nosy, but must understand your particular situation. Without a full knowledge of your circumstances, their advice might be incomplete or inappropriate.

- ❖ **Schedule regular portfolio reviews** as you and your advisor have agreed on, whether it's quarterly, semiannually, or annually. You should get a reminder telephone call, note, or postcard. But if you don't, take the initiative and call your advisor to schedule the appointment yourself.

- ❖ **Respect the hours during which your advisor schedules appointments.** Not all advisors are willing or able to meet with clients on evenings and weekends. If the hours a particular advisor keeps are a problem for you, perhaps you should review your expectations or choose another advisor. But talk with your advisors, and give them the first opportunity to address your needs. If they can't, they should say so and help you make a smooth transition to someone who can.

- ❖ **Show up for your appointments promptly.** An advisor's calendar is often packed. If you come late to an appointment, it can mean too little time to answer all your questions. If someone else comes late to his or her appointment, it can mean your appointment gets thrown off schedule— like what you've probably experienced at your doctor's office on occasion. Please, be polite by being prompt.

A successful and rewarding relationship with an advisor is based on trust. If you are less than forthcoming, it will have a negative effect on that relationship. If you don't feel you can be completely honest with a potential advisor, again, consider finding someone with whom you can be totally truthful.

Work with your advisor to develop a plan you will stick with, even when the market isn't doing so well. A good advisor puts this plan in writing. And you might not like this, but if you try to stray from the plan, be prepared for your advisor to pull that plan out of your file and remind you what you agreed to in a saner moment.

Finally, remember that the things your advisor asks you to do will probably be the opposite of what you think. For instance, if the bond portion of your portfolio has done well, she may ask you to take funds from those bonds and put it into stocks, which might not have done as well. It sounds backward, but it's a great way to keep your portfolio balanced and buy things when they are cheap. If you don't understand, then ask questions. Your advisor will probably find it refreshing.

Making Referrals

When you're happy with your advisor, make the highest and best compliment you can—tell your friends and colleagues to call her. The best advisor-client relationships turn into long-lasting friendships.

You are looking for an advisor you trust, you can tell anything to, and you enjoy working with. Well, advisors are looking for the same thing in a client. If you have a good relationship and enjoy working with your advisor, she probably enjoys working with you, too. And the most effective way for your advisors to meet other people like you is for you to make those introductions. They could be to anyone: friends, neighbors, colleagues, sorority sisters, fraternity brothers, people who are members of the same clubs as you, people whose children go to school with yours, or people you go to for other services (hairdresser, manicurist, interior decorator, dry-cleaner, mechanic, and so on).

Remember to Say Thank You

As your mother taught you, always remember to say thank you. Most advisors work hard to serve their clients well. If you feel your advisor is working hard for you, take a moment to say thank you. You could call, send a card, or send a small gift. For instance, one client explained to her daughter, Kristin, that we were making it possible for her to go to college. So Kristin drew a picture of her pre-school to say "thank you." That picture now hangs on the office door. It reminds us of the profound responsibility we have to our clients, and the incredible positive effect we have on their lives. Talk about job satisfaction! That small but heartfelt gesture means we're more willing to make an extra effort for these clients.

So if you want some special treatment from your professionals, remember to say "thank you." It doesn't have to be anything large or expensive, but it does need to be sincere.

The Bottom Line

Financial success is a journey, not a destination. Start taking the steps necessary to begin your journey.

Chapter 13

Understanding the Fundamentals

Capsule Outlook

Don't be a stranger to money and investment talk. Learn some of the basic terms and concepts, and you begin to understand how the world of investments can work for you.

Investing can sometimes seem like a foreign language. And if you don't know some of the basic terms, then communicating with someone about your money can be quite confusing. So in order to make sure we all understand each other, let's review some basic investment terminology. This will also give us the chance to make sure that we have the same understanding of some key concepts that will be important in making your portfolio fit your needs.

Basic Investment Styles

As in many other areas of life, investing has different styles. Some may be more appropriate for your portfolio than others. But you have to know what these styles are, how they differ, and how they are similar, in order to make an informed decision. This can be a bit like ordering coffee at Starbucks. Sometimes there are only a couple of characteristics that need to be named, like when you order a "tall coffee of the day." Other times, there are many more qualities that you need to describe, as when you order a "tall, extra-hot, no foam, decaf, vanilla, skim latte." What we're trying to get across here is the investment world's difference between the various styles. And just as you may like or dislike certain types of coffee, you may also prefer certain types of investment styles.

Privately Held vs. Publicly Traded

Some companies are owned by private individuals. One famous example is the M&M Mars Company, makers of M&Ms, Mars, Snickers, Milky Way bars, and Ethyl M Chocolates. The company was started by the Mars family back in 1911, and it is still owned by family members today. Most folks in the United States today work for privately held companies, many of them small businesses. Some of these companies offer stock purchase plans, but not all. When shares of private stock are sold, the company most often buys it. Publicly traded stock, on the other hand, can be bought and sold by anyone.

Other companies that started out private have "gone public" and sold shares to the public. Once they have done this, they are publicly traded on the New York, the American, or the NASDAQ exchange. Anyone who wants to own part of the company can buy shares. You can look on the television or in the newspaper and see what the company's share price is—it's public information. These publicly traded companies are the ones that make up the mutual funds so many investors buy.

Asset Classes

On the most basic scale, there are three types of publicly traded investments: stocks, bonds, and cash. Each of these "asset classes" can be divided further. For example, stocks, or equities, can be divided into domestic and foreign. Under these headings you can find large companies, medium-sized companies, and small companies. Sometimes you'll also hear "giant" and "micro." These terms refer to the largest of the large and the smallest of the small. Plus, you can choose companies by using a certain style: growth or value. Bonds can be divided into categories like Treasuries, agencies, and corporate bonds. Corporate bonds can be broken down into high-quality and high-yield.

Larger, more sophisticated portfolios often include additional asset classes, such as private equity, commodities, and real estate, but these are beyond the scope of this book.

Market Capitalization

A company's market capitalization, or *market cap,* is simply the current share price multiplied by the number of shares outstanding. There are many different definitions of what makes up large, medium, and small companies. Be sure you check how the research or mutual funds you use define these terms. For instance, Morningstar may use one set of definitions, while Valueline uses another. So be sure to clarify how these terms are used in the research you read. One common definition is ...

Large-cap	More than $10 billion
Mid-cap	$1.5 billion to $10 billion
Small-cap	Less than $1.5 billion

Remember that "giant" companies are the largest of the large-caps, usually those with over $50 billion in market capitalization. And the "micro" companies are the smallest of the small-cap companies, typically those under $500 million in market cap. Generally speaking, the smaller the company you choose to invest in, the more risk you take. But all stocks contain risk. There is no guarantee that any company will be profitable or that its stock will perform well. The stock market, throughout its history, has been littered with good companies whose stock has behaved dismally. But also, the stock market over time has consistently outperformed both bonds and cash. So even though stock performance is not consistent over the short-term, it is a far better performer over the long-term.

Industry Sectors

There are also industry sectors to think about when looking into investments. There are ten widely accepted sectors, as defined by Standard and Poors: utilities, energy, financials, industrial cyclicals, consumer durables, consumer staples, services, retail, health care, and technology.

Many of these sectors seem self-explanatory, but some of them are similar enough to cause some confusion, so let's review them:

❖ **Utilities.** This sector includes electric utilities, natural gas utilities, and water utilities. Examples include Dominion Resources, Duke Energy, Consolidated Edison, and PG&E. Think about the utility companies in your area that you depend on for electricity, gas, and water.

❖ **Energy.** These companies are engaged in mining, oil and gas, and oil/gas service. Examples include Chevron, Exxon-Mobil, Halliburton, and Schlumberger. Companies you recognize as being in this sector are probably service stations where you fill your gas tank, but this group also includes companies that provide equipment (like pipeline equipment, hoses, and pumps) and services (like exploration) to the oil companies.

❖ **Financials.** These companies include banks, insurance companies, mortgage lenders, brokerage firms, real estate investment trusts (REITs), and asset management firms. Examples here include Citicorp (bank), Allstate (property insurance), Jefferson-Pilot (life insurance), Countrywide (mortgages), Boston Properties (REIT), and Alliance Capital (asset management). As you can see, this sector covers a wide range of business activities.

❖ **Industrial cyclicals.** This sector covers a wide area, too. Here you'll find companies engaged in industries such as aerospace (Boeing), paper (Boise Cascade), paint (Sherwin-Williams), household supply (Eastman Kodak), home construction (Centex), and forestry/wood products (Weyerhaeuser). These companies represent heavy industry, and their profits are more subject to the ebb and flow of the overall economy.

❖ **Consumer durables.** This sector includes products you buy as a consumer that last a fairly long time. Examples include automobiles and auto parts manufacturers (Ford, Daimler Chrysler, General Motors), luggage (Samsonite), furniture (Ethan Allen), washers and dryers (Maytag), china (Mikasa), toys (Hasbro), sporting goods (Callaway Golf)—even pianos (Steinway).

❖ **Consumer staples.** Just as you would think, these are the items that don't last as long as their "durable" cousins, either because they wear out or you consume them. Examples here would be soft drinks (Coca-Cola), alcoholic drinks (Anheuser Busch), cosmetics (Estée Lauder), house-hold cleaners (Clorox), food (Keebler), and tobacco products (Philip Morris). You will probably have an easier time identifying companies and products in this sector because it's the one we all have the most daily contact with.

❖ **Services.** Included in this sector are companies that provide services you can't or don't want to do yourself. They include radio (Infinity Broadcasting), publishing (Martha Stewart), personal services (Jenny Craig), hotels (Marriott), casinos (MGM Mirage), airlines (Southwest Airlines), entertainment (MGM), cable TV (Liberty Media), broadcast TV (Fox Tele-vision), wireless telecommunications (AT&T Wireless), restaurants (Olive Garden), rentals (Hertz), rail or road trans-portation (CSX or Yellow Freight), and waste disposal (Waste Management).

❖ **Retail.** As you would suspect from the name, these are com-panies that sell things: groceries (Winn-Dixie), electronics (Best Buy), department stores (from Wal-Mart to Neiman-Marcus), clothing (Gap), drugstores (CVS), jewelry (Tiffany & Co.), home improvement (Home Depot), books (Barnes and Noble), and even coffee (Starbucks).

The distinction between consumer durables, consumer sta-ples, and retail may seem a bit fuzzy. Just remember, con-sumer durables and consumer staples are the companies that *make* the items we buy. Retailers are the companies that sell us the items we buy. So consumer durables/staples are the things we buy, and retailers are the places we go to buy them.

❖ **Health care.** This sector relates directly to your physical health: physicians (Healthsouth), pharmaceutical drugs (Pfizer), nursing homes (Manor Care), medical equipment (Bausch and Lomb), first-aid and personal care products (Johnson & Johnson), and biotechnology (Amgen).

❖ **Technology.** Last, we have the technology sector. These companies were the darlings of the market in 1999 and the dogs of the market in 2000. This sector includes printed circuit board makers (Jabil Circuit), telephone network equipment providers (Redback Networks), online information (Yahoo!), computer systems (WebMethods), data storage (EMC Corp.), computer switching equipment (Sun Microsystems), wireless equipment (Motorola), software (Microsoft), and semiconductors (Intel).

Market Capitalization: An Example

Take a look at investments you already own, and try to identify what size and sector each item is. Don't rely solely on the name because mutual fund names can be confusing, and stock names don't always tell the whole story.

For instance, let's look at General Electric, which is a huge company. You already know that, but there is also the mathematical reason, which we discussed earlier. GE had nearly 10 billion shares outstanding at the end of 2000, with a price of roughly $50 per share. That gives us a market capitalization of ...

$$10,000,000,000 \times \$50 = \$500 \text{ billion}$$

Since $500 billion is higher than the $10 billion cut-off point, that makes GE a large-cap company. It's also larger than the $50 billion definition of a mega-cap company.

So what industry sector does GE belong in? If you asked your grandmother, she might say it's a utility or energy company because it makes light bulbs. But that's not all it makes. Someone else might say it's a consumer durables company because it manufactures appliances like refrigerators, dishwashers, and clothes dryers. Well, that's true, too, but, again, that's not all it makes. And someone else might say it's a media services company because it owns NBC and MSNBC. That's true, too. In fact, most analysts classify GE as a financial firm or an industrial cyclical company. So, you see, even among people who research companies for a living, there is room for different conclusions on something as simple as what sector a company falls into.

Consolidation vs. Diversification

Do you remember your mother saying, "Don't put all your eggs in one basket"? Well, she was right. But she didn't tell you to keep all your chickens in different henhouses, did she? This is the difference between consolidation and diversification.

Consolidation

Consolidating completely would mean putting all your money in one single investment—one stock, one bond, or one mutual fund. That's not a good idea because your one stock could miss earnings, or your one bond could default, or your one mutual fund manager could retire, and then where would you be? In a mess! Just like putting all your eggs in one basket and dropping it on the way to the market.

Consolidating in a practical sense is a way of making your life easier. This way, your variety of stocks, bonds, and mutual funds are in a few accounts at one firm so you can track them more easily. This is a big advantage, especially at times like your annual financial checkup or tax time.

Diversification

Diversification is a little bit trickier. To diversify completely would mean holding only a few dollars in each of dozens of different investments, all of them from different institutions. This arrangement would probably drive you crazy. You would be flooded with statements from many different sources. If your money were all in taxable accounts, doing your tax return every year would truly be a nightmare—with 1099s from every one of those places for a few dollars each. This is what we mean by "keeping all your chickens in different henhouses."

Admit it! Are you one of those people who go to a different bank every year and open a new individual retirement account (IRA) because you want to be diversified? Well, unfortunately, you're not diversified! You own a bunch of different IRAs, with each one probably invested in a certificate of deposit. And the statements are likely more than you can manage.

Another important distinction to know is the difference between imagined or perceived diversification, and real diversification. Many people do what we just described, and buy a few dollars' worth of many mutual funds, all from different families. What most people tend to forget is that mutual funds are only a mechanism for you to invest in stocks and bonds. And with more mutual funds out there than there are stocks on the New York Stock Exchange, mutual fund companies are bound to own some of the same things. You need to know how much overlap there is in your mutual funds. Do they own the same things? We once had a client come into the office, swearing that she was diversified because she owned 18 mutual funds. When we dug into what companies were owned in each fund, we found that 14 of them were nearly identical. So she wasn't nearly as diversified as she thought.

Before you become too devoted to one particular mutual fund family, understand that every family has its stars and its dogs. Some families have more stars, and some have more dogs. You need to be very particular about which fund from each family you want in your portfolio. Of course, we would prefer it if the family you choose to deal with has more than just one good fund. That way, if you need to switch to another fund, there is an alternative within the family you can use.

It would be smart to consider consolidating your investments into a few accounts with a reputable firm. This does not mean all your mutual funds should come from the same family. In fact, they probably shouldn't if you don't want all your eggs in one basket. But consolidating yourself with a single firm helps a lot. You have only one kind of statement to learn to read. Your statements show everything you own in one place. There are fewer 1099s to deal with. And you have one firm to deal with for advice, questions, and paperwork.

Investment Performance Does Not Replace Savings

Think of yourself as a business: Smith, Inc. You work all year long, you earn money from your job, and you deserve to be profitable at the end of the year. That's how companies are evaluated. And your company is no different. Sure, you can reinvest your earnings in yourself—like buying a home or taking a well-deserved vacation. But excess spending is a quick way to financial trouble. And just like the CEO of a company has to answer to his or her shareholders, ultimately, you will have to answer to yourself for those decisions. In short, you owe it to yourself to save and invest.

With the performance of the U.S. stock market between 1995 and 1999, many people assumed that becoming wealthy was easy. All you had to do was buy technology stocks, and everything would grow at 50 percent a year, and you didn't have to save any more money. If the year 2000 has taught us anything, it should be that no stock or sector is without risk, that nothing grows at 50 percent a year forever, and that you do have to make additional contributions to your investment accounts. Remember, investing is a marathon, not a sprint!

The stock market can often be unpredictable, as it was in 2000. So how do you make money in a market like that? Two ideas: First, stick to the investment plan you put together, and second, use the *dollar cost averaging* method. Dollar cost averaging means investing a specific dollar amount on a regular basis, most often monthly. Depending on how often you are paid, you can dollar cost average as often as weekly and as seldom as quarterly. You invest regardless of the share price. So you're buying more shares when the price is lower, and you're buying fewer shares when the price is higher. While dollar cost averaging doesn't guarantee you'll make money, it sure improves your chances.

What Kind of Money Are You Investing?

Remember, your goal is to make the most efficient use of your money as possible. Therefore, you want to take advantage of opportunities for tax-advantaged savings whenever possible. In a nutshell, there are four types of dollars you can use to invest: pre-tax matched, pre-tax unmatched, after-tax/tax-deferred, and taxable. Think of these money types as buckets that should be filled in a certain order. Each bucket has a limit on how much you can put into it. So put everything you can in bucket #1 before you put anything in bucket #2, and so on.

Also, keep in mind that when you will need your money will help you decide which bucket to focus on. For example, if your child will be going to college when you are only 40 years old, then you will need to focus on buckets three and four (in the following sections) to avoid the stiff early withdrawal penalties that may apply to buckets #1 and #2.

Bucket #1: Pre-Tax Matched Money

In this category, you get to save money before state and federal taxes are deducted. Plus, for every dollar you contribute to this account, your employer gives you additional money to go along with it. I don't know about you, but if someone is going to give me free money, I'll take it! You have money withheld from your paycheck and don't pay taxes on it. This is great! And you don't lose any of your Social Security or Medicare benefits. Because this money never makes it into your paycheck, it's much easier to save.

With a matching provision, for every dollar you contribute to the plan, the company gives you some money to go along with it. Sometimes it's a few cents for every dollar you contribute. Sometimes it's much more generous. In any event, there's always a limit to this corporate generosity. Check your company's plan to see what its matching policy is. Usually, it's described something like this: Employee contributions are matched 50 cents for every $1 contributed up to the first 5 percent of salary deferred. So if you work for this company making $30,000/year, and contribute 5 percent of your salary, you will contribute $1,500/year and the company will give you $750 (subject to vesting).

In bucket #1, you get three benefits: pre-tax contributions, matching money from your employer, and tax-deferral on all your investment earnings. First, your contribution is made before federal and state income taxes, so you have to earn only $1 to contribute $1. (See the taxable section to compare.) Second, since you put your own money in, your employer will give you free money to go with your own contribution. Whether you get to keep this employer contribution if you quit this job depends on whether you are "vested" at that time. Third, you pay no income tax until you make withdrawals from these accounts.

To invest with pre-tax matched money, you need to have access to a 401(k), 403(b), SIMPLE, or the federal Thrift Savings Plan (TSP) (as a federal government FERS employee).

One question that often comes up is whether contributing to these kinds of plans has any effect on your Social Security or Medicare benefits. The answer is a definite no because you still pay both Social Security and Medicare taxes on the money you contribute to the plan. There is no reduction in these benefits.

A Word About Vesting

You always get to keep your own contributions to the plan, plus whatever amount that money has grown to. Once you are vested, you get to keep the company's contributions, too. Each 401(k) plan has different rules about when an employee becomes vested. The schedule is either *cliff* or *graded*.

With a cliff vesting schedule, once you have been employed with a company for a specified length of time, you're vested. For instance, with a three-year cliff-vesting schedule, once you have three years of "time in service" with your employer, you are fully vested. If you quit after two years and 364 days, you are not vested at all.

With a graded vesting schedule, you become progressively more vested each year. For example, with a four-year vesting schedule, you become 25 percent vested each year. After four years, you are fully vested.

So before you decide to take a new job, be aware of what you might give up in unvested benefits. And if you're close to meeting the vesting requirement, consider staying at that job until you do. It could make a big difference in your ability to meet your retirement goals.

Bucket #2: Pre-Tax Unmatched Money

Funds in this category still get the tax deduction, but your employer doesn't give you free money to go along with it. You still get tax-deferred growth, however. The pre-tax aspect is a big benefit, so be sure to take full advantage of it. If your employer matches you on only the first 5 percent of your contribution, bucket #2 would be everything over 5 percent, up to the maximum 15 percent you can put into the plan.

Depending on your adjusted gross income (AGI) and whether you are covered by a retirement plan at work, bucket #2 could include your traditional IRA contribution. If you make less than the IRS limits, you can deduct your traditional IRA contribution. If you make more, you can still make a traditional IRA contribution, but it won't be deductible.

Bucket #3: After-Tax/Tax-Deferred Money

In this bucket, you don't get a tax deduction, but your money still grows, and you don't pay taxes on those earnings each year. You pay income tax on these funds only when you withdraw from the account.

The kinds of accounts you find in bucket #3 include Roth IRAs, fixed annuities, variable annuities, and traditional IRAs for people over the AGI limits for deductibility.

A Roth IRA works much like a traditional IRA, with a couple of notable exceptions. First, to be eligible for a Roth as of 2001, your AGI must be under $95,000 as a single taxpayer or below

$150,000 as a married taxpayer filing jointly. Married taxpayers who file separately are not eligible to have a Roth IRA. Remember, as your divorce proceeds, you will probably move from married filing jointly to married filing separately to filing as a single taxpayer. So pay close attention to which type of IRA you are eligible for, and which one you're contributing to. Second, you can't ever deduct your $2,000 annual Roth IRA contribution. Roth contributions are by definition after-tax money. Third, when you are age $59^1/_2$ or older, and if you have had your Roth IRA for at least five years, you can withdraw from your Roth and owe no income taxes. And unlike traditional IRAs, a Roth IRA has no required minimum distribution when you reach age $70^1/_2$. This is a huge benefit. If you are eligible for both a Roth IRA and a deductible traditional IRA, talk with your financial advisor about which would be best for you. You can put a total of only $2,000 into an IRA each year, regardless of type, so it is important to make the most of that limited contribution.

If you have a traditional IRA, and your AGI is below $100,000 regardless of marital status, you can convert that traditional IRA to a Roth. However, you have to pay income taxes on the amount you convert. This can be an expensive proposition, so be sure to talk with your financial advisor and accountant before converting anything.

Bucket #4: Taxable Money

This category is usually the one most people think of first when they think of investing. Included are some important assets you will accumulate over the course of your life, like your home, your "rainy day" money market account, your company's employee stock purchase plan shares, and your qualified or incentive stock options. These are important pools of money to collect. But you have to be aware of the effect federal and state taxes have on how you manage these assets. To begin with, if you are in the 31 percent federal income tax bracket, you have to earn $1.44 to have $1 to invest after you've paid your 31 percent in federal taxes. Obviously, state taxes add to this burden.

Risk vs. Risky

In a portfolio, *risk* is the possibility that you will choose to invest your money at a peak in the market, and the investment goes down shortly afterward. This is a possibility, even if you're buying a blue chip stock, a well-known mutual fund, or even a bond. Any financial asset is subject to changes in price. Keep in mind that your concern is not what your investment does in the days, weeks, or even months after you buy it. Your real concern is what it does over a much longer period of time—years or longer. If you stick with quality in what you buy, any short-term price drops should not be a source of worry.

Risky, on the other hand, is choosing to buy some little company you've never heard of before because you heard about it at the water cooler at work and it sounded neat. "Tips" like this are often picked up from people like those you talk to in Internet chat rooms, your hairdresser, or your grocery store checkout clerk. The problem with these sources is that you don't know where the person you're talking to got their information. In Internet chat rooms, you often don't even know who you're talking to.

The key difference between *risk* and *risky* is quality—the quality of the company, the quality of the mutual fund manager, and the quality of the information you use to make your investment decision.

It Doesn't All Have to Match

When we were little, we learned that when you set the table for dinner, all the plates and silverware had to match. Many people approach their investments the same way, particularly with mutual funds. They believe that all your funds have to come from the same family. Well, as we said earlier, every family has its good funds, mediocre funds, and not-so-good funds. So don't limit your portfolio to just one fund family. Check out the fund family to see where its strengths are. Some are better at small-cap funds while others are better with large-caps. Go with the best funds that family has to offer.

Your portfolio doesn't have to be all mutual funds, either. You can branch out to having individual stocks and bonds in your portfolio, too.

Growth vs. Income

As you build your portfolio, it will likely include a collection of part stocks, part bonds, and part cash. The proportions depend on several factors, like your ability to deal with investment risk and the amount of time you have. These proportions also depend on how much you expect your investment to earn. This is the core trade-off in investing. You take more risk with stocks, but you have a greater potential return. You take less risk with bonds, but you have a lower potential return. You take the least risk with money market accounts, but you get the lowest potential return. In a nutshell, the greater the potential short-term price fluctuation, the greater the potential payoff.

Stocks and stock mutual funds provide growth. When investing in this category, you put $1,000 into a fund and expect it to grow. The amount of growth varies from year to year, but over time the idea is that your $1,000 will become much more.

Bonds, on the other hand, give you more predictable income. You know exactly when they pay interest and when they mature. The amount of interest you get is steady and dependable, but your money won't grow as it does with stocks. If you put $1,000 into a bond, when it matures you get only your $1,000 back, plus the interest it's paid you since you bought it.

But remember, with long-lasting goals like retirement, which can last 30 years or longer, your biggest risk is outliving your money. And you can't avoid that risk without growth. So stocks should be part of your portfolio, even during a "conservative" period of life like retirement—you probably will want conservative stocks instead of aggressive-growth stocks, but still stocks. Think of someone who retired 20 years ago in 1980. At only 3 percent inflation, her $30,000 income in 1980 is worth only about $16,000 a year now. That's quite a drop in purchasing power.

If you want to maintain your standard of living, you have to be able to give yourself a raise during retirement to keep up with inflation. Growth gives you a way to do that.

Investment Styles: Growth and Value

There are basically two schools of thought on how to choose stocks to invest in: growth and value. One style might do better for a while, then the other one outperforms it. Unfortunately, you never know which style will be the better choice in a given year, so it is wise to include both styles in your portfolio. That way, no matter what is doing well, your portfolio will be participating.

Think of your investments as a garden where you're trying to always have something in bloom. If all you have is growth, your investment garden will be bare when value is in bloom, and vice versa. By having some spring plants and some fall plants in your garden, and some growth and value in your portfolio, you will have something flowering all the time. And remember to be patient. You don't pull up all your mums (which flower in the fall) during the summer just because they're not flowering, do you? Of course not! Keep that same thought process in mind as you build and review your portfolio.

Growth is the more aggressive strategy of the two. It refers to the fact that a company is growing its revenues, its market share, or its earnings. However you look at it, the company is growing. It is this growth, and the anticipation of future growth, that causes the stock price to rise. The catch is that if a growth company has disappointing news, its stock can be punished harshly.

Value is the more conservative strategy. In this case, a company's stock might be considered undervalued because of some other event. It could be a poor earnings report, a negative piece of news, a change in management, or not being in the currently "hot" sector of the market. Whatever the reason, value is sometimes thought of as buying stocks when they are on sale. If you're familiar with Warren Buffett, value is his style. Keep in mind that this style requires patience on your part. The stocks in a value portfolio have to be given time to turn themselves around and get some positive attention from the market.

The Bottom Line

Understand the basic concepts and the language of investing to build a portfolio that fits your specific needs, beliefs, and style.

Chapter 14

Goal-Setting

Capsule Outlook

Your goals are the foundation of your financial plan—use them to become the master of your money.

You might be thinking, "Oh no! Not another chapter on goal setting." Well, this chapter isn't quite what you might think it is. We're not going to tell you what your priorities should be. We'll leave that judgment to you. Now that you're single, you don't have to answer to anyone but yourself about your priorities, financial or otherwise.

But once you've decided what those priorities are, how do you set a meaningful goal that will help you actually achieve it? That's what we're going to cover here.

Go back to that fantasy list of financial goals you put together in Chapter 12, "Now What?" Now we will start giving that list some structure. There is a commonly held notion that goals are nothing more than dreams with a deadline. We're going to work on the criteria that need to be set to give your dreams some definition and deadlines.

The mark of a well-defined goal is that it is ...

❖ Specific.

❖ Measurable.

❖ Realistic.

So let's take these elements in order.

A Well-Defined Goal Must Be Specific

You may have begun this process by saying things like ...

❖ I want to retire comfortably.

❖ I want my children to have a college education.

❖ I want to be financially independent.

Some of these phrases are probably on your "fantasy" goal list. They are wonderful sentiments, but they aren't specific—to say nothing of being measurable or realistic. So how can we make these relatively vague ideas into concrete goals? By making the thought more specific in the following terms:

❖ How much will this goal cost you today?

❖ How much will inflation apply to this goal?

❖ How many months or years do you have until this goal needs to be met?

❖ How long will this goal last?

❖ How much have you already set aside for this goal?

❖ How much will your investment grow while you're still saving? And after you stop saving?

❖ How much are you currently saving each month toward this goal?

The first four items on this list tell you how much you need to meet your goal. The last three tell you whether you're on track to meet your goal or you're behind.

For instance, let's use the retirement example. "I want to retire comfortably" becomes ...

❖ I make $35,000/year now, and estimate that I'll need about 85 percent of that, or $30,000/year, once I retire.

❖ I assume inflation will average 4 percent/year.

❖ I am 40 and want to retire at 65, so I have 25 years remaining to continue saving and investing.

❖ I assume I will live until age 85, which means I will spend 20 years in retirement.

❖ I already have $50,000 in my 401(k), and $30,000 in my IRA account, for a total of $80,000.

❖ I assume my investments will grow at 9 percent/year before I retire and 7 percent after I retire.

❖ I currently save $150/month in my 401(k) and $100/month in my IRA.

We will work through the math on this a bit later. For now, organize these seven characteristics for each of your goals. Use the goal blocks in Chapter 12.

A Well-Defined Goal Must Be Measurable

You will notice that several of the previous characteristics relate to making your goal measurable—both in current terms and in future terms. If you can't measure how much you want or will need, then you can't tell whether you're on track to meet this goal or whether it's realistic.

Going back to the previous retirement example, a $30,000 annual income at 4 percent inflation 25 years from now is an annual income of nearly $80,000. To draw that income for 20 years without annual cost of living increases during retirement requires a nest egg of nearly $850,000 when you retire at age 65. To give yourself a 4 percent raise each year to keep up with inflation will require just over $1.2 million. Remember, that nest egg will continue to grow during the 20 years after you retire, but you will also be making withdrawals from your income stream as you go along.

In this example, the $80,000 already saved, plus the $250/month being saved, growing at 9 percent per year will be worth just over $940,000 in 25 years when you expect to retire.

From there the math is fairly simple:

Anticipated actual nest egg

Minus Anticipated needed nest egg

Equals Retirement excess or deficit

$940,000 – $1,200,000 = ($260,000)

If you have a deficit, as in the example, then you should reassess your goal because you're not on track to meet it. There might be many reasons you could be in a position of playing catch up. Now let's talk more about making your goals realistic.

A Well-Defined Goal Must Be Realistic

You might not be saving enough or you might be investing too conservatively to meet this goal. Maybe your assumptions are out of line. Stocks in general have averaged about 10 percent per year since before the Depression. So in spite of the returns you probably saw during the late 1990s, don't assume you're going to get 30 percent a year—that's unrealistic. In fact, most of the goal calculators you find on the Internet don't allow more than a 10 to 12 percent assumed rate of return. Also, don't assume you're going to make 10 to 12 percent per year unless you are prepared to endure the fluctuations that go along with investing in the stock market. If you were invested in the stock market (through either mutual funds or individual stocks) during 2000 and 2001, you know exactly what we're talking about!

But that said, don't be frightened of stocks, either. Most retirement plan participants, especially women, have a tendency to invest most of their money in CDs, money markets, and guaranteed investment contracts or stable value funds—as Charlie Brown used to say, "AAARRRGGGHHH!" Even if you have a relatively long period of time until you retire, these instruments are incapable of growing at the rate you need. Odds are that if you use them too heavily, your nest egg won't grow large enough to support your goals.

Remember, stocks are like people—there are conservative ones, aggressive ones, and a whole variety of those in between. I'm sure your circle of friends and acquaintances contains lots of different types of people. Well, so should your investment portfolio.

If you're one of those people that says you only want a steady 5 percent, and believe that everything will be alright, consider this. If you put $1,000,000 in a 5 percent fixed investment, it would generate $50,000 per year. Keeping pace with inflation, you would be completely out of money just 15 years into your 30 year retirement.

If you are a more conservative investor, you should understand that the primary risk is that you won't accumulate enough to meet your goal. Safety comes with a lower potential payoff. If you are a more aggressive investor, you should understand that your primary risk is poor market return in the short run. Higher potential return comes with no guarantee. The trick is to find the balance that allows you to have enough safety to let you sleep at night, but a high enough return to give your money the chance to grow enough to achieve your goals.

Doing the Math

Let's go back to the previous retirement example and work through the math. You might need to use a financial calculator or one of the goal calculators available on the Internet. But before you start doing any estimates, you need to know how the numbers are calculated.

Let's say you have invested $1,000 and it grows at 8 percent a year for 10 years, compounded annually. That means at the end of the first year, your $1,000 is worth 1.08 times what it was worth at the beginning of the year. Then repeat the process nine more times:

$1,000 × 1.08 = $1,080

$1,080 × 1.08 = $1,166

$1,166 × 1.08 = $1,259

$1,259 × 1.08 = $1,360

$1,360 × 1.08 = $1,469

$1,469 × 1.08 = $1,587

$1,587 × 1.08 = $1,714

$1,714 × 1.08 = $1,851

$1,851 × 1.08 = $1,999

$1,999 × 1.08 = $2,159

This is exactly the same process credit card companies use to calculate the interest they charge on your account balances, only they compound the interest each month!

Benjamin Franklin is credited as saying that compound interest was the "Eighth Wonder of the World." So stop letting the credit card companies use it against you, and let your investments make it work for you.

Checking Your Progress

If working through the math in the previous section is more than you are comfortable with, then take advantage of the tools available on the Web. Most of the brokerage firm and mutual fund Web sites have calculators available that will help you determine whether you're on track or behind schedule. Take a look at the respective lists in Appendix B, "Resources." Also, if your 401(k) or 403(b) at work provides Internet access, there may be calculators available there as well.

Goal Calculators on the Internet

If you want to use the Web for checking your progress, there are a variety of resources to choose from. Just about every mutual fund family, brokerage firm, and bank has a goal calculator on its Web site. Take a look at the resource list in Appendix B.

Setting Priorities—a Case Study: Margaret

If you're like most people, you're not doing things one at a time. Like most people, your life is one big multitasking exercise—and you thought only computers could do that! Everything is happening at once or close to it. The problem is that all your goals seem to come due at the same time.

Let's look at an example that comes up more and more frequently these days: college versus retirement. Margaret didn't have her son until she was nearly 40, which means she will be paying for David's college education when she is between the ages of 60 and 64. Her plan was to retire at 65. That's two expensive goals coming due right at the same time.

So the conflict becomes which of these two goals takes priority? The first place you need to look is your definition of the two goals vying for your attention. In this case, they are "paying for college" and "retirement."

You might not agree, but during divorce settlement negotiations, courts most often consider a college education a generous gift—not an entitlement. If you pay for your child to go to college, he or she is very fortunate indeed. If you don't, you're *not* a bad parent. Legally, unless it's part of your property settlement agreement, you don't "have to" pay for college. In your heart, however, you may feel a different obligation. Remember, there is a big difference between a legal obligation and a self-imposed one. It's important that you keep those differences in mind and plan accordingly.

Most parents approach the issue of college with the thought that they will pay for four years of undergraduate school anywhere the child wants to go. But public colleges and universities aren't cheap, and private schools are downright expensive. So you could revise the goal so that you pay for your child to attend a public school. If you need to control costs even more, you could stick to only in-state schools.

If your situation requires further adjustments to the college goal, consider the following possible ideas:

- ❖ Your child could take a summer job with the earnings contributing to the cost of college.

- ❖ Your child could participate in a work-study program during the school year.

- ❖ Your child could compete for an academic or athletic scholarship.

- ❖ You could revise your goal so that you pay for some fraction of the total cost.

Whatever you decide to do, be sure to discuss it with your child so that he or she doesn't apply to Harvard when all you can afford is the state university. Note also that some state university systems have joined together to form regional networks so that students from anywhere within the area pay in-state tuition. Check with your state to see if it participates in a regional network of this type.

Then there's the issue of your retirement. With the timing in Margaret's case, the big expense of college is coming right at what will likely be her peak earning years just before retirement. That timing might convince Margaret that she "can't afford" to contribute to her retirement plan while she's paying college expenses. But the question really is can she afford not to? Remember, when you don't contribute to your employer-sponsored retirement plan, you're probably giving up the company matching contribution, in addition to any amount you could have contributed. That's why the question really is, "Can you afford not to contribute?"

We don't want Margaret to sacrifice everything for David's college education and then not be able to retire. Depending on how much she spends on college, she may have to retire later, possibly years later than she intended.

For people with more than one child, this conflict compounds quickly. In one family we know, the parents absolutely insisted on putting all five of their children through whatever school the children chose to attend. Now, both parents are still working, and probably will continue to do so well into their 70s—all because they chose the goal of college at the expense of their own retirements. So weigh carefully whether you want to be working that late in your life.

What Margaret finally decided to do was to alter her lifestyle a bit to allow her to make full contributions to her 401(k) at work, her Roth IRA, as well as a special college fund. She doesn't spend as much on eating out as she used to, and she will just repaint her kitchen instead of remodeling it like she originally planned to. But these adjustments will allow her to put aside the amounts she believes will be needed to pay for both college and retirement. And when David goes to college, it will likely be a state school.

Take a Look at Your Spending

A final note on spending and prioritizing: It's often difficult to prioritize your present desires—a fancy car, dinners at nice restaurants, expensive clothes, and so on—against future goals such as college, retirement, or a dream home. You can get immediate gratification by spending money on desires, but you don't get that same immediate satisfaction by saving for a future goal. Unfortunately, in our society, we have been led to believe that we need it now or it isn't any good.

People become rich because they live below their means. People are amazing creatures who can live on whatever their paycheck turns out to be. If you had to live on less money, you could. If you lost your $50,000/year job, and the only other job you could find paid just $40,000/year, you could endure that 20 percent pay cut. With the commitment to savings we're talking about, you get to keep the $50,000 job and save the extra $10,000 by living below your means. What a great deal!

What does it mean to live below your means? It means being smart about how you spend your money. The wealthy didn't get drawn into a lease just so they could have the fanciest car in town. A lease is nothing more than an arrangement to make car payments but give back the car at the end of the leasing period. The truly wealthy buy a good car, pay nearly all cash for it, and drive it until the wheels fall off before buying another one. They buy a home to build equity and get a tax write-off, and don't throw money out the window every month on rent. They contribute everything they possibly can to their 401(k)s and contribute another $2,000 a year to IRAs—every year! They save more on top of that. They don't eat peanut butter and jelly every day, but they don't go out for every meal either.

They run their family finances like a business. Revenue or income is nice, but truly wealthy people are looking for the savings, investments, and profits that are left after the expenses are paid. That is how to create financial wealth both in a business and in your personal life.

Let's look at the example of the car. Cars are depreciating assets, which means they go down in value as they age. Because of this depreciation, and because you can no longer deduct interest on a car payment, it is far better to pay cash than to finance a car. If you want to buy a particularly nice car, then save for it and pay cash if possible. Then drive it for a good long time. Don't trade a car in every few years.

Here's one particularly successful story. Bob wanted a BMW, so he started saving. While he was saving, he looked for a demonstrator of the right model. A year or so later, he found a company executive's car that had been driven for about a year and was going to be sold. Because the car wasn't completely new, he paid only $16,000 for what would have been a $25,000 car if he had bought it new. He paid about half down and financed the other half for four years. He made extra payments on it and paid the note off almost six months early. It's now 16 years later, and he's still driving the same BMW. And he's had no car payment for over a decade! How would you like to have no car payment and be able to save that money for something else? Yes, he'll probably buy another BMW in a couple of more years. But he'll save most or all of the purchase price before he does, and he'll probably drive it for 15 or 20 years.

How much have you spent on your car lease or purchase payments over the past 20 years? If you have a car payment of $400 per month for four years, and you buy a new car every five years, it works out like this:

$400/month × 12 months × 4 years × 4 cars over the 20 years = $76,800

How much of that money would you rather save for your retirement, your kids' college expenses, or a vacation home? We can't change what you've already done, but we can change how you do things in the future.

And what would you do with the $400/month for the year you didn't have a car payment? Would you save it? Probably not, but why not? Your budget already includes the car payment. But instead, it might be absorbed into the regular monthly cash flow. So let's do the math and see what you would save:

$400/month × 12 months × 4 years = $19,600

And that doesn't count any money market interest that could be earned, which comes to nearly $1,000 a year! That much should be in your savings and investment accounts.

This is what we mean when we say, "You work hard for your money. Be smart with it!"

The Bottom Line

Your long-term goals will be the hardest to focus on, but they are the greatest financial successes you will achieve. Pursue your goals without fear or shame, and enjoy them when you have achieved them.

Chapter 15

Post-Divorce Decisions

Capsule Outlook

Financial planning doesn't come with a schedule—You'll have to create your own schedule.

Once your divorce is final, there are a host of decisions you need to make. Don't assume that because there are no deadlines for completing these items, you can let them slide. Failing to take care of these issues can be a big mistake.

When you got married, your spouse became a built-in primary "go-to" person for many items:

- ❖ Who do you want to leave your money to?
- ❖ Who do you want to be able to make decisions for you if you're incapacitated?
- ❖ Who do you trust to make decisions about money you leave for your children's benefit?
- ❖ Who do you want to benefit from your insurance policies when you die?

When you were married, the answer to these questions and others was probably "my husband or wife." You wanted to leave your money to your spouse. You trusted your spouse to make business and health care decisions for you when you couldn't. You believed your spouse would honor your wishes. The government even gave you certain tax and gift benefits together.

Now that you're divorced, you probably don't want to leave that kind of power and control, or those benefits, in the hands of your ex-spouse. When you die, do you really want your ex-spouse to get your retirement money? Do you want your ex-spouse making decisions about your health care? Do you want your ex-spouse deciding whether or not to withdraw life support for you? With this change in marital status, the answer to these questions is probably no. And your ex-spouse probably doesn't want to leave you in charge of those issues for him or her.

This is true regardless of how you feel about your divorce and your ex-spouse. Hopefully, things were cooperative, not acrimonious. But even if your divorce was cooperative, your ex is probably not the person you trust with those powers and benefits anymore.

Plus, your situation could change dramatically. For example, Terri was a divorced mother with no intention of ever remarrying. But within five years, she had remarried, had become a stepmother to two more children, and was enjoying her new life thoroughly. If these kinds of changes take place in your life, it's only right that you want to include your new family in your financial plans. So be sure to take the needed steps to do that.

Beneficiary Designations

Several categories of assets transfer by beneficiary designation when you die, not by your will (we'll talk about your will later on). They include your retirement assets (IRA, 401[k], profit-sharing, money purchase, and pension), life insurance policies, and trusts. You need to make special efforts to be sure your wishes are reflected in these types of assets.

Beneficiary Designations for Retirement Accounts

A beneficiary designation is made by completing a form. This paperwork is available from your employer, retirement plan provider, brokerage firm, mutual fund company, or life insurance company. You will need to fill out a new form for each retirement account and life insurance policy you own. Usually you are asked for your beneficiary's name, Social Security number, address, and relationship to you. If you don't have someone's Social Security number, or some other piece of information, get it ahead of time. That way you can complete the beneficiary designation forms and won't have to remember to provide some missing element later on.

Many firms give you the opportunity to name both primary and secondary beneficiaries. As the names imply, your primary beneficiary gets the proceeds. But if your primary beneficiary dies before you do, the proceeds go to your secondary beneficiary.

Also, keep in mind that you can name more than one person as beneficiaries of the same stature. For instance, let's say you're married and have three children. While you're still married, you would likely list your husband as your 100 percent primary beneficiary and the children as secondary beneficiaries. After you're divorced, however, you can choose to leave all three children equal portions as primary beneficiaries. You can also leave them different amounts in whatever proportions you choose.

When Your Spouse Must Be Your Beneficiary

While you are married, you must name your husband as your 100 percent primary beneficiary on all Employee Retirement Income Security Act (ERISA) qualified retirement plans (401(k), 403(b), profit-sharing, money purchase, and pension). Equally, your spouse must do the same for you. This is not a requirement of your employer; it's a federal law.

The idea is to provide at least some degree of protection for spouses. You might consider that unfair and feel that it's your money, and you should be allowed to leave it to whomever you choose. There's obviously some merit to that argument, but consider this: It would be highly unfair for a wife to find out only after her husband has died that she isn't the beneficiary. Before this law was in effect, that happened. It would be particularly terrible if she had counted on those funds for support but was left destitute. Again, before this law, that happened, too.

By allowing someone else to be named as beneficiary while you are married, you are essentially giving up those funds. Because your consent is required, however, you at least get some advance notice that you won't be getting that money if your spouse dies. And if you don't give your consent, you can't be forcibly cut out until after a divorce.

How to Name Someone Else While You're Still Married

While you're married, unless you consent, your spouse must name you as the 100 percent primary beneficiary on their ERISA qualified retirement accounts. The same holds for you. But even while you are married, you can name beneficiaries other than your spouse if you get his or her consent.

Consent involves two things: a signature and a notary of that signature. The consenting spouse has to show identification and sign in front of the notary. So if you are consenting to a beneficiary other than yourself, be sure not to sign the form until you are actually in front of the notary. Most banks, brokerage firms, attorneys' offices, and libraries have notaries available. They may charge for their services, so be sure to ask.

Understand that consent for your spouse to name someone else gives him or her only one opportunity to do so. Your spouse can use that opportunity to name the kids instead of you, for example. If your spouse has a mind change and wants to name someone besides the kids, however, then he or she must get your consent again. Remember, the same holds true for you. If you want to name someone other than your spouse, you have to get your spouse's consent.

Both the new beneficiary designation and your spouse's notarized signature go on the beneficiary designation form. In most cases, you can get that form from your employer, the investment firm that handles your account, or your insurance company. Be sure to complete the form in its entirety and return it to the appropriate office. Many people think they're done when the form is filled out and forget to file it, so make sure you don't make that mistake.

How to Change Your Beneficiary After the Divorce

You will notice that the previous examples talk about beneficiary designations while you are still married. Once the divorce is final, no spousal consent is required because technically there is no spouse. You are single. So when you are officially single again, complete a new form and submit it as soon as possible.

Beneficiary designations are used only when you are deceased. Whether you're still married or already divorced, if you wish to change your beneficiary designation, be sure to complete the process in its entirety. After you die, the latest beneficiary designation on file for your account is the one that's used. Whoever is listed on that form receives that asset, so if your current designations aren't what you want them to be, you've got some work to do.

Beneficiaries of Trusts

Trusts are private legal documents. If you have any trusts, be sure to reread them regularly to be sure they still fit your situation. With a divorce, these trusts might need some revision. Don't try to revise these documents yourself, however. Consult with an attorney who specializes in trusts and estates if changes need to be made.

A Word About ERISA

The Employee Retirement Income Security Act (ERISA) was passed in 1974. In it, Congress spelled out specific rules that apply to certain employer-sponsored retirement plans, such as 401(k), profit sharing, money purchase, target benefit, and defined benefit pensions. In essence, ERISA works to protect workers from employers who would try to provide the majority of benefits to the owners, while leaving rank and file employees out in the cold. Most of the rules relate to the employer's obligations to its workers, including reporting and testing requirements from the Internal Revenue Service and Department of Labor. Some of the rules create protections like the spousal consent rule. For more information, check out the Department of Labor's Web site at www.dol.gov.

Insurance

Practically everyone carries insurance, whether it's life insurance, health insurance, or disability insurance. Usually, people get these benefits through their employer. Sometimes, most often with life insurance, additional policies are bought in addition to the coverage offered through your employer.

Insurance for You

Sometimes insurance gets lost in the frenzy of activity surrounding a divorce, but it is an important part of your financial planning, especially as you transition back to a single status. Many people assume they can't afford it or don't need it. Still others choose to ignore it because they don't understand it.

Insurance is essentially a method of transferring risk to someone else. The price of insurance is called a *premium*. And in exchange for a premium, the insurance company takes the risk that you will collect on the policy. There's an expression that explains this concept quite simply:

> Don't refuse to pay a relatively small premium to avoid a relatively large risk.

Think of it this way: How financially devastated would you and your family be if you suffered a long illness, a lengthy disability, or, worst of all, if you died unexpectedly? These are the very kinds of events that insurance is intended to help you deal with.

On the flip side, don't complain that you have spent a year's worth of premiums for insurance and you didn't get anything for it. If this has happened, then you have had a year of good health and good fortune. Be thankful for it.

Initially, you need to figure out:

- ❖ The types of insurance you need for yourself.
- ❖ The types of insurance you need on your ex-spouse.
- ❖ How much coverage you need.
- ❖ Where you can get that coverage.

Let's review these issues.

What Kinds of Insurance Do You Need for Yourself?

There are three basic types of insurance coverage we're talking about here: life, health, and disability.

Life insurance is just that—a policy that pays a death benefit to your beneficiaries when you die. You can purchase two types of life insurance: term and permanent. With *term life insurance,* you are covered as long as you pay your premium. If you fail to pay, the coverage is cancelled. It is generally the least expensive form of life insurance. But the older you get, the more expensive the premium becomes. Typically, the life insurance offered through your employer is term insurance.

Permanent life insurance is more expensive, but it allows you to build up cash value, which can be invested in a variety of ways. Also, the cost of insurance is not subject to increase. If you don't or can't pay the premium, it could be paid from the accumulated cash value in your policy. Or the amount needed could be automatically loaned to you, depending on the provisions in your particular policy.

There are many types of permanent life insurance, including whole, variable, universal, variable universal, and adjustable. All of these types allow for policyholders to accrue cash value within the policy. That cash value is then invested in either a fixed account or mutual funds, depending on the type of policy. These kinds of insurance are highly sophisticated and can be very complex. Be sure you are well-informed and comfortable with any permanent insurance policy you have. If you aren't sure, ask questions.

Most often, you get some term insurance provided by your employers at their cost. You can usually buy additional term coverage through your employer, but you pay the additional premium. If those coverages aren't enough, you can buy more permanent or term life insurance on your own.

When you buy life insurance, you are providing for the possibility that your death will result in a loss of earnings or cause taxes to be due. The specific amount of coverage you need depends on the many variables that make up your particular situation. It is advisable that you consult a professional to determine precisely how much life insurance you need. One rule of thumb says to begin with a death benefit of 7 to 10 times your annual earnings and make adjustments from there.

Health insurance covers costs associated with doctor visits, hospitalization, and prescription drugs. You can get traditional fee-for-service coverage or an HMO/PPO policy. Most often, people have health insurance coverage through their employers because as part of a group, premiums become more reasonable. Also, some employers pay a portion of the premiums for their employees, which makes the coverage that much more affordable. With fee-for-service policies, you can see any doctor you like and pay a set percentage of the expenses, usually 20 percent. Then the insurance company pays the rest. HMOs, or Health Maintenance Organizations, require you to visit their clinic to see a doctor. PPOs, or Preferred Provider Organizations, work like HMOs, except patients see physicians on the PPO list to get maximum benefits. Some PPOs allow you to see doctors not on their list at a slightly reduced benefit. In exchange for these restrictions, the company should provide coverage without the usual claim forms and reimbursement processes.

Disability insurance is most often forgotten. It provides a replacement for income lost when you can't work. There are two types: short-term and long-term. Each becomes effective after an exclusion period and lasts for a certain length of time. Like life insurance, disability insurance is most often provided through an employer. Smaller firms and self-employed individuals frequently do not have access to disability coverage at a reasonable price and must go through another organization, like a trade association. As you investigate your own coverage and needs, be aware that disability insurance typically replaces only a percentage of your income, usually 50 to 75 percent. Policies that cover 100 percent of your income are very expensive. Pay close attention to the policy's definitions of things such as what's considered a disability, how long you have to be unable to work before benefits are paid, and how long the exclusion periods are.

Where to Get Insurance

Many married couples engage in what we call "benefit swapping." You use your employer's health insurance benefit and your spouse's life and disability benefits, for example. Unfortunately, when you get divorced, it's now up to each of you to get your own coverage. If you work for a large employer, you probably have access to most or all of the insurance you need and want.

If you are a small-business employee or are self-employed, you might have to go through an organization that has set itself up as a group, like a trade association, labor union, or professional society. Call the groups to which you belong and find out what kinds of insurance they can help you find.

If you are unable to get coverage immediately following your divorce, you may choose to use COBRA coverage. This is only temporary coverage available for a maximum of 36 months, and it's usually more expensive. Under COBRA you still get the insurance at the company's group rate, but now you pay the full cost with no help from the company. If you need to use COBRA coverage to stay insured immediately after your divorce, that's fine. But be sure not to procrastinate. Make finding replacement coverage for yourself and your family a priority.

Insurance for Your Children

Your children's health insurance coverage will likely be a point of negotiation in your divorce. If both you and your ex-spouse have access to health insurance through your employers, either of you can keep the kids on your insurance. If both of you do so, it might be a relatively large expense for relatively little additional benefit. Be sure to review the costs and benefits of the policies available, and then make your choice.

Insurance on Your "Ex"

If you are awarded child support, spousal maintenance/alimony, or both, you might want to insure your ex-spouse against a disability or premature death.

One of the biggest issues here is payment of the premium. If you will be receiving alimony and child support payments, you may want to pay the premiums yourself so you can ensure that the policies stay in force. If alimony is your only income, however, the cost of that insurance could be an overwhelming portion of your budget.

One alternative is for your ex-spouse to pay an additional amount of alimony so that you can make the premium payment. This method tends to work because alimony payments are deductible for the payer and taxable for the recipient. It's a small price for the peace of mind that comes from knowing the premium will be paid.

A trust can be used in this situation as well. You might not be comfortable trusting your ex-spouse to make the alimony payments, and he may not be comfortable trusting you with a sizeable insurance policy on his life. With a trust, you can use a neutral person or a corporate trust department as the "trustee" who would then administer the trust. The trust can be structured to give you only a continuation of alimony and child support benefits in the case of your ex-husband's death or disability. Both of you would have to agree on the disposition of any remaining funds once the alimony and child support obligations have been fulfilled.

Let's look at an example of how a trust with a life insurance policy would work. Remember, this is only an example. Your numbers will be different. Jane and Matt decide to get a divorce. At the time, they have two sons, ages six and two. Matt is to pay as follows:

$1,000/month in alimony for 15 years,

$600/month in child support until the eldest child is 18, and

$400/month in child support until the youngest child is 18.

Jane and Matt choose to establish a trust containing a $500,000 life insurance policy on Matt, with a corporate trustee. This policy will cost $1,200/year, or $100/month. They agree to split the cost of the policy, so Matt increases his alimony payment to $1,050/month.

Over the intervening years, Matt continues to pay alimony and child support, but is killed five years later in an automobile accident. Ordinarily, Jane would be unable to collect her income. With the trust, however, her alimony and child support payments are then paid from the $500,000 death benefit in the trust. Those payments to her continue, just as if Matt were living, until the obligations have been paid. And once those payments are finished, the remaining money is paid out according to the terms of the trust. That could include paying for the boys' college expenses, helping them buy their own homes, or additional items that Jane and Matt were willing to pay for as stated in the trust document.

You can see how this kind of arrangement would help you and your ex-spouse be more comfortable with potential alimony and child support payments. If it is a possible solution for you, be sure to consult with an experienced trust and estate attorney so that the appropriate documents can be drafted along with your divorce papers.

Your Basic Legal Documents

There are four documents that most attorneys consider essential to your legal well-being: a will, a power of attorney, a living will, and a power of attorney for health care. During your marriage, these documents probably centered on the two of you. Now that you are divorced, you probably don't want to leave your ex-spouse with that degree of power over your final affairs.

Updating these documents requires a consultation with your attorney. We highly recommend that you retain someone who specializes in trusts and estates. We have seen the negative consequences of poorly drafted trusts, which has led me to the opinion that this is one of those areas in life where it doesn't pay to skimp. A good estate-planning attorney is worth his or her weight in gold.

Will

A will gets filed with the local probate clerk, and addresses the transfer of any assets not in a trust, the custody of minor children, and the disposition of personal property. This is a public document that can be accessed and read by anyone requesting to do so, once it has been filed with the clerk after your death. This availability to the public has resulted in people using trusts to maintain privacy. But just because you have a trust does not mean you should ignore having a will drafted or updated. If you have neglected to transfer a particular asset into your trust, its distribution will be handled in your will. So have your will drafted and signed, and keep it updated.

Power of Attorney

A power of attorney document gives someone else the ability to perform tasks and conduct business on your behalf. This power can be durable or nondurable. *Durable* refers to the power staying in effect even if you become incapacitated. A *nondurable power* would become void if you became incapacitated. In either event, a power of attorney becomes void when you die.

Your power of attorney can become effective immediately or when you become disabled. Your documents will specify exactly how your disability is defined and when the power of attorney goes into effect. Most often, powers of attorney that become effective when you become disabled are referred to as "springing" powers because they spring into being when needed. To go into effect, they require a letter from one or more of your physicians stating that you are unable to handle your own affairs.

Consider carefully who you name as your power of attorney and when those powers become effective. Be sure the person you name is both willing and able to perform those duties, and name an alternate in case your first choice later becomes unable or unwilling to serve. Remember that asking someone to be your power of attorney is a large responsibility. Don't be surprised or offended if they decline. It could put someone in an awkward position with the rest of your family. Some people might not feel qualified to do a good job, and still others may be afraid of the decisions they will be asked to make. When you ask someone to be your power of attorney, he or she tends to think seriously about whether he or she can do a good job for you. So if the person you choose decides not to be your power of attorney, use the opportunity to find out why and ask who he or she would suggest you consider instead.

Living Will/Power of Attorney for Health Care

A living will and power of attorney for health care are often combined and are referred to in some states as an *advance medical directive*. These documents describe the types of medical treatment you do not want to have administered and give a specific person the authority to make medical decisions for you if you are unable to do it yourself.

Again, this is a big responsibility. Be sure to talk with your designee in great detail to make sure he or she will honor your wishes. This designee will have a great deal of power when you're in a vulnerable position. Choose someone worthy of the task.

A Successful Estate-Planning Story

This subject is not a happy or fun one, but having estate-planning issues thought through, expressed, understood, and in place is crucial to having your estate handled the way you want. The following example is about a married couple, but it will show you the importance of having your estate plan in place.

Mr. and Mrs. B had been married for nearly 50 years. Both were devout Catholics. In putting together their estate plan, they consulted with an attorney who encouraged them to talk about what they wanted and what they didn't want. He also encouraged them to discuss these issues with their children, other family members, and their parish priest. After doing so, they met with the attorney again to draft the documents that would allow their wishes to be carried out.

Unexpectedly one morning, Mrs. B didn't call her husband to breakfast. She had suffered a stroke. He called the paramedics and went with her to the hospital where the doctor informed Mr. B that his wife had suffered a stroke that was so massive that it would be fatal in a matter of hours or days. Because Mr. and Mrs. B had discussed these issues and had their plan in place, Mr. B not only had the authority to tell the doctors what he wanted done for his wife, but also knew he was doing exactly what she wanted. Because of her faith, her primary concern was that she received last rites before her death. With the paperwork in order, the hospital made arrangements to bring in a priest, while the doctors kept her alive and comfortable. She received last rites and was allowed to pass away quietly as she had instructed.

It's not a pleasant topic, we know. But it's far better to discuss something unpleasant now than to leave your family wondering whether they're doing the right thing for you later.

The Bottom Line

Check your beneficiary designations, insurance coverage, and legal documents to be sure they reflect your new single status. These are just the documents that will protect you when you become vulnerable, and will assure that your wishes are followed.

Chapter 16

Post-Divorce Financial-Planning Issues

Capsule Outlook

People don't plan to fail. They fail to plan.

Once your divorce is final, there are several financial-planning issues you will need to go over again. They basically break down into the following categories:

- ❖ College planning
- ❖ Retirement planning
- ❖ Elder care/long term care planning
- ❖ Estate planning

For you to have the greatest opportunity for success, you should make definite plans, including the steps you need to take to meet your goals. Outlining the process also enables you to check your progress to see if you are on track to meet those goals.

College Planning

Most people are concerned about their children's education. Parents consider it a top priority, even above their own retirement. However, most states do not consider a college education a child's "right." They consider it more of a highly generous gift. As such, money for a child's college education usually comes about only from a parent making such savings a priority. But before you start plowing cash into a savings or investment account, let's take a look at the goal of paying for college and understand how we can work through it.

Three Basic Alternatives: Before, During, or After

Regardless of where your children go to college, as their benefactor, you have three choices about when and how to set aside money for tuition, fees, and other expenses. You can save before they go, you can pay the tuition bills as they come in, or you can make loan payments after they have graduated. The question is which way is right for you?

If you figure you won't be able to pay your children's college expenses from your income, you should look at saving in advance. Even if you can afford to pay for college out of your regular income, saving and investing before your children graduate from high school is still the least expensive way to pay. If you start investing early in your children's lives, you have more time for that money to grow before you need it. This way, the total cost of college is paid for partly with your savings and partly with the growth of that money.

When paying tuition bills during your children's time in college, you are paying from your current income. As the money comes in from your regular paycheck, you will be writing a check back out to the school. With a payment plan, you still pay the total cost, but you get to spread that expense out over a series of payments made throughout the year. For instance, some public universities have a plan where you pay the cost of a year's tuition, fees, room, and board from roughly May through the following April. So by the end of a given school year, you have finished paying for it. Some schools charge interest, but others don't. Check with the schools you and your children are thinking about to see what's available.

Your third alternative is to take out loans while your kids are in college, and pay those loans back after they graduate. Depending on how you apply for those loans, they could be your responsibility or your children's. The problem with this approach is that it is expensive in terms of added interest, and the interest expense is generally not as tax-smart as other alternatives. At most, you will be able to deduct part of the interest on your loans. At the moment, only the first $5,000 in interest is deductible, and refinancing does not extend that amount. Your loans will probably cost much more than $5,000 in interest over the life of the loan. Repaying these loans can sometimes take years. And having big loans to repay can be a serious obstacle to other goals your children may have, like buying a home of their own.

Some limited tax benefits are available, such as the Hope Credit and the Lifetime Learning Credit, but they are fairly small amounts compared to the cost of a college education. Also, as the parent, your income is typically much higher than your children's income right after they graduate. If your income is too high, you might not even qualify for these deductions. Since the income limits change each year, check with your accountant, or look at the IRS Web site at www.irs.gov for current information and more details.

What Do You Have to Cover?

There are lots of different expenses associated with going to college. You have tuition, fees, room, board, books and supplies, laundry money, pocket money, fraternity/sorority dues, car expenses, and travel costs to go back and forth from home. How much of this do you really have to cover? If you live in California and your child is going to school in Florida, you're going to have to cover airfare back and forth, but probably only once or twice a semester, not for every long weekend. Regardless of how far away school is, paying for a fraternity or sorority is definitely optional. Those costs might be one of the things your children have to pay for out of their summer earnings.

Another idea to consider is that you don't have to pay the entire bill. There are various ways for a parent to cut back on the cost, including paying for a portion of college costs, for example, half instead of all. And in some cases, it just might not be possible for you to pay for any of your children's education. For instance, if you have several children at home and aren't making much money, you may not have the luxury of extra money to pay these costs. If so, that's okay. Just remember to support your children in whatever way you can—letting them live at home, helping them learn to juggle their work and school schedules, and being there for them to talk to when they need you.

Where Will They Go?

If you're trying to keep expenses down, the first two issues that usually come up are public versus private and in-state versus out-of-state. First of all, private schools are significantly more expensive. According to the Peterson's Undergraduate Database (1999), here's how it breaks down:

Average Ivy League School

Tuition	$20,927
Fees	$1,019
Room	$4,172
Board	$3,018
Total	$29,136

Average Private School

Tuition	$10,707
Fees	$352
Room	$2,687
Board	$2,330
Total	$16,076

Average Public School Out-of-State

Tuition	$5,446
Fees	$426
Room	$2,219
Board	$1,793
Total	$9,884

Average Public School In-State

Tuition	$2,409
Fees	$426
Room	$2,219
Board	$1,793
Total	$4,012

You need to think about whether the additional cost of a private or Ivy League experience is worth it. Some people feel strongly that it is. Others think a school's prestige is more important at the graduate level. Still others feel that it doesn't matter where you go to school; it's what you do with the education that matters.

Regardless of your public/private or in-state/out-of-state decisions, geography can be an issue in another way. Some schools are in cities like Chicago, San Francisco, and New York, where it is expensive to live. So you might need to look at schools in less expensive cities like Des Moines, Iowa; Greensboro, North Carolina; or Spokane, Washington.

Another way to use geography to keep costs down is to have your children go to school close enough to live at home, at least for the first couple of years. But weigh this decision carefully before you choose. A college education is only partially about what you learn in class. It is also about learning how to live on your own. And if your children are living at home, many of these lessons can be lost.

Another thought for keeping costs down is to look at a college as opposed to a university. Many colleges are less expensive than traditional universities because there are no graduate programs.

Students tend to get more direct contact with the professors, instead of being taught by teaching assistants or graduate students, as at many larger universities. There is also the option of going to a community college or junior college for a year or two, which is significantly less expensive, and then transferring to a four-year school.

Sharing the Cost

Most parents approach the question of sharing the cost of college with the idea that they will pay 100 percent of the cost wherever their children choose to go, and that if they don't, they have failed. That's a crock. Plenty of people have had to put themselves through college, and many of them would tell you they're better off for the experience. Sure, paying for 100 percent is a great gift if you can do it, but it's not the one true sign of a great parent.

As we said earlier, if college costs are part of your property settlement agreement, then you know how much both you and your ex-spouse are required to pay for. Remember, that property settlement agreement is a legally binding document.

Let's say your property settlement agreement says your ex is obligated to pay for one third of the cost, but you are not obligated to pay anything. You might want to pay for a third of the costs and have your children cover the last third through scholarships, work/study, and summer jobs.

Perhaps you are able to cover only 25 percent of the cost. That's fine. Just be upfront with your children about what you can and can't do. Help them figure out how to pay for the rest of college.

In either case, decide what your goal is, and work backward to determine how much you need to set aside to meet that goal.

Doing the Math

College planning is a small scale version of retirement planning. When you do the math for a college-funding plan, there are several items to keep track of. First of all, how much does the school you're looking at cost today? And how much have those costs increased from year to year? Remember, the average costs of tuition, fees, room, and board in 1999 were:

Average in-state public	$4,012
Average out-of-state public	$9,884
Average private	$16,076
Average Ivy League	$29,136

Those costs have gone up by nearly 10 percent a year for the past 10 years. Many schools have realized recently that these price increases may be too much for most people to afford, and that it's a great source of frustration to see tuition go up nearly twice as fast as inflation. Therefore, many schools have made a conscious effort to keep their tuition hikes to a minimum.

Keeping Money in Your Name

So you've decided to start saving and investing a little bit each month. Should you keep that money in your own name, or should you put it in your children's names? The answer to this question is highly personal and depends on several things, such as ...

❖ How likely are you to need this money yourself?

❖ How many children are you responsible for?

❖ How much do you trust your children?

If you put the money in your children's names, it is an *irrevocable* gift to them, meaning you can't take it back to pay for rent, credit card bills, groceries, car payments, or vacations. It has to be spent for the children's benefit. If you think you might run into budget problems and need the cash for your own use, then keep it in your name. Don't put anything in your children's names that you aren't prepared to live without.

If you have more than one child, you might want to keep more of the money in your name to give you more flexibility. For instance, let's look at a four-child home: Amy, Billy, Cathy, and David. If you put most of the money in Amy's name, and she goes to a fairly inexpensive school, you would want to use the rest of the money for Billy, Cathy, and David—but you can't. Actually, Amy would have to make that decision. And if the amount is over $10,000, gift taxes might be involved. And if Billy and Cathy have extra money left after their college years are paid for, they would have to make a gift to David as well.

UGMA vs. EIRA

Okay, you've decided to put money in your children's names. How should you do it? The most frequently used account is the Uniform Gift/Transfer to Minors Account (UGMA or UTMA). An account for someone who lives in California would be titled "Mary K. Smith, custodian for Suzie P. Smith (UGMA/CA)." There is no limit to the amount that can be deposited into UGMA/ UTMA accounts. You can invest in stocks, bonds, mutual funds, or money markets on behalf of your children, but the earnings in this account are taxable each year at the custodian's tax rate. Once the child reaches age 14, the investment earnings are taxable at the child's rate. This is what's often called the "kiddie tax." It's intended to keep the super-wealthy from hiding assets in their children's names. Once the children reach the age of majority in their state of residence, the money is theirs. In some states that age is 18; in others it's 21.

An education IRA (EIRA) was limited to an annual contribution of $500 per child per year, until the child reaches age 18. That contribution limit has now been increased to $2,000 per child per year. So if both parents set up EIRAs for the same child, the total annual contribution is $2,000, not $2,000 per account, and not $2,000 per parent. The benefit to this type of account is that the investments grow tax-deferred. When funds are used expressly for college costs, there is no tax upon withdrawal. For a child born today whose receives the maximum of 18 contributions of $2,000 each, assuming 10 percent annual growth, you will accumulate just over $90,000. While that amount may not cover all of your child's four-year education, it will cover a lot.

Also, the contributor to an EIRA must qualify by having an adjusted gross income of less than $150,000. If you don't qualify, perhaps a grandparent or other relative does.

State Prepaid Plans and Section 529 Plans

Another way of dealing with college costs is to use a state prepaid tuition plan. Check with your state, since some cover only tuition, while others also cover room and board expenses. The concept is simply that you freeze the cost of tuition by committing to the prepaid plan. Also check on whether the tuition paid to one state is transferable to another state, if your child chooses to attend another university.

A Section 529 plan is sponsored by a particular state and run by an investment manager like a mutual fund family. It allows you to invest a much larger amount than you can in an EIRA and these funds also grow tax-deferred. Money withdrawn to pay for college is taxed at the student's rate, not the parent's. Any remaining balance is transferable to another child. However, you have no control over how the money is invested. If that bothers you, then you might want to make other arrangements. Also, don't use a Section 529 plan if you might need these funds for a noneducational purpose, like your own retirement.

Getting Help from Grandparents

If grandparents or other relatives can help out with college expenses, make sure to have them pay the school directly. This arrangement allows them to make unlimited gifts without the usual $10,000 annual gift limit and potential gift tax.

Retirement Planning

Retirement is on just about everyone's list of financial goals, but the prospect of meeting this goal is daunting and often overwhelming. It is a big one, but don't let that confuse or discourage you. In fact, for those of you with several years left before retirement, you have a great opportunity to take charge of this monumental goal and make it your own.

As with any goal, you need to use the "MRS" principle: Make it *measurable, realistic,* and *specific.* We'll talk about the specific and measurable aspects in a moment. But before we do, let's do a quick refresher on being realistic. Ultimately, only you can be the judge of whether your goals are realistic. With a goal as long term and large as planning for your retirement, being realistic takes on special importance. Go into retirement planning with the idea that you will maintain your standard of living after you stop working. Don't think of retirement as a fantasy in which you'll suddenly start living like royalty. Remember, if you've just been getting by, don't expect to retire like Ivana or Donald Trump.

Now, on to the specific and measurable components ... The two characteristics go hand in hand, so let's look at them together. Specific refers to the fact that there is a number involved. Measurable refers to the unit of measurement you will use to get your specific number. These units may be currency, time, cost, or investment growth rate.

When Do You Plan to Retire?

This is a simple two-part question:

❖ How old are you now?

❖ At what age do you plan to retire?

Subtract the two, and you will know how many years you have to work with.

For example:

I'm 40 years old.

I want to retire at age 65.

That gives me 25 years to plan.

How Much Income Will You Need?

The general rule is that you will need around 80 percent of your pre-retirement income to maintain your standard of living after you stop working. For some people, this percentage is too much; for others, it is too little. To figure out how much you will need, take your regular monthly budget, and imagine that you're not working. What expenses will you no longer have, like commuting, parking, clothing, and dry cleaning? And what expenses will you have that you don't already have, like traveling to visit the grandchildren every year?

For this example, let's say you now make $50,000 a year. At retirement, 80 percent of that is $40,000 a year.

What Are Your Assumptions?

There are three assumptions you need to define:

- ❖ What do you expect inflation to be?
- ❖ What rate of growth do you expect from your investments before you retire?
- ❖ What rate of growth do you expect from your investments after you retire?

One way to answer the inflation question is to see what inflation has done in the past. Between 1925 and 2000, inflation has averaged 4 percent. Remember, inflation will be an issue both before and after you retire.

The growth rates you expect depend on how your retirement money is invested. If you are invested more in stock, you might want to plan on closer to a 10 percent return. If you are invested more in bonds, you may want to use something closer to 6 percent. Regardless of what you figure for your pre-retirement return, you will probably want to assume something a bit lower for the post-retirement period because most people get a bit more conservative with their investments after they stop working. But don't expect to ever be completely out of growth-oriented investments, even after you've retired, because you've still got to keep up with inflation.

So in our example, let's make our assumptions like this:

Inflation will be 4 percent.

Asset growth before retirement will be 10 percent.

Asset growth after retirement will be 7 percent.

How Long Do You Plan to Live?

We're not trying to be cute here. The biggest risk you run in retirement planning is outliving your money. So look at how long people in your family tend to live. Right now, men and women are expected to live until about age 85. But that number keeps getting larger. A woman who makes it to age 50 without heart disease is expected to live to age 92.

For our example, let's plan on living to age 85.

How Much Have You Saved?

Get your statements together and figure out how much you have already saved.

In our example, let's say you've accumulated:

$100,000 in your 401(k)

$30,000 in your IRA

And you currently save:

$7,500 a year in the 401(k) (15 percent of your $50,000 salary)

$2,500 a year in 401(k) match from your employer (dollar-for-dollar match on the first 5 percent of your $50,000 salary)

$2,000 a year in the IRA

Case Study

Now that we have been specific about the retirement plan goal in our example, let's run the numbers. First, the $40,000/year in retirement income needs to be adjusted by 4 percent inflation for 25 years. That makes the desired retirement income just over $106,000.

Next, what will the money already in your 401(k) and IRA accounts be worth in 25 years? That's $130,000 ($100,000 in the 401[k] plus $30,000 in the IRA), growing at 10 percent for 25 years. That gives you $1,400,000.

But remember, you're adding to these accounts each month. So what will your additions grow to? That's $12,000 ($7,500 in the 401(k), $2,500 401(k) employer match, and $2,000 in the IRA), growing at 10 percent for 25 years. That gives you another $1,180,000. So in total, going into retirement, you will have $2,580,000.

When you retire, how long will that nest egg last? With a 4 percent inflation rate and only a 7 percent growth rate, you will notice that things get a bit tighter. So that $2.5 million nest egg will support a $106,000 income for 43 years, even adjusted for inflation. Another way to look at this example is to see how much you will need to support your $106,000 income until age 85, and see if there is a shortfall in your savings. To maintain that income for 20 years, from age 65 to age 85, requires a retirement nest egg of $1,600,000. Without any one of the three elements (401[k] contribution, employer match, or IRA contribution), the plan is much less able to support you.

To help you work through the numbers for yourself, we've included a simplified work sheet in Appendix A, "Forms," courtesy of the American Funds group of mutual funds. Take a few minutes to work through your own numbers and see if you are on track, or if you need to do some catching up.

Elder Care Planning

It is a commonly stated goal that older folks don't want to be a burden on their children. The only way to achieve this goal, however, is to plan for it. There are essentially two ways of dealing with the potential costs: buying a long term care insurance policy, or saving and investing especially for possible costs related to growing older.

Remember, elder care issues apply not only to you, but also to your parents and other family members, if you will be expected to help care for them as they get older. You must think about how much you will be able to do yourself and what other activities will be competing for your time. For instance, if you have young children and must work, that's two full-time jobs right there! Being responsible for an aging parent makes it three full-time jobs, which doesn't leave any time for you.

It used to be that people moved from their homes straight into nursing homes. Now there are a variety of living arrangements available, including in-home care, assisted living, and full-time skilled nursing care (the traditional nursing home). In-home care and assisted living have helped keep costs down by offering a lower level of care for a lower cost. But not all long term care insurance policies cover these types of care. And Social Security does not cover what they call "custodial care" or care that relates to your "activities of daily living," such as bathing, dressing, and feeding yourself.

Even so, elder care is not cheap. The average assisted-living facility costs around $1,600 per month, and the average nursing home runs nearly $4,600 per month. Multiply that by the average stay of two years, and you're looking at a significant expense.

Also, families have different ideas about what kinds of living arrangements are acceptable and which are not. We would urge you to keep an open mind on this issue. You might think that anything short of staying in your own home is unacceptable, but there may come a day when staying home alone is not the best solution. Be flexible and willing to look at another option if your current living arrangements don't work out.

Make Sure You Know Your Definitions

If you choose to purchase an insurance policy, read it! The whole thing. Know how your policy defines when your benefits will be paid, what kinds of care these benefits will cover, and how long they will pay. These definitions can be vastly different from policy to policy.

A word of warning: Medicare, the age-65-and-over federal health insurance program, does not cover care required to help you with *activities of daily living,* which include dressing, bathing, eating, and toileting. If you need help with these activities but otherwise do not need medical assistance, Medicare will not help you. If you do need medical care and are fully disabled, but aren't yet age 65, there is a two-year waiting period before you can apply for Medicare based on that disability.

Medicaid will help you in either case, but requires that you spend down all your assets in order to qualify. In other words, you have to be almost completely broke to get Medicaid assistance.

Who Will You Have to Cover?

Obviously, you want to have your own long term care needs met, but you might be responsible for other family members. Who will be depending on you for their care later on? Your parents? Brothers and sisters? Aunts and uncles? Extended family members? And how will you provide that care?

These are not easy conversations to have. But you will be much better prepared to handle whatever needs arise if you have discussed them well in advance. You don't want to be making decisions about long term care under duress. The situation will be stressful enough when it arises. Do yourself a favor and work out the details now, both for your care and for the care of those who will depend on you.

Where Can You Get Insurance Coverage?

Many larger employers offer long term care insurance as an employee benefit, and some of these programs enable you to add other family members to your coverage. Frequently, these policies do not require a physical exam, but do require answering a brief health questionnaire. This group form of coverage can provide an affordable way to get long term care insurance, but these policies might not cover everything you want or need, like a private room.

Buying Insurance vs. Personal Savings

If the coverage through your employer is not enough, or if your employer doesn't offer long term care insurance, you can look into buying a policy directly from an insurance company. Going this route usually requires a physical exam and answering some pretty in-depth health questions. If the person you're trying to get a policy for has been sick, he or she might not be able to get the insurance, or it could be too costly. Even if you're in pretty good health but over age 50, the premiums can get expensive. And the older you get, the more expensive the premiums become. So in some cases, the cost of insurance may just be too high.

If you apply for a policy when you're younger, then it will be cheaper. That's just because you're less likely to make a claim at age 25 than you are at age 55. The advantage of this plan is that you'll be able to lock in the cost of your insurance, so even if you become uninsurable later (because you've gotten sick), you'll still have this insurance coverage. In fact, to take the most advantage of this plan, some people choose to buy a long term care policy for their children or grandchildren as a graduation gift. This way, the children can be covered for the rest of their lives at the lowest possible cost because they are young and healthy.

If the cost of insurance is just too high, then it might not be a realistic option for you. In that case, you need to look at funding the cost yourself. In any event, consider how long your family members have lived and needed either assisted living or nursing care. For instance, Anne's grandfather lived until he was 95, had been in assisted living from age 85 to age 94, and moved to a nursing home the last year of his life. That's 10 years of care. Her parents are now in their 80s and still living on their own, so she prefers to plan for them living to age 95 instead of the usual 85. And she is planning to cover four or five years of assisted living and nursing home care, not the usual two or three years.

Choosing a Carrier

Long term care insurance is a relatively new kind of insurance. Because of this, no insurance company has yet been in the position of having to pay lots of claims. The baby boomers are over 70 million strong, and they have changed the face of the U.S. economy as they have moved through their lives. We seriously doubt that long term care will not be affected by the demands these boomers put on the health care system. They will be the ones who test the care providers' and the insurance companies' abilities to meet massive needs.

Look at yourself. You are considering buying an insurance policy that you won't, you hope, have to make a claim on for many years. When you do need those benefits, however, you will be in a vulnerable state.

With these thoughts in mind, a long term care insurance company isn't the place to cut corners. You need a dependable, well-funded company that will be there when you need it. Quality is of the utmost importance here.

Estate Planning

Estate planning is a serious-sounding term for a simple question: "Who do you want to get your assets when you die?" It is not just for the rich. Estate planning is for those who want to have some control over what happens to their children and their money when they die. Your plan can be relatively simple or highly complex, depending on your needs. The more money you have, the more detailed your estate plan tends to be. If your estate is below the level at which you will owe estate taxes, then your estate tends to be simpler from a tax perspective, but could be more complex for other reasons. The laws and taxes that come into play with an estate can be complicated.

Some people say you can write these documents yourself. We don't believe you can. We mentioned earlier that long term care insurance was one of those items where skimping on quality wasn't really worth it. Well, this is another one of those items. Good estate-planning attorneys are worth their weight in gold. They can make suggestions you never thought of. They can help you deal with a problem you don't know how to handle. And having seen both well-written trusts and poorly written trusts, we wouldn't wish a bad estate plan on our worst enemies.

If you're worried about the cost of using an attorney to write a "simple" will, consider this: Throughout this book, we have suggested using attorneys intelligently. Use a lawyer for what you really need a lawyer to do. Well, writing a will is one of those things you really need a lawyer to do. No matter how good you are at your job—whether it's being a mom or being a CEO—you still aren't an estate-planning attorney. And just as you have spent years honing your craft, they have, too. A good estate-planning attorney more than makes up for the cost of legal fees by helping you avoid mistakes and make a better plan.

To get started on the process for yourself, think about who you want to leave money to. It could be people, such as children, grandchildren, nieces, nephews, and parents. It could also be organizations that are important to you, like a charity, your church, a hospital, or a social cause.

Keep in mind that it is important to get your estate plan right because you get only one chance at it. The plan you have in place at the time of your death is the one that is used. And after you've died, that's pretty much it. Things get firmly set in stone once you're gone. That said, understand that you can always make adjustments to your estate plan as you go along. And you should reread your estate-planning documents regularly to be sure they still do what you want them to. You probably don't want to leave your family with a messy estate to settle. To avoid that, you should talk with an estate-planning attorney and put together a plan that fits your needs, whatever they may be.

What Is the Point of Your Estate Plan?

As we said earlier, the point of your estate plan is to leave your assets to the people and organizations you have selected. One big factor to consider is that as a single person, you can only leave $1,000,000 (as of 2002) to someone other than a spouse. When you were married, you could leave twice as much without estate taxes. Those amounts sound like a lot, but if you have contributed to a 401(k) and an IRA regularly for many years, and your house is paid off, then you may already be close to that amount.

Think more generally here, instead of "I want to leave $10,000 to cousin Emma." What is important to you? Knowing that your children or grandchildren get a college education? Protecting money from a spendthrift in-law? Do you have special needs children who require additional care because of a physical or mental handicap? Lots of estate plans start out something like this:

> Well, my son by my first marriage is grown, and there are two grandchildren ages 10 and 12 that I'd like to help with college costs. But my first obligation is to my children by my second marriage, who are now only six and eight. I need to make sure their college costs are taken care of first. And my father was very ill before he died, but the people at Metropolis Hospital were very good to him. And I have worked on many projects to feed the homeless, so I'd like to do something there, but that's not my first priority.

Depending on how large your estate is, you may or may not be able to achieve all these goals. But from the previous statement, the priorities would be:

1. Take care of your six- and eight-year-old children.
2. Help with college costs for your 10- and 12-year-old grandchildren.
3. Donate to Metropolis Hospital.
4. Donate to a homeless shelter.

Documents Needed

The four documents usually prepared by estate-planning attorneys are as follows:

❖ Will

❖ Durable power of attorney

❖ Living will

❖ Durable power of attorney for health care

Sometimes, the living will and durable power of attorney for health care are written as one document and called an advance medical directive. These documents help you address questions such as ...

- ❖ Who gets custody of your minor children if you die?
- ❖ Who can make business decisions for you if you are unable to yourself?
- ❖ What medical procedures do you want or not want in case of an accident or lengthy illness?
- ❖ Who can make medical decisions for you if you can't do it yourself?
- ❖ Who do you want to leave your assets to when you die?

Take a look at Chapter 15, "Post-Divorce Decisions," for more details on these basic documents.

Using Trusts

Generally, trusts are used when you don't want to leave an asset to someone outright. There can be many reasons for this, ranging from tax planning to protecting assets from someone you don't trust completely. Here are some common types of trusts and a brief description of what they are used for:

- ❖ **Revocable living trust (RLT).** This trust is used primarily to void probate as much as possible. Assets in an RLT are easily accessible during the owner's lifetime, and disposition instructions can be changed at any time.
- ❖ **Irrevocable life insurance trust (ILIT).** An ILIT is a sophisticated tool that is used to maximize gifts by using the gifts to purchase a life insurance policy. When the life insurance policy pays its death benefit, the trust directs how those proceeds are to be spent.
- ❖ **Generation-skipping trust (GST).** Large, complex estates use a GST to minimize estate taxes when leaving money to grandchildren and other beneficiaries who are two generations younger.
- ❖ **Special-needs trust.** This type of trust is used to house funds needed for the care of someone with physical or mental handicaps.

❖ **Spendthrift trust.** If you don't have confidence in someone's ability to handle an inheritance, then a spendthrift
trust may help. It is intended to put limits on what will be
paid out of the trust, and may put someone other than the
beneficiary in charge of the trust.

Updating and Maintaining Your Plan

You know how some women buy clothes for a special occasion?
They buy a fabulous dress when it's on sale and they aren't under
pressure to buy anything. But then they go home and hang it in
the closet, waiting for a special occasion to come up. The plan
works great, until the special occasion comes up and you run to
the closet, only to find out that the dress doesn't fit anymore.

Well, your estate plan is not too far off from this analogy. Your
best planning happens not when you're under stress or pressure,
but when you have the time to think things through completely.
You can always make changes as your circumstances change, but
you need an estate plan in place, just in case something does
happen. And to make sure the plan still does what you want it to,
you have to take it out of the "closet" and reread it from time to
time. In other words, make sure it still fits.

The Bottom Line

There are several financial-planning issues you need to address following your divorce. Get started on them now. You can always make
adjustments as you go along.

Chapter 17

Portfolio Planning

Capsule Outlook

All the planning in the world accomplishes nothing until investments are made and money is put to work.

Now that you have your goals and priorities in order, let's look at some of the topics that will come up as you take action, implement your plan, and build your portfolio. In many respects, this is the most important step, because all the planning in the world won't get you anywhere if you don't finish the process and invest. We mentioned earlier that the process is simple: Earn money, save money, and invest money. It takes all three steps. Be sure to follow all the way through.

A word about portfolio planning: We believe strongly in stocks—not an individual stock that you think will make you rich overnight—but diversified, managed portfolios of stocks. It is through the growth available from these diversified and managed stock investments that real wealth is created.

Allocating Your Assets

Part of investing is deciding how to divide up your investment dollars. This process is called "asset allocation." It's just a fancy way of saying that you shouldn't put all your eggs in one basket. This division of dollars will be into different "asset classes" with different "styles" in each class. Every asset type is intended to do a different job, depending on your needs.

Think of it this way: Your entire portfolio is like a dresser. It holds everything and keeps it all organized so you know what clothes you have. Your particular stocks, bonds, mutual funds, and money-market funds are like the contents of the drawers: socks, shorts, and shirts. When you get dressed, you need all three. But if it's springtime, you'll choose differently than if it's fall. Or if you're going to a fancy pool party, you'll wear something different than you would wear to the beach. The specific investments in your accounts serve the same purpose: to be sure you have enough different items in your portfolio so you always have something to meet your needs.

Essentially, there are three basic asset classes: stocks (or equities), bonds, and cash.

Investing in Stocks or Equities

Stocks are ownership in a company. Despite what people came to think in the late 1990s, stocks are not lottery tickets. They are not intended to make anyone rich overnight. However, over an extended period of time, stocks have historically outperformed every other asset class. Most important, stocks have provided investors with their best defense against inflation and the best opportunity to create meaningful new wealth. Unfortunately, stocks do not come with guarantees. But then again, neither does life. We can't guarantee that the sun will come up tomorrow, but we're pretty sure it will. There might be a rainstorm, but then the sun will return. Sometimes the rain lasts a few minutes or a few days, and sometimes it lasts for weeks. But if you understand that the rain does come, you can make the rain work for you and be glad for it. Similarly, when the stock market has its rainy days and other investors are complaining, you can use your dollar-cost averaging plan to buy quality stocks and mutual funds at a lower price—and laugh all the way to your goals.

Stocks need to be a part of a well-balanced portfolio. And they should be part of your portfolio, no matter what your age or stage of life. Stocks provide capital appreciation for growth investors who are still trying to create their nest egg, and they provide an inflation hedge for more income-oriented investors who don't want to have their lifestyle compromised by inflation. Very conservative investors may choose to own a much smaller portion of stocks or to use more conservative types of stock to meet their growth needs. As an investor, you need to choose how you wish to own them: in a self-directed account, with input from an advisor, with a private portfolio manager, or in a mutual fund. The main differences between these types of ownership are who is making the daily buy and sell decisions, and how much control you have over the portfolio as a whole.

Making Money from Owning Stock

Stock ownership gives investors the opportunity to make money in two ways: dividends and capital gains.

If you own stock, you own part of the company. As an owner, dividends are your share of the company's profits. Remember, dividends are the last thing a company can pay each quarter. The company is required to pay interest on bonds and interest on any preferred stocks that are outstanding before they can pay a dividend. So any company that has a good dividend-paying history is generally considered to be pretty stable. But remember, there are companies that have cut or discontinued their dividends altogether. For instance, Woolworth's eliminated their dividend in the late 1990s, and as a result, the market punished their stock price severely. Dividends are declared by the Board of Directors and are paid out to shareholders on a specified date each quarter. Many companies pride themselves on the fact that they pay regular dividends, have done so for years, and have raised their dividends on a regular basis. Dividends are declared per share. If you're thinking of buying a stock that is close to paying its dividend, look for the "ex-date." If you buy on or after this date, then you don't get the dividend.

At the end of the year, you will get a Form 1099 from every firm where you have a taxable account. This 1099 reports to you and to the IRS how much you were paid in dividends for the year. You must report this income and pay ordinary income taxes on it each year. These ordinary income tax rates are higher than the long-term capital gains rate. Any state income tax is in addition to the federal tax. So some investors, especially those in the higher tax brackets, may not particularly want a stock to pay dividends because it is relatively tax-inefficient.

Not all companies pay dividends. For instance, technology and other growth companies often choose to reinvest their earnings back into the company. Also, the company doesn't have to pay out every penny they earned. They can keep some of their earnings in anticipation of future expenses. Any earnings a company keeps and doesn't pay to shareholders are called "retained earnings."

There's a second reason that dividends are tax-inefficient. Not only does the shareholder have to pay tax on the dividends they receive, the company has to pay corporate income taxes on their total earnings, before dividends are paid out. You may have heard the expression "double taxation." Well, that's the drawback of dividends. Both the company and the stockholder have to pay taxes on those dividends. So there's a lot less money left once Uncle Sam has taken his cut.

Capital gains are actually what most people think of when they think of stocks. This is where you buy a stock for $30 per share and expect that price to go up. It is important that you keep track of your cost basis—the total amount you paid for a stock, including any reinvested dividends—so you can properly report your capital gains. Actually, there are two types of capital gains: short-term and long-term. The difference is the way you are taxed. Short-term gains are taxed as ordinary income. Long-term gains are taxed at a maximum rate of 20 percent. The difference is your holding period. If you held a stock for a year or longer, it's treated as long-term. If you held it for less than a year, it's treated as short-term.

As you can see, these calculations can get complex, especially if you've reinvested dividends over the years. Keep a sharp eye on your records. Also, we recommend using a top-notch CPA. One client, Lyn, did her own taxes for years. When she sold her home of many years, she wasn't comfortable with her own ability to handle accounting for that sale properly on her tax return, so she hired an accountant. She recently remarked that the accountant had not only lifted a huge burden from her shoulders, but that the accountant had also reduced the amount of taxes she was now paying to nearly nothing. Now Lyn wonders how much more she could have saved by using an accountant earlier. How much could you save?

Where Stocks Trade

Stocks trade on a variety of exchanges. The best known are the New York Stock Exchange (NYSE), the American Stock Exchange (AMEX), and the National Association of Securities Dealers Automated Quotation (NASDAQ). Not long ago, the AMEX and NASDAQ merged to create the NASDAQ/AMEX market site. Most of the stocks you will likely be considering will trade on one of these two exchanges. Each has its own nickname:

Stock Exchange	Nickname
New York Stock Exchange	The Street
American Stock Exchange	The Curb
NASDAQ	Over the Counter

The terms "The Street" and "The Curb" are references to where trading took place in the late 1800s as the markets were just getting started.

There are regional exchanges in places like Boston, Philadelphia, and Chicago. They often specialize in a particular sector and have established indices to measure them. For example, Philadelphia has its Semiconductor Index.

Because of the large number of stocks traded on the NASDAQ, it has been divided into parts. The NASDAQ National Markets is where you find companies that are popular with investors, such as Microsoft. It used to be that being a NASDAQ stock meant the company couldn't get listed on the NYSE. Today, however, companies are making the conscious decision to be listed specifically on NASDAQ and not pursue listing on the NYSE. There are a number of reasons for making this decision, including the cost of listing on the NYSE and the caché that has arisen from the numerous reputable and powerful companies that are listed on NASDAQ.

For companies with lower levels of investor interest, there are the NASDAQ "Pink Sheets." Stocks trading here tend to be lower priced (less than $5 per share) and are often penny stocks. Equities traded in the pink sheets also tend to have very low daily volume. Only a few shares a day will actually change hands. The name comes, as you would guess, from the fact that quotations were originally printed on pink paper, a practice that continues today. Don't spend a lot of time looking for the next Microsoft here. You're not likely to find it.

There are also a of exchanges in other countries, such as France, Germany, Hong Kong, Japan, and Mexico. This is where the shares of companies based in those countries would trade. However, better-known foreign firms may also be available on the NYSE as "American Depositary Receipts" or "ADRs." This is a convenience mechanism to make sure foreign shares more accessible. Before you write off the idea of investing in foreign companies, take a look at some of the products you use (listed in the following table)—you may be surprised at how many of them are produced by foreign-based companies. You'll probably also be surprised at companies that you thought were foreign actually being part of a U.S.-based company.

Foreign Stock Exchanges

Product	Company	Country
Whopper	Burger King	United Kingdom
Lucky Strike Cigarettes	British American Tobacco	United Kingdom
Red Man Chewing Tobacco	Swedish Match AB	Sweden
Lea & Perrins	Groupo Danone	France
Jaguar	Ford	United States
Rolls Royce	Volkswagen/BMW	Germany
LensCrafters	Luxottica Group	France
Shell Gasoline	Royal Dutch Petroleum	Netherlands
Columbia Pictures	Sony	Japan
Stouffer's Lean Cuisine	Nestle	Switzerland
Hawaiian Punch	Cadbury Schweppes	United Kingdom
Jeep	Daimler Chrysler	Germany
Frigidaire Refrigerator	Electrolux PLC	Sweden
7-11 Convenience Stores	Southland Corporation	Japan
Ben & Jerry's Ice Cream	Unilever NV	United Kingdom
Maybelline	L'Oreal ADR	France
Gerber Baby Food	Novartis AG	Switzerland
Dove Soap	Unilever PLC	Netherlands
Los Angeles Dodgers	News Corporation	Australia

Market Capitalization

We discussed in Chapter 13, "Understanding the Fundamentals," how companies come in different sizes and how those sizes are defined in terms of "market capitalization." As you build your portfolio, you will want to include a little bit of each size company among your holdings.

❖ **Large-cap companies.** This tends to be where you will find your "blue-chip" companies. These are firms that have been around long enough and are established enough to have definitive market share, relatively stable profits, and often, a history of paying dividends. The names of these firms are usually easily recognized, and you probably use their products and services in your daily life.

❖ **Mid-cap companies.** You may recognize some of these companies' names as well, even though they are a bit smaller than their larger cousins. Sometimes these are large companies whose stock price is currently depressed. At other times, they are formerly small-cap companies that are now successfully expanding.

❖ **Small-cap companies.** This is the most aggressive of the sizes. Many small-cap stocks have a small number of shares available in the market. Often, they don't trade many shares each day. This can make it tough for a stock's price to appreciate meaningfully.

Choosing Stocks

Choosing stocks is like choosing a wardrobe. Not everything will match. Nor does it have to. You will have a variety of styles for different occasions. For instance, you probably have clothes that are appropriate for work, others that you would wear on the weekend, and still others that you would wear to paint the house or mow the lawn. But you probably have something really fancy for when that special occasion comes up. Think of your stocks in the same way. You will probably have some that are defensive, some that are aggressive, and some that are good, old-fashioned, everyday stocks.

There are several schools of thought about how to choose stocks successfully. Going back to the wardrobe analogy, just as different

styles go in and out of fashion, so, too, do stock selection philoso-
phies. One year, the fashion is formal business dress; the next year
it's business casual. But when business casual became all the rage,
did you throw out all your business clothes? No! Again, think
about your stocks the same way. One year, large-cap growth is in
fashion, then it's small-cap growth, then it's international stocks.
You have no idea what is going to be in fashion next, but in order
to participate in the growth of the "hot" style, you have to own
something in that style. But you don't throw out everything else
and own just one type of stock. To do so would be gambling, not
investing!

Deciding When to Sell a Stock

Most investors don't even think about selling their stocks. They
think that figuring out what to buy and when to buy it is the hard
part. But at some point you will probably have to consider selling
for a variety of reasons. For example …

❖ The stock you bought isn't performing well, and you don't
see any prospects for improvement.

❖ You identify another stock with better potential.

❖ The stock you bought has performed extremely well, and it's
now too much of your portfolio.

❖ You need cash to make a different investment (either another
stock or possibly a bond).

❖ The stock no longer meets your criteria (for example, the
growth rate is too low, the P/E ratio is too high, and so on).

❖ The company has had a change in management or corporate
philosophy to a team or point of view that you don't agree
with.

❖ You need cash for an immediate expense.

Have a discipline for selling and stick to it. Know what criteria will
have to be met for you to sell. It sounds a bit odd to be ready to
sell a stock the moment you buy it, but if you have those requirements in mind at the beginning, you will be much less likely to
hold on to the wrong things.

Whatever the reason, you can't expect to hold a stock forever. Go back to that wardrobe analogy for a minute. Your clothes wear out. They go out of fashion. You gain or lose weight, and they don't fit anymore. You retire and just don't need those work clothes. If you never cleaned out your closet, you would have a roomful of smocked dresses from the fourth grade. Your stocks are no different. At some point they just may not fit your needs anymore. When that happens, you need to consider selling. You don't want a portfolio full of the wrong things because you had no sell discipline.

Understanding Fundamental Investment Selection Styles

Fundamental analysis refers to the inherent, basic qualities of a company: sales, profits, earnings per share, competitive position, market share, and the like. Among the fundamental styles, there are basically two:

❖ **Growth investing.** In this style, dividends are not so important. What is important is how quickly a stock is growing. To measure this research analysts look at things like at earnings growth, market share growth, revenue growth, or new product growth. Sometimes, the growth rate is not as important as the acceleration rate of the growth.

❖ **Value investing.** Value investing is almost the opposite of growth. Here, you are looking for the "K-Mart blue light specials" of the market. You are looking for stocks whose prices have been depressed but still represent fundamentally good companies. This takes patience because you will usually have to wait a fair amount of time to see the kind of results you are looking for.

You should have some of both styles in your portfolio.

Understanding Technical Analysis

Another way of evaluating stocks is to use technical analysis. With this method, you study the chart patterns of stock prices. Technical analysts believe these charts point to patterns of behavior that indicate whether a stock is strong or on the verge of falling apart. There are several different types of charts that can be plotted, and each requires a particular method of analysis that is beyond the scope of this book. If you are interested in using technical analysis, there are several books available.

Many people use a combination of fundamental and technical analysis. The fundamental is used to figure out what to buy, and the technical is used to determine whether this is a good time to buy or sell.

Picking the Style That's Right for You

The style you will be comfortable with will depend largely on your ability to handle risk. There is a style, or more appropriately a mix of styles, out there for virtually every investor. Among stocks, we have the following major styles: large-cap growth, large-cap value, mid-cap growth, mid-cap value, small-cap growth, small-cap value, and international. The following list provides an overview of investor attitudes and how those attitudes affect a portfolio:

❖ **Conservative.** Investors in this category are often more comfortable with value-oriented investments and large-cap companies for the stock portion of their portfolio. Understand, though, that "lower risk" doesn't mean "no risk." These stocks can still go down. Also, if you are only willing to accept a small amount of risk, know that you should also expect a more moderate performance. You won't be telling the great stories at the office water cooler about how your stock tripled. Also, the conservative investor will tend to have a heavy proportion of their overall portfolio in bonds.

❖ **Moderately conservative.** This investor is willing to add some growth style and some small- and mid-cap companies to his stock portfolio—but just a sprinkling. His overall portfolio will typically include some bonds, but not a majority.

❖ **Moderately aggressive.** This investor is willing to fully diversify his stock portfolio to include all sizes and styles, including international. He will have about equal division between the growth and value styles. And even though he is seeking higher returns, he is doing so with a disciplined plan. His overall portfolio will also have some bonds, but, again, not a majority.

❖ **Very aggressive.** This investor is also willing to diversify her stock portfolio to include all sizes and styles, including international. She, however, is also willing to allocate a higher percentage to the more aggressive small-cap, mid-cap, and international choices, usually with a strong tendency toward the growth style. Her portfolio will likely not include many, if any, bonds. She recognizes that this portfolio may have a bumpy ride at times, but with a longer time horizon, she is looking to be rewarded for her aggressive posture with additional return.

Your actual style will likely be a combination of these styles. You may be comfortable with the conservative stock portfolio but choose not to own any bonds. Or you may choose the more aggressive stock portfolio with a heavy allocation to bonds. Which style suits you?

Flirting with Day Trading and Market Timing

Day trading and market timing have been the subject of a great deal of media attention over the past couple of years. They are undoubtedly highly aggressive, highly speculative styles of trading. But we caution you strongly, even vehemently, against attempting these trading methods. Many people have lost substantial amounts of money this way. Day trading violates the basic characteristic of the stock market being a *long-term* entity. No one knows what stocks are going to do in the short-term. Anyone who tells you they do know is highly suspect. If anyone had figured out how to time the market by now, then all investors would be doing it this way, and they don't.

Not timing the market also means not pulling your money out of stocks just because the market is having a bad spell. No one knows when the market is going to turn, and if you're on the sidelines in a money market fund, you miss the ride up. Again, if anyone had figured out how to time the market this way on a consistent basis, then that guy would be managing everyone's money. And if you're a value investor, you should be turning cartwheels at the opportunity in a bear market. This is your chance to buy stocks at greatly reduced prices.

How do the rich manage their money? The wealthiest individuals and families in the world buy quality stocks and have them professionally managed. So if you want your family to be the next Rockefeller, take a lesson …

Where to Go to Buy Stocks

Where you will be most satisfied buying stocks will depend on the type of service you need. If you need advice, help with research, and someone to counsel you, find a good full-service broker. Most full-service brokers provide the ability to do your trades over the phone with them or through the Internet.

If you're more of a do-it-yourselfer, you may be happier with a discount brokerage firm. Sometimes there are brokers you can talk to, sometimes not, depending on the firm. Even when there are people to consult at a discount firm, recognize that you often don't get the same person. Because the research and the results are your responsibility, the commissions are discounted. Fee-based accounts are not generally available from discounters. And don't be taken in by advertisements that say trades are free. There is always a cost. None of these companies is in the business of charity. They're in business to make money. You may not be able to see how, but know that they are making money on your trades.

Paying for Stocks

In Chapter 12, "Now What?" we discussed the difference between commissions and fees. Take a few minutes to go back and review these alternatives and decide which one you are more comfortable with. Also know that some advisors have chosen to run fee-only practices. Be sure to ask any advisor you are considering working with how their practice works.

A Word on IPO Investing

Initial public offerings (IPOs) are when a company that has never had stock traded in the market before first makes it available. IPOs have a reputation for going up wildly, and everyone wants shares. Be aware that IPOs are highly aggressive, because the companies involved are relatively unknown entities. They do *not* all go up 1,000 percent the first day, but the ones that do will make the evening news. You probably know a few of them by name. And if you got shares, you probably talked about the stock's price rocketed up on opening day. But you probably also left out that you only got 10 shares and that you got so wrapped up in the hype that you didn't sell when the stock took a tumble a few days or weeks later.

Unfortunately, many investors are unaware of the pecking order at firms that do IPOs. Many believe they are entitled to as many shares of the "hot" deals as they want. However, the IPO market has its own unique requirements. It is not reasonable to simply demand IPO shares from your investment representative. Clients who have supported all of the firm's offerings will probably get more generous amounts of stock directed to them. Clients who have significant portfolios and pay significant asset management fees will also probably get more generous IPO allocations. And many times, nearly the entire IPO will go to institutional clients (mutual funds, pension funds, municipalities, and the like). Understand where you fit in the hierarchy, and set your expectations accordingly.

If your investment representative's firm is not the lead underwriter on a particular deal, don't expect them to get you shares of another firm's IPO. Think about it. If you were in charge of a new issue that everyone wanted, you would keep all the shares at your own firm for your own clients. Wall Street is no different.

Also on especially "hot" deals—the ones that are hyped in the popular media—your investment representative may not get any shares for her clients at all. If this is the case, don't hold a grudge. Go to work on the next issue.

If, as an individual investor, you don't rate as much IPO stock as you'd like, consider owning a mutual fund that does a lot of

IPOs. There are several that participate to a fair degree, and a few that focus on IPOs in particular.

Investing in Bonds

Bonds play a part in any well-balanced portfolio. They provide current income for more conservative investors and ballast for balanced investors. Very aggressive investors may choose not to own bonds until their investment posture changes to require a more conservative approach. Other investors may not use them at all. You need to choose how you wish to own them: outright or within a mutual fund. Remember that bonds have less risk than stocks, but they also have less potential return.

Where stocks represent ownership in a company, bonds represent a creditor relationship with a company. If you own a bond issued by General Motors, then General Motors owes you a debt. As a bondholder, you will receive interest payments, usually every six months. In addition, you can reasonably expect to get back the face value of the bonds you hold on their maturity date.

Bonds are not very glamorous, especially when compared to stocks. But investors find them appealing because of their more conservative natures. Bonds provide three characteristics that are different from stocks: income, safety of principal, and lack of correlation with stocks.

❖ Bonds provide income—more than three times more income than stocks. But remember, bonds are for income and stocks are for growth.

❖ Bonds provide safety of principal. This depends on the issuer's credit strength, but bondholders can reasonably expect that their principal, the face amount of the bond, will be paid back in full on the maturity date. If you sell the bond before maturity, though, you take your chances that the market price of the bond may be more or less than what you paid. Bond prices and interest rates have an inverse relationship. When interest rates go up, bond prices go down. Similarly, when interest rates go down, bond prices go up.

❖ Bonds lack of correlation with stocks. This means that stocks and bonds usually behave differently at any given time. The idea is that when your stocks aren't performing well, you bonds hopefully will be, and vice versa.

These three benefits come from two primary characteristics: a set interest rate and a maturity date. Because of that set interest rate, bonds are often called "fixed-income securities." As we mentioned earlier, typically bonds make their interest payments to holders every six months. To determine when a bond will make interest payments, look at the maturity date. If it's June 15, one interest payment will be made on June 15, and the other will be made six months later on December 15.

The maturity date is the date on which the bondholder will get the face amount of the bond, assuming the issuing company is able to pay.

Credit Ratings and Risk

To give investors an idea how reliable a bond may be, there are several firms that issue credit ratings. The best-known are Moody's and Standard & Poors. Their ratings are listed in the following table.

	Standard & Poors	Moody's
Investment Grade	AAA	Aaa
	AA	Aa
	A	A
	BBB	Baa
High Yield or Junk	BB	Ba
Below Investment Grade	B	B
	C	C

Just as a bank chooses how to lend money based on people's credit history, investors, in part, choose which bonds to own based on the company's credit rating.

With any bond, there is a possibility that the issuer will fail to pay off the bond at maturity. This is *default risk*. This is why many people give strong consideration to credit ratings. In exchange for increased risk of default, an issuer will have to pay more in interest to make their bond more attractive and make up for their higher potential default risk.

The Relationship Between Interest Rates and Bond Prices

The company that issued a bond will always pay interest at the coupon rate. Since that coupon rate is fixed, a bond's price will move up and down in order to make the bond's yield more closely reflect current interest rates. Therefore, the relationship between a bond's price and its current yield are inverse. So if interest rates go up, the bond's price will go down. And if interest rates go down, the bond's price will go up.

For instance, consider a bond with 1-year left until maturity and a 5 percent coupon rate. At maturity this bond will return $1,000. If the interest rate for 1-year bonds is 5 percent, then the bond will trade at "par" or 100. That means the price of the bond is 100 percent of face value. If interest rates for 1-year bonds go to 6 percent, then the bond will trade at a "discount," or less than par. If interest rates for that maturity drop to 4 percent, then the bond will trade at a "premium" or more than par.

The current market interest rate is shown in the following table.

	Market Interest Rate		
	4%	5%	6%
Face value	$1,000	$1,000	$1,000
Coupon	5%	5%	5%
Current price	125.000	100.000	83.333
	$1,250.00	$1,000.00	$833.33
	premium	par	discount
Current yield	$50 ÷ $1250 = 4%	$50 ÷ $1,000 = 5%	$50 ÷ $833 = 6%

Notice that the current yield and the market interest rates are the same. The price of the bond changes to make the coupon more reflective of the current interest rate environment.

Interest rate risk runs in two directions:

❖ The possibility that interest rates will rise, causing a bond to decrease in price when the investor needs to sell. This will cause a capital loss.

❖ The possibility that interest rates will fall at the time a bond matures, causing the investor to re-invest in another bond at a lower interest rate. This will produce a lower income stream from the same amount of invested funds.

Who Issues Bonds?

Generally, bonds are issued by one of three types of entities: corporations, the federal government and its agencies, or state and local government entities. Interest paid by corporate bonds is always taxable. The federal and state governments have a reciprocal deal. The federal government doesn't tax state bond income, and the state governments don't tax federal bond income. So interest on Treasury bills, notes, and bonds are taxable federal income but are not taxed by the states. State bonds, on the other hand, are exempt from federal income taxes. And if you live in the state that issued a municipal bond, you won't pay state or federal taxes on the interest from that bond. Because you don't pay state or federal tax, the interest rates on municipal bonds is lower than on taxable bonds. So how do you compare interest rates between the two? By calculating the "taxable equivalent yield" or TEY.

Let's say you're in the 28 percent federal and 5 percent state tax brackets and are considering a municipal in your own state with a 5 percent yield. Taxable bonds with the same maturity are yielding 7 percent. Which is better?

TEY

$= 5\% \div (1 - 0.28 - 0.05)$

$= 5\% \div 0.67$

$= 7.46\%$

In this case, you would be better off with the tax-free 5 percent municipal bond than with the fully taxable 7 percent bond.

Managing Maturity Dates

Managing the maturity dates of your bonds becomes very important as the proportion of bonds in your portfolio and your dependence on income from those bonds grows. When one of your bonds comes due, you have to invest in a new bond to keep the income stream flowing. Odds are that interest rates have changed over the time you owned that bond. If rates are higher when it's time to buy that new bond, you'll get more income from that new bond, but the rest of your bond portfolio will likely be down in value. If you hold all your bonds until maturity, that increase in interest rates is great. But rates may have dropped, and now that you have to buy a replacement for the bond that just matured, you may be looking at less income for investing the same amount of money. For that reason, you obviously don't want to have all your bonds coming due at the same time. So what do you do? One commonly used strategy for dealing with bond maturities is "laddering." This means that when you initially set up your bond investments, you stagger the maturities. This can be for a few months or for several years, depending on your needs. Looking at a $100,000 10-year ladder, it would contain $10,000-worth of 10 bonds, each maturing in a successive year. The first of these would mature next year, and the last 10 years from now.

Laddering will not save you from having to replace a maturing bond at a lower interest rate. It will help guard against having to do so with your entire bond portfolio. Laddering also allows you to go farther out on the yield curve, without having to lock all your money away for too long.

Bond Insurance

Bonds can come insured. The best-known insurers are MBIA and AMBAC. Any bond insured by one of these firms is automatically rated "AAA." However, this insurance only guarantees that the bond will make its interest payments on time and that it will pay the face amount upon maturity. Insurance doesn't guarantee an investor will make money on a bond. Remember, as interest rates move, the price of bonds will move. You may experience negative returns, precisely because of those price fluctuations, especially if you sell the bond before its maturity date.

Bonds serve a valuable and useful purpose in any balanced portfolio, and an important one in an income-producing portfolio. It is important to be aware of the risks involved. Despite their conservative nature, bonds are not risk-free. By using bonds to balance your portfolio, you can diversify your investments and smooth out your return. By using bonds to provide you income, you can create a well-structured income stream.

Investing in Mutual Funds

Mutual funds are a convenient way to get professional management of your stock and bond investments. There are a variety of funds available from a variety of sources. Especially for smaller investors, mutual funds provide a more cost-effective way to invest than trying to purchase individual securities.

You've decided that you need to own both stocks and bonds, but you aren't comfortable with your ability to choose the individual securities. Or maybe you are starting from scratch and don't have a lot to invest. Or perhaps you want to invest a set amount each month and need an easy way to do so. Well, a mutual fund may be what you're looking for. So what is a mutual fund exactly? It is a collection of your money and other investors' money that is given to a professional money manager who invests according to the terms in the fund's prospectus. The manager decides what securities get bought and sold and, in exchange, is paid a management fee. In addition, mutual funds have trading expenses, which vary depending on how often the portfolio is traded, and advertising costs. All the fund's expenses are subtracted from its net asset value (NAV) or price. As a fund shareholder, you won't see those costs itemized out on your statement. You'll have to read the prospectus to find out how much the management fee is. Because they are variable costs, the advertising and trading expenses are only reported after the fact in a fund's annual report. So how much are these charges? For specific information on an individual fund, you must refer to that fund's prospectus.

A fund's prospectus is the document that governs how a fund is to be run. It says whether a manager can buy stocks, bonds, or both. It details what style the manager is supposed to use. The Securities and Exchange Commission (SEC) regulates mutual fund prospectuses heavily. Every one must be submitted to the SEC for approval. However, the SEC does *not* endorse any mutual fund or any other investment product. They simply work to assure that the prospectus meets all current legal requirements. Because they are legal documents, prospectuses have had a reputation for being hard to read, especially for people who aren't securities lawyers. So, in the last few years, a more user-friendly introductory section has been introduced. You may find this section is easier to read. Use it as your starting point and get an initial feel for the fund. But read the rest of the prospectus to find out all the details.

The other term we've used is "net asset value" or NAV. This just means the price of a mutual fund. It is calculated by adding up the value of all the stocks and/or bonds in a fund at the end of the day and dividing by the number of shares of the fund that are outstanding.

What happens to the dividends, interest, and capital gains that a mutual fund recognizes throughout the year? They are credited to the fund and are distributed to shareholders, usually once a year in December. However, some funds, like bond funds, make distributions more frequently. Unfortunately, mutual-fund shareholders have no control over how much those distributions are going to be.

Dollar Cost Averaging

Most mutual funds and investment firms can set you up to "dollar cost average." This is the process where you invest a specific amount of money on a set schedule, regardless of what the market is doing. This works to your benefit because you are making disciplined investments, which is half the battle for most people. Dollar-cost averaging is also beneficial because it automatically buys more shares when the price is lower, and fewer shares when the price is higher. And you don't have to have lots of money to do it. Some fund families offer this service for as little as $25 per month. All you have to do is fill out a couple forms and provide a voided check or deposit slip for the account your money will be coming from.

Measuring Performance

Total return measures how much you made from both the dividend and capital gain in a particular stock, bond, or mutual fund. It is most often expressed as a percentage of your initial investment amount. For example, if you paid $20 a share for a stock, it went up to $22 when you sold it, and you received $0.50 per share in dividends during the one year that you owned it, your performance would be as follows:

Capital gain: ($22 − $20) ÷ $20 = 10%

Dividend yield: $0.50 ÷ $20 = 2.5%

Total return: 10% + 2.5% = 12.5%

Individual Securities Versus Mutual Funds

So what's the difference between owning individual stocks and owning a mutual fund? First, it's the decision-making. If you own stocks in your own account, you make the buy and sell decisions. With a mutual fund, the manager makes those decisions for you. Second, it's the tax issues. If you own stocks, you can control how much you recognize each year in gains or losses. With a mutual fund, you don't have that control because the fund manager is not available to work with you on those decisions. Third, it's a question of what you own. With your own account, you know exactly what you own. It's printed on your statement. With a mutual fund, you can only know what the fund owned as of its last report. And since then, the fund could have sold positions you liked or bought positions you disliked. Finally, it's a matter of cost. If you have a substantial portfolio, you may be able to have your assets managed for less than the cost of a mutual fund by using private portfolio management.

Private Portfolio Management

What is private portfolio management? In this model, you work with an advisor who helps you establish your overall investment plan. Then, to implement your various stock and bond investments, you use a Registered Investment Advisor, or RIA, who focuses on the particular size and style of stock that you need. With nearly 30,000 of these RIAs to choose from, making a selection can be tough. And most RIAs have extremely high minimum account sizes if you go to them directly. When looking for an advisor to help you with such a method, look for someone who will provide a comprehensive process such as ...

❖ A rigorous selection process that requires RIAs to show a definable and repeatable investment process.

❖ A review of the RIA's business to be sure they are financially sound.

❖ A selection of RIAs that can provide all the styles you will need.

❖ Oversight of your RIA to be sure he's sticking to the style.

❖ Performance reporting.

The private management arena always works on a fee basis. A commission arrangement is not available here. The fee is on a declining scale. The more money you have in such a program, the lower the percentage will be. It is this mechanism that allows some investors to better control expenses, as opposed to using mutual funds.

More Sophisticated Asset Classes

There are several additional asset classes that are appropriate for larger, more sophisticated portfolios and investors. While an in-depth discussion of them is beyond the scope of this book, we thought you might like to know generally what they are and how they work.

Before you even consider the following strategies, your financial plan must be in place. You must be completely funding that plan through your 401(k) and IRA. You must have a full cash reserve for emergencies. This is mandatory, because you must be able to walk away from whatever money you commit to these more advanced strategies and lose it all without having that loss destroy your entire financial plan. These strategies are speculative, some of them extremely so. They require much more skill, much more nerve, and much more money than most people have. When they pay off, they pay off big. But when they fail, they fail big, even catastrophically. Remember at the end of the movie *Trading Places,* the heroes became incredibly rich and the villains lost their entire financial empire.

Just because you take more risk, you will not automatically make more money. You very well may lose money. If you aren't willing to live by those rules, the following strategies aren't for you. If you choose not to use any of these methods, you are not a bad investor. There are plenty of fabulously wealthy people out there who have never touched these strategies and never will. You can be a successful investor with or without these methods.

❖ **Margin.** Margin is the right to borrow against the stocks, bonds, and mutual funds in your portfolio. You can use that borrowing power to buy stock for which you don't have enough cash to buy outright, to short stocks, or to participate in very aggressive strategies like options and futures. Check with your advisor, because not all securities are not "marginable." In its simplest terms, margin allows investors to get more "bang for their buck." But if you use margin to buy a stock that goes down, that bigger "bang" will blow up because you not only have the loss on the stock, but you still owe the money you borrowed to buy it.

The most basic use of margin is to borrow money from the firm in order to purchase stocks or bonds. The SEC's Regulation T allows you to borrow no more than $0.50 for every dollar of stock that you buy. There is also a maintenance requirement of 25 percent equity, or no more than

75 percent borrowed money. This allows the price of the margined stock to fluctuate, as it will on a daily basis, but limits the degree to which your borrowing can go. Different firms have higher maintenance requirements than the SEC. And some firms won't let you borrow against certain stocks at all. Be sure to check with your advisor to see what the firm's specific requirements are.

❖ **Selling short.** Making money in stocks is often described as "buy low, sell high." You can also do this in reverse—"sell high, buy low." This is known as "shorting" or "selling short." You borrow stock you don't own from the firm, sell it, and buy it back later, hopefully at a lower price. To do this, you must have margin privileges in place. Shorting stocks is subject to the same Regulation T requirements as buying stocks. But because you're shorting, it's 100 percent plus the Regulation T 50 percent, so you have to have 150 percent of the current value of the stock in cash to start. Needless to say, unless you have plenty of cash handy, this is not a strategy you are going to want to tackle.

❖ **Futures.** Futures are contracts to buy or sell a given commodity at today's price by a particular date. There are all kinds of commodities that have futures traded: metals, currencies, agricultural products, and natural resources. All futures contracts expire on the third Saturday of a given month. So the last day to trade them is the Friday before that. At expiration, you must be prepared to take physical delivery or purchase a contract that closes out the position. One reason that futures are only appropriate for certain investors is that, because they are highly leveraged, so you can lose more than you put in. Also, don't overlook the issue of physical delivery. Are you prepared to have a tractor trailer back up to your garage and unload several tons of gold, or corn, or pork bellies? My freezer can't hold all that! Buying futures is also subject to margin requirements.

Large companies with one big expense most often use futures. For example, a huge part of an airline's expenses come from fuel costs. So many airlines engage in futures trading to control their fuel costs. And they may actually take delivery of several thousand gallons of jet fuel. They would certainly be better equipped to handle that delivery than the ordinary investor.

❖ **Options.** Options are most commonly sold on stocks and the stock indices. There are two types. A *put* is the right to sell a specific stock at a particular price, called the strike price. A *call* is the right to buy a specific stock at the strike price. Option rights also expire on the third Saturday of each month. One option contract covers 100 shares of the underlying stock, so remember to multiply. The price of an option is called a "premium." So if the option you are considering buying sells for $3 and you buy one contract, it will cost you $300 (ignoring transactions costs). If you buy 10 contracts, that covers 1,000 shares (10 contracts × 100 shares), and it will cost you $3,000.

Futures options are puts and call on futures contracts. As the name implies, they are a hybrid of futures and options, and, therefore, are exceedingly aggressive. You may have heard of "triple witching" day on the nightly business report. That's the last day that options, futures, and futures options contracts trade before their expiration on Saturday. The markets tend to be very volatile during that week, and particularly on that Friday, as traders scramble to prepare for positions to expire, get called for exercise, or be delivered.

❖ **Private equity.** Large investors can participate in pools that invest in privately held companies. These private companies can be anything from consulting firms to print houses to advertising agencies to retail stores. Since the underlying companies are not publicly traded, these investments are very illiquid, meaning their value can't be calculated easily, and thus they can't be sold for cash easily. In fact, the mere act of selling shares in such a pool may cause the seller to suffer a significant loss because of this illiquidity. Generally, there are substantial minimum investments to participate in private equity and certain investor qualifications that must be met.

❖ **Real estate.** Aside from your home, real estate is often an investment. Some real estate is residential, but there are also opportunities in commercial venues like shopping centers, office buildings, and industrial parks. Like private equity, real estate is also subject to a large liquidity risk—the risk that you won't be able to sell it when you need to, or for enough money.

If you want to invest in real estate but don't have the cash to buy a whole shopping center, you can use Real Estate Investment Trusts (REITs). REITs are companies that are established expressly to allow investors to participate in real estate ventures that are otherwise out of their reach. Pay attention next time you pull into your local shopping center. On the bottom of the welcome sign is probably a mention of "Owned and operated by Metropolis Realty." If it's a publicly traded company, that may be a way to address your desire for more real estate in your portfolio.

To reiterate—and this can't be emphasized enough—you have to earn the right to be an advanced investor. Any money you choose to invest in things such as options and futures must be completely disposable money. The greater the risk, the greater the potential reward, but also the greater the potential loss. You must have your complete financial plan in place, funded, and working. You have to be able to lose all of the money that you put toward these speculative investments without having that loss destroy your overall financial plan. It isn't that you're more skilled if you pursue these strategies, it's that you're taking more risk.

Finding an Advisor

If you need to, review the section in Chapter 12 on deciding whether to work with an advisor and how to select an advisor. There are many ways to find an advisor, such as on the Web or through credentialing organizations. Unfortunately, these methods only give you the impersonal facts about a person's resumé, and you need to know more. You will probably be much more comfortable asking friends, neighbors, and your other advisors who they know. Ask several people for a recommendation. You will want to interview several advisors before you make your selection. Remember, professional competence is only half of the equation. You need to find someone you are comfortable with, someone you can talk freely with, someone you trust implicitly. Go back and look at the various credentials that are available, and decide which ones are important to you.

As we've said before, when you choose an advisor, always remember to be a good client. Both you and your advisor should benefit from your relationship.

Types of Investment Firms

You will find advisors in many different places filling a variety of advisory roles. Most often, your financial advisor will work for a wire house, a regional firm, or a boutique firm, or they may be independent. With the recent merger activity in the financial services industry, some of the firms you know have changed their name or have now been bought by someone else. So don't let the specific names confuse you. The big difference between firms like these and say a mutual fund company is that they represent a wide variety of potential investments, not just one. Let's review what kinds of places these are:

- ❖ **Wire houses** are the largest of the brokerage firms and are international in scale. They have extensive research, trading, operations, and training capabilities.

- ❖ **Regional firms** can also be quite large but limit themselves to a particular geographic region of the country. The large regional banks now own most of these. There are a few remaining that are free-standing, but given the consolidation now underway, we would expect most of these to be merged into another firm over the next several years.

- ❖ **Boutiques** are small, high-end firms that cater to a particular type of investor. They typically have high minimum account requirements and take on fewer clients. They also often have limited research and training capabilities.

❖ **Independents** are those people who hang out their own shingle and practice without an affiliation to a particular firm. Out of necessity, these independents will execute their trades through a particular firm, whose name will sometimes appear on your statement.

❖ **Discount brokerage** houses are different from the preceding firms in that they don't offer advice in the same sense as full service firms. Because of the demand from investors for advice, they are now adding that service to their repertoire. However, there is an important distinction between the type of "advice" you receive from a discount firm versus a full service firm. With a discounter, you must initiate the communication, you must ask the questions, and you must sort through the planning options. That can be especially tough to do when you don't even know what questions to ask. Our general rule of thumb is that if you only use a toll-free telephone number, a Web site, and a voice-response system to access your account information, then most likely you aren't getting personalized investment advice from a single advisor who knows you well, will help you sort through the things you don't know to ask about, and make specific recommendations.

Carpe Diem

Now that your divorce is final, take advantage of the opportunity you have been presented with. Seize the day! Control your money. Decide on your goals. Set your priorities. Start your dollar cost averaging plan. Get professional advice. Invest. Build your own advisory team.

The Bottom Line

You're about to embark on a wonderful journey. Decide where you want to go, and take those first steps. You'll be there before you know it ...

Appendix A

Forms

The Personal Information Form is an efficient tool for use in organizing essential information. This form can be used by you alone or by any professional you may work with in the divorce process.

Personal Information

YOUR NAME:

First	Middle Initial	Last

ADDRESS:

_____

_____

_____

PHONE NUMBERS:

Home: _____

Work: _____

Fax: _____

Cell: _____

YOUR E-MAIL ADDRESS:

_____

SOCIAL SECURITY NUMBER: _____ - _____ - _____

DATE OF BIRTH:

Month	Day	Year

DATE OF MARRIAGE:

Month	Day	Year

DATE OF SEPARATION:

Month	Day	Year

Employment Information

YOUR PLACE OF EMPLOYMENT:

_____

_____

_____

_____

HOW OFTEN ARE YOU PAID:

Once a week   _____

Every two weeks   _____

Twice a month   _____

Once a month   _____

DATE OF HIRE:

_____   _____   _____

Month   Day   Year

WHAT WILL YOUR SOCIAL SECURITY INCOME BE?

$_____

To find this information, look on your Personal Benefit
Statement from your place of employment. You might have
to ask your employer for this information.

Spouse's Personal Information

SPOUSE'S NAME:

| _____ | _____ | _____ |
| First | Middle Initial | Last |

ADDRESS:

_____

_____

_____

PHONE NUMBERS:

Home: _____

Work: _____

Fax: _____

Cell: _____

SPOUSE'S E-MAIL ADDRESS:

_____

SPOUSE'S SOCIAL SECURITY NUMBER:

_____ - _____ - _____

SPOUSE'S DATE OF BIRTH:

| _____ | _____ | _____ |
| Month | Day | Year |

Spouse's Employment Information

SPOUSE'S PLACE OF EMPLOYMENT:

_____

_____

_____

_____

HOW OFTEN IS YOUR SPOUSE PAID:

Once a week   _____

Every two weeks   _____

Twice a month   _____

Once a month   _____

DATE OF HIRE:

_____   _____   _____

Month   Day   Year

WHAT WILL YOUR SPOUSE'S SOCIAL SECURITY INCOME BE?

$_____

To find this information, look on the Personal Benefit
Statement if this statement is provided by the employer.

Children's Information

CHILDREN'S NAMES, CURRENT AGES, AND DATES OF BIRTH:

First Name	Age	Month	Day	Year
First Name	Age	Month	Day	Year
First Name	Age	Month	Day	Year
First Name	Age	Month	Day	Year
First Name	Age	Month	Day	Year

ARE THERE ANY SPECIAL MEDICAL OR EDUCATIONAL EXPENSES FOR ANY OF YOUR CHILDREN?

YES _____ NO _____

If YES, please explain:

_____

_____

_____

_____

_____

CUSTODY ARRANGEMENT:

Sole Custody ____ Shared Custody ____ Split Custody ____

If you chose Shared Custody, indicate the number of days for each parent (total of 365):

Mother: _____ Father: _____

OTHER DEPENDENTS LIVING IN YOUR HOUSEHOLD:

_____

Health Insurance Information

AT PRESENT, WHO PAYS FOR HEALTH INSURANCE?

Husband: _____   Wife: _____

WHAT IS THE <u>MONTHLY</u> COST FOR THE FAMILY PLAN?

_____

WHAT IS THE <u>MONTHLY</u> COST FOR THE SINGLE PLAN?

_____

IF THERE ARE MINOR CHILDREN, WHO WILL BE PAYING FOR THEIR HEALTH INSURANCE?

Husband: _____   Wife: _____

AFTER THE DIVORCE, WHAT WILL BE THE FUTURE <u>MONTHLY</u> COST OF HEALTH INSURANCE?

Husband: _____

Wife: _____

Mortgage Information

1. Term: _____ years
   For how many years is your loan?

2. Loan Type: _____
   Adjustable rate mortgage or fixed?

3. Interest rate: _____%

4. Date of purchase: _____

5. Amount of loan: _____

6. How many years remain on the loan? _____

7. Fair market value of your house: $_____

8. Purchase price: $_____

9. Balance due on this mortgage: $_____

10. Address the mortgage is for:

    _____

    _____

    _____

11. Name of mortgage company:

    _____

Automobile Information

AUTO #1:

Make: _____

Model: _____

Year: _____   Mileage: _____

Retail value: _____   Trade-in value: _____

PLEASE CHECK ANY OF THE FOLLOWING OPTIONS:

Power steering ____   Power brakes ____   Power windows ___

Power seats   ____   Power locks ____   Cruise control   ___

Leather interior ____   Moon roof   ____   Sun roof   ___

AM/FM stereo   ____   Cassette deck ____   CD player   ___

Custom paint job ____

ANY OTHER OPTIONS:

_____

_____

PLEASE CHECK THE CONDITION OF THIS AUTO:

POOR _____   FAIR _____   GOOD _____   EXCELLENT ___

BALANCE OWED: $_____   MONTHLY PAYMENT: $_____

PURCHASE DATE: _____
INTEREST RATE: _____

NAME THAT APPEARS ON THE TITLE: _____

Automobile Information

AUTO #2:

Make: _____

Model: _____

Year: _____   Mileage: _____

Retail value: _____   Trade-in value: _____

PLEASE CHECK ANY OF THE FOLLOWING OPTIONS:

Power steering ____ Power brakes ____ Power windows ____

Power seats ____ Power locks ____ Cruise control ____

Leather interior ____ Moon roof ____ Sun roof ____

AM/FM stereo ____ Cassette deck ____ CD player ____

Custom paint job ____

ANY OTHER OPTIONS:

_____

_____

PLEASE CHECK THE CONDITION OF THIS AUTO:

POOR _____ FAIR _____ GOOD _____ EXCELLENT ____

BALANCE OWED: $_____ MONTHLY PAYMENT: $_____

PURCHASE DATE: _____
INTEREST RATE: _____

NAME THAT APPEARS ON THE TITLE: _____

Retirement Plans

(Please furnish **copies** of current benefits statements.)

CSRS (Civil Service Retirement System), FERS (Federal Employee Retirement System), TSP (Thrift Savings Plan), IRA (Individual Retirement Account)

FOR YOU:

    CSRS ____   FERS ____   TSP ____ (U.S. government employees)

    401(k) ____   IRA ____   Defined Benefit Pension ____

FOR YOUR SPOUSE:

    CSRS ____   FERS ____   TSP ____ (U.S. government employees)

    401(k) ____   IRA ____   Defined Benefit Pension ____

DATE OF SERVICE (Date you started employment):

    YOU: _____

    SPOUSE: _____

Separate Property

Are there any assets that are separate property, such as money or property you owned before the marriage or gifts/inheritances received during the marriage?

YOU:

_____

_____

_____

_____

Please explain the source of the funds being claimed as separate.

SPOUSE:

_____

_____

_____

_____

Please explain the source of the funds being claimed as separate.

Asset Information

ASSETS include all cash, stocks, bonds, mutual funds, annuities, real estate (other than personal residence), and businesses. Do not include household furnishing or jewelry unless of investment grade. Please furnish **copies** of current statements.

Description	Value
_____	$_____
_____	$_____
_____	$_____
_____	$_____
_____	$_____
_____	$_____
_____	$_____
_____	$_____
_____	$_____
_____	$_____
_____	$_____
_____	$_____
_____	$_____
_____	$_____
_____	$_____
_____	$_____
_____	$_____
_____	$_____
_____	$_____
_____	$_____
_____	$_____
_____	$_____

If necessary, continue on a separate sheet.

Debt Information

Joint debts: List all jointly owed debts. Fill in the name of the company or person debt is owed to (Creditor), the balance (Balance), the monthly payments (Pay), and the interest rate (Rate). Please furnish **copies** of current statements.

Creditor	Balance	Pay	Rate
_____	$_____	$_____	_____%
_____	$_____	$_____	_____%
_____	$_____	$_____	_____%
_____	$_____	$_____	_____%
_____	$_____	$_____	_____%
_____	$_____	$_____	_____%
_____	$_____	$_____	_____%
_____	$_____	$_____	_____%
_____	$_____	$_____	_____%

Separately owed debts: List all separately owed debts and indicate whether each debt is yours or your spouses. Please furnish **copies** of current statements.

Creditor	Balance	Pay	Rate
_____	$_____	$_____	_____%
_____	$_____	$_____	_____%
_____	$_____	$_____	_____%
_____	$_____	$_____	_____%
_____	$_____	$_____	_____%
_____	$_____	$_____	_____%
_____	$_____	$_____	_____%
_____	$_____	$_____	_____%
_____	$_____	$_____	_____%

Asset and debt division: On a separate sheet, please provide a listing or statement describing how you would like to divide the assets and debts. It can be as simple as a listing of assets and debts for each person. Also, state how you would like to handle arrangements for the house, with details of selling and splitting the net proceeds **or** arrangements for one person to buy out the other's share of equity.

Future lifestyle: On a separate sheet, please provide a statement describing the custody arrangement for minor children (sole, shared, split), anticipated monthly rent of apartment or house, and details (price, financing, and so on). List also if large purchases such as an auto are anticipated in the near future.

The following items will be required for you and your spouse:

❖ Tax returns from the past five years

❖ W-2s for the past five years

❖ Current pay statement

Appendix B

Resources

Please use the following sources to become more educated about your financial situation before and after divorce. These Web sites and books are a great place to start. Many sites allow you to email questions, request investment literature, and search for professionals you may wish to contact in your local area.

Mutual Fund Web Sites

www.americanfunds.com

www.fidelity.com

www.putnam.com

www.oppenheimerfunds.com

www.aim.com

www.alliance.com

www.vanguard.com

Bank and Brokerage Firm Web Sites

www.vankampen.com

www.wellsfunds.com

www.msdw.com

www.painewebber.com

www.ml.com

www.citibank.com

www.firstunion.com

www.bofa.com

www.lm.com

Other Sites

www.choosetosave.org

www.morningstar.com

Government Employee Web Sites

www.opm.gov

www.tsp.gov

Divorce Information Web Sites

www.Divorcesource.com

www.Splitup.com

www.DivorceResourceNetwork.com

www.Divorceinfo.com

www.Divorcelawinfo.com

Books and Magazines

Ahrons, Constance. *The Good Divorce: Keeping Your Family Together When Your Marriage Comes Apart.* New York: HarperCollins, 1995.

Friedman, Gary, and Jack Himmelstein. *A Guide to Divorce Mediation: How to Reach a Fair, Legal Settlement at a Fraction of the Cost.* New York: Workman Publishing Co., 1993

Ricci, Isolina. *Mom's House, Dad's House: Making Shared Custody Work.* New York: Fireside, 1997.

Trafford, Abigail. *Crazy Time: Surviving Divorce and Building a New Life*. New York: HarperPerennial Library, 1993

Weintraub, Pamela, and Terry Hillman. *The Complete Idiot's Guide to Surviving Divorce*. Indianapolis: Alpha Books, 1999.

Wilson, Carol Ann. *The Financial Guide to Divorce Settlements*. Columbia, MD: Marketplace Books, 2000.

Divorce Magazine (A quarterly publication for separated, divorced, and those considering. Also available as an online subscription at www.divorcemag.com.)

Appendix C

Glossary

401(k) plan   A plan offered through your employer that allows you to set aside up to 15 percent of your earnings on a pre-tax basis into an account that grows tax-deferred.

alimony   (Spousal Maintenance) Payments made by cash or check that enable the receiving spouse to live independently of the paying spouse.

alternate selection   A method used to distribute personal property by which each person takes a turn choosing from a list of items which both party wish to receive.

annuity   An insurance contract that allows you to invest after-tax dollars on a tax-deferred basis, above and beyond any IRA or Roth IRA contributions you may make.

appreciation   The increase in the value of your assets.

asset allocation   The division of your assets among different investments with the intention of reducing risk.

asset classes   Because of characteristics these assets are divided into real estate, personal/family businesses, career, retirement, or liquid.

bear market   A market where the stock indices are generally falling. Technically, the market must fall 20 percent from its previous high water mark before being considered a true bear market.

beneficiary   The person you designate to receive assets upon your death.

bonds   Represent debt owed by a company.

bull market   A market where the stock indices are generally rising.

business valuator   Usually an accountant or CPA who examines the assets and financial documents of a business and places a monetary value for which the business could be placed for sale.

capital gain   The difference between the purchase price and the sale price on a particular asset.

cash flow worksheet   A report that estimates taxes and calculates either a deficit or excess of cash after deducting or adding payments of child support, alimony, and living expenses.

child support   A dollar amount approximation of monthly basic living necessities for a child or children.

community property   Property to which both spouse's have a claim and is usually divided equally.

compliance conference   A meeting to ensure that requested actions have been completed.

consolidation   The idea that you can keep your assets in a few accounts so you can keep better control of them.

cost basis   The amount paid for an asset or the purchase amount remaining after deducting depreciation claimed for tax purposes.

counterclaim   Response to an action or allegation.

coupon   The interest rate at which a company pays its bondholders. The coupon on a bond does not change once issued. For example, a 5 percent bond would pay $50 on each $1,000 worth owned by an investor.

defined benefit pension   A qualified plan under which employees receive an income for life upon retirement. The amount of income depends on how long the employee worked at the company.

demand for interrogatories   Written questions to be answered under oath.

dependency exemptions   A specific amount allowed to be deducted from taxable income for a child, parent, or other relative who depends on you for more than half of their total support.

deposition   Information taken under oath, by either party's attorney.

disability insurance   A contract that pays a percentage of income upon your disability. Coverage may be for short-term or long-term disabilities.

discount on a bond   The amount under par value paid for a bond. For example, a bond that cost $900 carries a $100 discount.

discovery   The process of uncovering all the pertinent facts concerning a case. In divorce, this may include furnishing statements and completing forms concerning the assets, debts, income, expenses, and other aspects of the situation.

diversification   The idea that you can reduce risk by investing in a variety of different investments.

dividend   The stockholder's proportional share of corporate profits.

dollar-cost averaging   The process of investing a set dollar amount in a particular investment on a regular basis, regardless of the investment's performance at that moment.

Domestic Relations Order   A court order that awards a portion or whole of a retirement account titled in the name of a spouse.

durable power of attorney A document that allows you to name someone else to make business and other nonmedical decisions for you when you are unable to do so yourself.

equitable distribution The distribution of asses and debts may vary depending upon the factors of the marriage.

equity See *stocks*.

ERISA Employee Retirement Income Security Act of 1974. This is the law that governs qualified plans offered by an employer.

filing status The designation used by the Internal Revenue Service for calculation of taxes owed in a given year.

Final Decree of Divorce A document, issued by the court and signed by the judge, in which the terms of the Settlement Agreement are accepted and the marriage is dissolved.

financial disclosure Exchange of all financial information in a case.

health insurance A contract that pays specified benefits for health care costs incurred by the covered persons. Benefits may be fee for service, HMO, or PPO.

Hold Harmless Letter A document executed so that one party assumes sole responsibility and releases another party from future actions.

insurance premium The price of continuing insurance coverage under a particular policy. This applies to life, health, and disability policies.

interest rate risk The possibility that interest rates will change in the marketplace, thereby affecting future prices and yields on available bonds.

IRS Form 8332 A form submitted to the IRS, which allows a noncustodial parent to claim a child or children as dependents.

itemized deductions Amounts for certain items such as property tax, mortgage interest, and charitable contributions that are deducted from taxable income before calculation of taxes owed.

legal custody   The right and responsibility to make decisions concerning the welfare of the child or children.

life insurance   A contract that pays a specified death benefit in exchange for a specified premium. Policies may be term or permanent.

litigation   A hearing in a court whether one or both parties are represented by legal counsel. Usually called trial, where a judge renders a decision after all the facts have been presented.

living will   A document that states what medical procedures you wish to have performed or not in the event of a medical emergency.

marital assets   Assets accumulated during the marriage. The accumulation period varies by state and may end at divorce or at separation.

market risk   The possibility that political events, economic events, or investor sentiment will change in the future, thereby affecting future prices.

Medical Durable Power of Attorney   A document that allows you to name someone else to make medical decisions for you when you are unable to do so yourself.

mixed assets   Items that possess properties of both marital and separation classifications.

modifiable alimony   Payments that made be changed by the court or by agreement or both parties.

money purchase plan   A qualified plan where the employer makes a contribution each year of a specified percentage of employees' earnings.

Monthly Income, Expense, and Debt form   A one-page listing of all monthly and expenses and debts detailed by category.

Motion to Compel   A request to the court to force disclosure or action.

motions An application to the court for granting a specific action.

net equity The value of an asset, calculated by subtracting debt owed from the fair market value.

net worth The value of all assets owned after deducting loans or debt.

nonmodifiable alimony Amount and term of payments that cannot be changed.

par The full face value of a bond, which is $1,000.

Pendente Lite A court order directing temporary child support, alimony, child custody, visitation, or temporary occupation of the marital home while the terms of the Settlement Agreement are being negotiated.

period alimony Payments made for a certain number of months or years, which terminate at the end of a designate term.

permanent alimony Sometimes called lifetime alimony, usually continue until either party dies or the remarriage of the receiving spouse.

Personal Information form A listing of personal information for you, your spouse, and children that includes listings of assets and debts and employment information.

physical custody The type of custody determined by the location and number of days the child or children reside.

pleadings Detailed papers that state the grounds for divorce or defense of the grounds.

predivorce checklist A listing of all essential information and documents concerning your legal, financial, and personal situation.

preliminary conference A meeting at which both parties and their attorneys set forth the issues of the case and schedule the exchange of financial information.

premium on a bond   The amount over par value paid for a bond. For example, a bond that cost $1,100 carries a $100 premium.

premium   The price of an option, futures contract, options futures contract, or insurance coverage.

present value   A method whereby a future stream of payments may be reduced to a lump sum amount. This is the amount of money required to make payments for a specific period, usually the recipient's life expectancy.

pretrial conference   A meeting, usually held in the judge's chambers, during which the attorneys inform the judge of the facts concerning their client's position.

profit-sharing plan   A qualified plan where the employer makes a contribution each year of a variable percentage of employees' earnings.

purchasing power risk   The risk that investment performance will not keep pace with inflation, thereby causing the investor to lose purchasing power. This is arguably the greatest risk investors face today.

qualified plan   A retirement plan that is qualified under ERISA. Examples include 401(k), profit sharing, money purchase, and defined benefit pensions.

quitclaim deed   A document by which one party relinquishes all ownership rights to a property or asset.

recitals   The first section of a Settlement Agreement, which contains personal information about both parties and their family.

rehabilitative alimony   Payments intended to enable the receiving spouse to increase his or her earning potential by attending college or obtaining additional training or experience.

retainer   A sum of money paid in advance for work or professional services to be rendered.

Roth IRA A tax advantaged account where individuals are allowed to deposit a limited amount each year. Growth on these funds is tax-deferred. If withdrawals are made after age $59^1/_2$, no tax is due.

separate assets Assets brought into the marriage by either party or gifts or inheritances from a third party during the term of the marriage.

Settlement Agreement A legally binding contract that contains the details of the divorce including the financial settlement, child custody, and future payments such as child support and alimony. Also called a Property Settlement Agreement or Marital Settlement Agreement.

shared custody When the child or children reside with each parent more than a minimum amount of days per year.

SIMPLE 401(k) A salary deferral plan not subject to ERISA.

Simplified Employer Pension (SEP) A self-employed or small business retirement plan not subject to ERISA requirements into which the employer makes a variable contribution of each employee's earnings.

sole custody When the child or children physically reside primarily with one parent.

split custody A situation when there is more than one child and the children are split in their physical residences.

Statement of Net Worth A form by which the court learns of an individual's income, expenses, assets, and liabilities.

stocks Represent ownership in a company and are traded in increments of shares.

Summons of Notice Notifies one spouse that the other spouse wishes to file of dissolution of the marriage.

total return The total amount of return an investor receives from an investment. It includes dividends, interest, and capital gains together to give a complete picture of how an investment has performed.

traditional individual retirement account (IRA)   A tax-advantaged account where individuals are allowed to deposit a limited amount each year. Growth on these funds is tax-deferred. Tax is paid upon withdrawal from the account.

UGMA/UTMA   Uniform Gift to Minors Account/Uniform Transfer to Minors Account. An account that allows an adult to serve as a custodian for a minor child.

verified answer   Pleading in which one party either admits or denies allegations in the verified complaint.

verified complaint   Pleading which contains the nature of circumstances of misconduct.

vesting   The schedule according to which you are eligible to take any employer contributions to a qualified plan with you when you leave that employer.

will   A document that outlines how your assets are to be distributed when you die. If you have minor children, it also names who will serve as legal guardian to the children.

working capital   Amount that remains after deducting taxes and expenses from salary and other income.

yield   The effective interest rate which an investor receives considering the premium or discount paid for a specific bond. For example, a bond that cost $1,100, and pays 5 percent coupon would yield $50 ÷ $1,100 = 4.54 percent.

Index

E

J–L

M